NUBIA

The Rise and Fall of African Empires
By Andre Samuels

Cover Art by Kathleen B. Stebbins

Dedication

This book is dedicated to my Mother, Sister, and Brother. Your unending support, faith, and encouragement compelled me to complete this book. Words cannot express my gratitude. I love you dearly.

Contents

THE EMPIRE OF KUSH

- The Conquest of Egypt
- Piankhy The Deliverer
- The Story of Shabaka
- Taharqa: The Greatest Nubian Pharaoh
- The Queen of Kush & War with Rome

CHRISTIAN NUBIA: The Indomitable Heirs of Kush

- Christian Nubia in History
- The Battle for Dongola
- Christianity Comes to the Nubians
- The Origin of Christian Nubia
- The Golden Age of Christian Nubia
- The Downfall of Christian Nubia

AXUM: The Divine Empire

- The Rock Hewn Churches of Lalibela
- Gondar: The African Camelot
- The Origin of Axum
- Mighty Axum: The Destroyer of Kush
- Axum's Conquest of Arabia
- The Year of The Elephant
- Axum: A Refuge from Oppression
- The First Hijra & The Wise Negus
- The Legend of Prester John

THE SWAHILI: Mansions, Merchants and Sailing Ships

- Swahili Cities: Through the Eyes of a Traveler
- The Myth of the Swahili Origins
- The Truth of the Swahili Origins
- The Zanj Rebellion
- The Swahili & The Chinese Treasure Ships

- The Fantastic Cities of the Swahili
- The Decline of the Swahili

GREAT ZIMBABWE: The Granite Cities of the Inland Empires

- The Granite Cities of the Inland Empires
- The Origins of Zimbabwe

GHANA, MALI & SONGHAI: The Empires of Gold

- Ghana: An Empire Built by Books
- The Origin of Ghana
- The Empire of Mali
- Timbuktu: The City of Scholars
- The Founding of Timbuktu
- Architecture in the Mali Empire
- The Marvelous Mud of Mali
- The Origin of the Mali Empire
- The History of the Mali Empire
- The Legacy of the Mansas
- The Kolokan Mansas
- The Army of the Kolokan Mansas
- The End of the Kolokan Dynasty
- The Reign of Souleyman
- The End of Mali & The Portuguese

SONGHAI: The Last Great Empire

- The First Great Emperor: Sonni Ali Ber
- A Man of Honor
- The Askia Dynasty
- The Black Sultan & The End of Songhai

THE GREAT TRIBES & KINGDOMS

- Life in Provincial Kingdoms
- The Skills of Early Slaves

BEAUTIFUL BENIN

- A City as Fine as Amsterdam
- The Benin Moat
- Trade In The Kingdom
- The British, Benin and The Aftermath of War
- The Origin of Benin
- The Forest Kingdoms & The Foundation of Benin

KANEM BORNU: The Black Knights

- The Origin of Kanem-Bornu
- The Rise of Islam & The Kanembu Tribe
- A King with a Vision
- The Kingdom of Bornu

THE HAUSA: The Chiefs of Indigo

- The Origin of the Hausa
- The End of The Hausa

AFRICANS IN ISLAMIC SOCIETIES

- Antar: The First of All Knights
- Blacks in the Life of Muhammad
- Muhammad's Black Generals & Advisors
- The African Protection of the First Muslims
- Blacks in Islam's Early Battles
- Blacks in Islamic Liturgy
- Blacks, Afro-Arabs & The Islamic Empire
- The Islamic Slave Trade & Arab Supremacy
- The Zanj Rebellion & Racism in the East
- Black Military Elite in the Islamic World
- The Battle of the Three Kings
- The Siddi of India & The Unconquerable Fort
- Race or Culture: The Quandary of the Afro-Arab

Introduction

If we are honest with ourselves, when we imagine African cultures our minds are filled with tribal images. We imagine the exotic. We imagine impoverished tribes, living in primitive huts, on the verge of starvation. We imagine primitive weapons, primitive art, simple fabrics, and unsophisticated culture. We imagine an Africa virtually devoid of high cultural achievements. The central focus of this book is to prove that this image of Africa is indeed a concoction of our imagination. It bears no resemblance to the Africa of old. This image of Africa was consciously created to justify slavery, the annexation of African lands and an unspeakable host of crimes against the entire continent. Nubia: The Rise and Fall of African Empires was written to encourage readers to evoke a new mental image of Africa's cultures and help readers reimagine the landscape of its history. Readers will be introduced to an Africa filled with sumptuous cultures, wealthy nobles and fantastically successful merchants. The "Africa" readers will become familiar with was once filled with tremendous, earth shaking armies. Black Knights clad in pitch black suits of armor once galloped through their domains, protecting their kingdoms from attackers. Wealthy black merchants once filled their sailing ships with an astonishing array of products and shipped them to their global trading partners. Grand African Empires built cities that rivaled the world's greatest capitals. The Emperors and Queens of Africa were known worldwide for their wealth, piety, and ferocity. Their armies enforced the will of their sovereigns against the Caesars, Khalifas, and Popes, leading the competitive nations of Europe and Arabia. Readers will come to know an Africa overflowing with books, universities, and some of the world's most well educated scholars. The sculptural art, poems and plays produced by Africa's highly educated classicists inspired and influenced the creativity of Europe's most acclaimed artisans. Readers will learn that there was once an Africa, filled with kingdoms that rivaled the glamor and grandeur of the world's most successful polities. Some of these nations hosted seaside mansions, ivory laden concert halls, stone mosques and churches that were architectural wonders. The remnants of most of these kingdoms are still accessible for travelers today to experience firsthand and with their own eyes. The most accurate portrait of Africa is not of a "Dark Continent" shrouded in mystery and disconnected from the world, rather it is of an Africa deeply integrated in the history of world affairs. African kingdoms were actors on the global stage as drivers of global currencies, participants in military engagements and the exporters of coveted products. The role of Africa in global affairs cannot be understood without replaying the major movements of history. Nubia therefore, is an integrated history that recounts, the history of many of the world's greatest non-African political powers. By reviewing the history of these non-African actors, we can begin to understand the role that African kingdoms played in shaping global events. Nubia attempts to place Africa in its proper context without embellishing or exaggerating the accomplishments of African culture. If Nubia: The Rise and Fall of African Empires postulates that Africa was once filled with incredibly powerful empires, it is incumbent on the book to also explain the demise of each of these once great nations. A large portion of the book is dedicated to describing the origins and rise of African polities, exploring the decline of these great kingdoms, and then concluding with an explanation of how Africa arrived in the modern world in its current state. Our most powerful sources in this re-examination of Africa are the firsthand accounts of European and Arab explorers. The reality is that in provoking a radical re-imagining of Africa, the integrity of our sources is of primary importance. We have not relied on biased sources, politically driven sources, or politically correct sources. Instead, we have used the archeological surveys, personal diaries, and firsthand accounts of those pre-disposed to discounting the incredible achievements of African civilization. These firsthand accounts, from men and women, report that they were astonished by the achievements of people that they often held in little regard. By relying on these hostile witnesses, we assure ourselves of accounts that lack exaggeration. We can screen for their bias, and build an accurate mental image of the Africa that once acquitted itself against the greatest powers of the ancient world. Our unabashed goal is to restore the respect deserved by African Civilizations. Lastly, in honor of West Africa's Griots, who preserve history through storytelling, Nubia is written in a narrative format. It re-tells the great battles, conquests, and achievements of Africa's most inspirational and infamous rulers. The Griot's were wise to select the narrative format because stories bring history to life. Hard to pronounce kingdoms become vivid and lush landscapes. Rulers with difficult names become real men and women, who strive for causes we intimately understand. The clang of steel and cacophony of war ring in our ears as we imagine battles with names we've never heard. Nubia: The Rise and Fall of African Empires is a compilation of accurate historical events, captured from the journals and travel logs of explorers, merchants, and travelers in the ancient world. Their narratives paint a vivid image of African Empires that once held significant sway in the world and their recollections transform our impressions of black civilizations.

The Empire of Kush

Today, the Sudan in Africa is one of the poorest regions on earth, but over 2,000 years ago, it was the birthplace of one of the world's wealthiest and most enduring empires (1070 B.C.-350 A.D). When we think about the Nile River and the region around it, Egypt springs to mind as the only great kingdom established along the banks of the world's most famous river. There were however, two major super powers in the region. The Kingdom of Kush was once a sophisticated and influential world power. Their military was large and formidable, having proved itself against many of the most powerful empires in history. The armies of world powers like Egypt, Rome and Assyria would all suffer defeat at the hands of Kush's Nubian armies. Kush was a cosmopolitan nation with numerous cities, fantastic wealth, and trade relationships with the most prominent empires in the world. Kush's sophisticated agricultural schemes fed a large population as the Nubians proved themselves capable of breathing life into the most challenging desert environments. Grand palaces and pageantry surrounded the Kings and Queens of Kush, who made the empire one of the longest lasting kingdoms in human history. The massive burial fields of their royal dynasties reflect the enduring legacy of the empire. The early leaders of Kush were buried in massive graves as large as football fields and then later they were buried in pyramids, taking their tremendous wealth with them into the afterlife. Archeologists combing through the desert sands of the Sudan have discovered the remarkably long extent of Kush's prominence. When the great world power of Rome was still in its infancy as a small city state, Kush was already a powerful empire and it remained a great power, until nearly the collapse of the unified Roman Empire. Researchers have learned since it's discovery, that the Kushites possessed libraries, multiple systems of writing, universities and fabulous artistry that influenced the fashions of Egypt. Kush and Egypt would compete for dominion, with each nation taking turns ruling the other. Despite the hostility of their relationship, trade, commerce, and common religion would define their interactions, resulting in twin cultures that may seem shockingly similar. Both nations would build pyramids and numerous temples in what is usually seen as the "Egyptian" style to worship a similar pantheon of Gods. The re-discovery of Kush unfolded over a long period. James Bruce was the first to report hints of the forgotten kingdom in 1772. The Scottish explorer reported seeing the faint outlines of Pyramids that he believed were the remnants of the ancient city of Meroe, written of in historic Greek records. Many years later Frederic Caillaud reported seeing numerous pyramids in his seminal book "A Trip to Meroe on the White River" in 1826. Unfortunately, his text simply incited the looting of the ancient sites by treasurer hunters. Explorers like Giuseppe Ferlini were given free reign to raid the extensive pyramid fields of Meroe, destroying the heritage of ancient Nubia. In his craven quest for riches, Ferlini destroyed 40 pyramids by blasting the peaks off them and lowering himself into the burial chambers to loot the gold and silver of black monarchs that were once revered. Ferlini absconded with the treasure of the Candace or

Queen Amanishakheto. He attempted to sell the relics but few in Europe would accept the notion that blacks could produce such wonderful artifacts. When early archeologists began to conduct legitimate examinations of Kush, they believed that they had found the birthplace of Egyptian Culture. Despite the evidence depriving them of this notion, the reports of fantastic temples, and unending pyramid fields still enthralled researchers. However, once researchers were confronted with the fact that these grand constructions were the work of the black Sudanese, whom they despised, interest in the culture waned. Egyptologists like Karl Richard Lepsius, furthered the damage to Nubian history by using his credentials to deny Africans credit for the grand civilization. He espoused the notion that Greek texts which referred to the Kushites as Aethiopians, were references to red skinned Caucasians, whom he argued built Kush. The Greeks, he vehemently asserted were definitively not referring to negros. George Reisner, another famed explorer is largely considered to be the father of Nubian archeology for his exhaustive research and the revelations they produced. He uncovered the names of Kush's entire line of monarchs and he defined the dates and order of their reigns (70 generations in total). There is a sad irony in the fact that the effective father of Kush related archeology also preferred to grant credit for its towering achievements to a race he defined as Egyptians and Libyans, rather than black men and women. He eventually even blamed black people for destroying Kush's civilization. The demise of Kushite culture was caused by intermarriage with darker skinned immigrants according to Reisner. Despite their unceasing efforts to deny local Sudanese credit for the creation of Kush, we can derive from the research of these early archeologists that prior to pillaging by explorers, Kush was an awe-inspiring kingdom. The personal diaries and research of each are still available today. They give first hand descriptions of the beautiful ivory discovered in looted pyramids and describe in detail, immaculate bronzes, celebrative statuary and gold jewelry with inlaid pearls. These hostile witnesses bear witness of the once great empire. Archeology of Nubian sites was made even more difficult by Egypt's construction of the Aswan Damn which effectively flooded most of the archeological sites in historic Nubia. Overtime, as the reality of Nubia's black origin set in, Kush's similarities with Egypt permitted some researchers to dismiss Kush as a mere imitation of Egypt. We know now that Kush was not a mere imitation of Egypt, in fact many aspects of Kushite Culture predated Egypt while other aspects of the culture developed simultaneously with Egypt. Today's scholars have largely moved beyond the old racist paradigms that limited the perspective of their predecessors. They have come to realize that the Nile River was not a one-way street of cultural influence. They have discovered that Kush was indeed influenced by Egypt but the equally ancient cultures of Nubia similarly inspired numerous aspects of Egyptian culture. Modern researchers realize now that early scholars were overly critical of Kush, viewing the nation through a distorted, purely Egyptian lens. When early 20th century scholars repeatedly encountered Egyptian references to Kush as "wretched" and "vile" they assumed it was a reference to the quality of Nubian civilization. They latched onto Egyptian negativity because it mirrored their own racial bias. Modern scholars realize that the animosities of the Egyptians were driven by the feeling that Kush was a persistent threat and competitive neighbor. Kush at various points was a world superpower that can boast of having reigned over Egypt, unifying the two kingdoms under a single crown, creating the world's largest empire (at the time).

The term Nubia or Nubian is often abused as a synonym or catch-all moniker for black Africans in general. Even in the title of this book, we have abused the term Nubia to refer to all African Kingdoms, when the term only properly applies to one. When used appropriately, the term Nubian applies narrowly to those black Africans that settled along the banks of the southernmost portion of the Nile River, in the modern Republic of Sudan. Their land was called Nubia, a reference to their fantastic wealth and the Egyptian word for gold (Nwb, or Nebu) and their empire was called Kush. Our understanding of Kush was revolutionized when researchers discovered an exciting narrative, written in complex hieroglyphs on the internal tomb of a prominent Egyptian governor. The narrative rewrote our understanding of the power dynamic between Egypt and Kush. The hieroglyphs were written during Egypt's 17th dynasty, 1575-1550 B.C, long before the given birth year for the empire of Kush. They recount the tremendous invasion of Egypt by Nubia, at the height of Egyptian power and development. The glyphs tell us that Kush swept over Egypt "without limit" at the head of a massive army. The Nubians it seems, led a broad coalition of cultures and races in attacking Egypt. They poured over the borders of Egyptian territory, conquering, and destroying everything within their wake. The Egyptians, like many powers were often prone to erasing events in their history that were less than flattering. The Tomb of Sobeknakht, the Governor of El Kab, only recounts the event as a memorial to the Governor because of his valiant efforts to protect his city. The history was also intended to be a warning to future generations. We learn from the glyphs that Kush's influence extended over much of the region. It reads, "**Listen you, who are alive upon the earth, Kush came, aroused along his length; he having stirred up the tribes of Wawat, the land of Punt and the Medjawe**". It goes on to describe the innumerable forces of the Nubians and their allies, and their total domination of Egypt. For his part, the governor rejoices in his success in managing to burn and repel some of the Nubian attackers. Kush, it seems, sacked a substantial portion of Egyptian territory. The assault crippled much of Egypt. After the Nubians concluded their punitive expedition, they returned to their own territory. The inscriptions brought new understanding to a host of Egyptian statues and artifacts found in Nubian graves. The artifacts were apparently evidentiary emblems of Nubia's dominance over its Egyptian neighbor.

The invasion of Egypt by Kush would have a lasting impact, especially in the minds of Egyptian leaders. The desire for revenge consumed the Egyptian Pharaoh Thutmose I who desperately wanted to avenge the destruction of his kingdom, a century earlier. In plotting his revenge, the Pharaoh was determined to launch an invasion of Nubia. His primary concern was the famed Nubian archers that defined the backbone of Kushite military prowess. Throughout the ancient world, Nubians were renowned for their skills with the bow and Thutmose worried that they could be his undoing. Although Thutmose I never conquered all of Nubia, his Egyptian campaign was more successful than any previous expedition. Thutmose drove deeper into Nubian territory than any other previous Pharaoh. Egypt would dominate Nubia for approximately 500 hundred years. Generations of Nubians would be enslaved or absorbed into Egypt's army. Many Nubians would be educated in the Egyptian court as officers in administration, the military, and as Nubian faces for the Egyptian administration within Nubian provinces. The Egyptians would turn to the power of religion to subjugate the Nubians. They revived worship of the ancient God, Amun-Ra among the Nubians to legitimize their control of Kush. A temple was built at the mountain of Gebel Barkal, where the god Amun-Ra was believed to reside. The head of a huge monumental cobra was carved into the mountains face to cap the mountain. A ceremonial city called Napata, would be built around the remote mountain in Nubia. Nubians were appointed as Governors and Viceroys and they would largely accept Egyptian culture as they were charged with extracting tribute from Nubian lands. Nubians at court and Nubian mercenaries in the military would master the administrative habits of Egypt and a truly Egyptianized black culture would emerge. In time, the Nubians grew frustrated with their circumstances. In 1070 B.C. they turned the cult of Amun-Ra against the Egyptians. Whereas, the Egyptians intended the worship of Amun-Ra to legitimize the subjugation of the Nubians, the Nubians used it to legitimize their uprising for independence. In 725 B.C the Nubians would use the Egyptian pantheon of gods to fuel a Nubian spiritual revival and justify their conquest of Egypt, as the rightful sons of Amun-Ra. The Nubian conquest is forever known to history as the establishment of Egypt's 25th Dynasty. In time, Nubian Pharaohs would gift as much to Egypt as Egypt gave to Kush. Kush would rebuild many of Egypt's monuments and temples which were crumbling from the inattention of an Egyptian culture that had, in many ways forgotten itself. Egypt had passed through the hands of several foreign powers and infighting amongst Egyptian rulers left Egypt weak, and cultural practices neglected. The Kushites would restore Egypt to its former decadent glory. Monuments were reconstructed and defunct Egyptian religious practices like pyramid construction (a practice which ceased for 800 years) were revived. By joining the ample territory of Kush and Egypt under one administration, the 25th Dynasty became the largest empire on earth. Kushite rule was noted for its efficiency and competency. The first Nubian Pharaoh, Piye called himself "The Deliverer" and in many ways, he and the Nubian Pharaohs did deliver Egypt from a self-inflicted decline. The Nubian Pharaohs were unusually distinguished, avoiding many of the negative behaviors that were common of monarchs throughout the world. The Kushites did not erase their predecessors from history or claim credit for their previous achievements which was a common practice. They banned executions and avoided treating former enemies with harshness. When Kushite dominion of Egypt ended and Nubian rulers were expelled from Egypt by an invading army, the Nubians would withdraw and continue to rule the substantial, remaining half of their kingdom from their spiritual capital, Napata. In 300 years, Nubians would leave Napata with its 3 palaces and hilltop location south to the forested region of Meroe.

The new capital of the Kush Empire would be a city called Meroe for the next few centuries of Kush's unusually lengthy history. The Nubians would move to the site of Meroe in 300 B.C and erect a large industrial city, after leaving their former capital City of Napata. Meroe is often referred to by historians as ancient Africa's Birmingham. The City and its Nubian inhabitants built one of the ancient world's greatest centers for iron production. At a time when much of the world was still utilizing bronze implements and the smelting of iron, was a science understood by few, Meroe would supply much of the world with the mysterious metal. An army supplied with iron weapons could tear through a military armed with the comparatively soft bronze. In studying ancient Africa, we must understand that the climate and landscape have changed dramatically over time. Meroe was founded in an area that was once covered in lush forests and rich in iron deposits. What is today a desert landscape was once an incredible thicket of African hardwoods, harvested to feed the massive blast furnaces that smelted Nubian iron. In time, Nubians would become universally regarded as some of the world's greatest iron workers. As demand for their products soared, black smoke from their bloomeries filled the skies of Meroe. Today, the evidence of industry is found in the black soot that still stains the desert sand near Meroe as a remnant of their industrial factories. The Nubians also traded their well-made cotton textiles, jewelry and gold with India, China, Rome, Egypt and the Middle East. The Nubians maintained numerous alliances with Middle Eastern Powers like Israel, The Phoenicians and early Palestinians and often served as a protector to these nations. Over time, the Nubians developed a strong central government that was unique in the world, not merely for its efficiency but for the essence of its structure. Kush was a monarchy but in this uniquely African system, the Queen was equal to the King. Nubia's queens often bore the official title of The Candace. The Pharaoh and Candace divided the demands of administration between the two offices. There are periods of Nubian history in which the Queen or Candace commanded the army. During other periods, women were primarily concerned with administration. During the period of Kushite dominance over Egypt, the administration of the state was primarily in the hands of women. Kush would be a progressive kingdom in many other ways. Kush would be one of the first empires in the world to build schools that were open to the common citizen (in Meroe). The temples of Kush would double as universities, in much the same way that later mosques and

European monasteries would serve as spiritual centers and institutes of higher learning. The Kushite system of writing developed out of its relationship with Egypt, and began with the Nubian adaptation of Egyptian hieroglyphs. The Nubians however would evolve their own-more advanced system of writing with an alphabet. The Nubians continued to innovate by adding a second cursive form of their alphabet at a time when much of the world failed to develop even a single system of writing. They made great use of their literacy, maintaining copious documentation of their civilization and extensive libraries. Our understanding of Kush remains limited because of our inability to decipher the Nubian script. Despite our inability to understand their extensive records, we know now that Kush was not a mere vassal of Egypt but a Nubian Kingdom as large and as powerful as Egypt.

THE CONQUEST OF EGYPT

Between 790-760 B.C. the Empire of Kush, would conquer Egypt, and unify the entire Nile Valley. Centuries of hostility would culminate in a massive invasion, at a moment of Egyptian weakness, intimately linking the course of both nations. In order to understand Kush and its triumphant moments, we must understand the history of Egypt. At the end of Egypt's 20th dynasty, in approximately 1077 B.C. the nation of Egypt was fracturing. Following the death of Ramesses XI, (the 20th dynasty's final ruler), the state of Egypt was divided into separate regions with different sovereigns. The immediate descendants of the Pharaohs would rule a separate region from the city of Tanis while the High Priests of Amun would rule the from the city of Thebes in the southern part of the country. Egypt would not be unified for another century. However, this reunified state was ephemeral and would soon pass away. Successive generations would vacillate between periods of disunity and stability and continuous warfare would define the interactions of local governors, chiefs, and particularly petty princes. Egyptian civilization would decline precipitously while myopic factions would struggle with each other for supremacy, without consideration for the long-term consequences to Egyptian civilization. The nation, its monuments, and its history were poised for catastrophe, as a result of a divided leadership that nearly destroyed Egypt. The destruction of Egyptian culture would continue with the eruption of a civil war in Thebes. For the Egyptians, the pattern of persistent warfare would become very familiar, and the disintegration of Egyptian culture would be severe. The Empire of Kush would step boldly into this chaotic power vacuum, halt the pattern of fragmentation, and restore Egypt to its former unified glory.

PIANKHY "THE DELIVERER"

The period of Nubian dominance would begin when the Nubian Pharaoh, Piankhy also referred to as Piye, conducted a campaign into Egypt during his 20th year as the sovereign lord of Nubia. Piankhy was the son of King Kashta and Queen Pebatma. Kashta, his father, as King had already extended his own influence over the region into the Egyptian city of Thebes. Kashta sought an alliance with Shepenupet, the Divine Adoratice of Amun (a high priest), in which she would adopt his daughter (Amenirdis), and name her as successor to the priestess. The Adoratice of Amun was also the sister of the ruler Takelot III. This mutually beneficial union, as well as other political maneuvers gave Kashta significant influence on Egyptian affairs. But Kashta would never claim the title of Pharaoh. Kashta's son and successor, Piankhy would trade his father's influence, for complete dominion of the region, by conquering and uniting all of Egypt. The Kushites, were not fond of the disorganized condition of their northern neighbor, however the war only began as a response to hostility towards them. The army of Tefnakhte, an Egyptian ruler from the western delta region, would foolishly march south, to attack the Kushites. Piankhy would meet the Egyptian, crush his forces, and take steps to stem the tide of disunity and cultural disintegration in the north. When Piankhy marched north (in 727 B.C.) extending his domain, he would defeat the combined military might of Peftjaubast, Osorkon IV of Tanis, Input II of Leontopolis and Tefnakht of Sais (Sais would be the city that future Assyrian rulers would rule from). Since its inception, Kush and Egypt were culturally similar, and the Kings of Kush would claim to be the rightful, albeit denied, heirs to the Egyptian throne. As a result of their claim and the cultural similarities between the two, Piankhy did not view himself as a foreign invader, declaring himself, to be the "Deliverer from Disunity". His victory led to the creation of a joint Nubian and Egyptian culture. He would reign for 31 years, between 747 and 716 B.C. Piye or Piankhy establishes the 25th dynasty and is succeeded by Shabaka (his brother) and then by his two sons Shebitku and Taharqa. Piankhy's victory was recorded on a round-granite Victory Stela, discovered in 1862, at the Temple of Amun, near the foot of Gebel Barkal (Napata- a mountain in Nubia). While Piankhy was successful in his invasion of Egypt, he chose to install the conquered kings as his royal governors. Instead of ruling from Egypt, Piankhy chose to return to Napata, an important Nubian ceremonial city. It should be noted that much of Kush now lies beneath a great lake, as a result of the construction of the Aswan Dam. The dam which supplies modern Egypt with the majority of its hydroelectrically produced power, and the crocodile infested lake it created, has rendered archeology impossible. The consequence of this construction is that we struggle to develop a complete understanding of the level of development in Kush. Despite the impediments, a constant stream of revelations from recent research has uncovered a vast kingdom. Recent research suggests that Kush was a highly-developed military super power. Its territory is much greater than researchers initially believed. It is interesting to note that after expending the effort to conquer Egypt, and deliver it from disorder, Piankhy showed very little interest in remaining outside of traditional Nubian territory. Despite his clear possession of both kingdoms, and consequently the cities of both states. Piankhy would never again return to Egypt.

The Nubian dynasty would distinguish itself through the proficiency of its administration, its respect for, and adherence to Egyptian religious orthodoxy, and its military strength (and the willingness to exercise that strength). The Nubians would also protect Egypt for nearly a century from the tenacious advances of the Assyrians. The Assyrian Empire was centered in Mesopotamia (modern day Iraq). It was a sophisticated military power house with expansionist ambitions. It is difficult to overstate the power, might and influence of the Assyrian Empire. In time, the mighty Assyrians would dominate the Babylonian Empire, the Phonecians, Israel, and Egypt. In time they would become the world's largest empire. The Assyrians fed their insatiable appetite for conquest with revolutionary iron weapons that were substantially more effective than the implements of their neighbors. Iron which was notoriously difficult to smelt represented a technological revolution in weaponry, which the Assyrians used to great effect. Assyrian chariots, lancers, cavalry, and bowman would combine with a corp of army engineers that produced siege towers and battering rams for the world's most aggressive force. The Assyrian Kings inspired an unmatchable sense of terror throughout their world by filleting the flesh from the bodies of their enemies. They produced a spectacle of gore and violence that swept across the ancient world as their tremendous army ran roughshod over countless enemies. Historians are fond of saying that the Assyrian Kings bathed the world in blood. Despite their aggressive posture towards Egypt, and the fact that average Egyptians reviled the Assyrians, the Egyptian rulers (that governed before Nubia conquered Egypt) seemed determined to appease the encroaching menace. The establishment of Nubian leadership in Egypt however, would be built on a posture of strength, and would end the policies of appeasement. At every turn, the Kushites would stand as a road block to the ambitions of the Assyrian hoard.

THE STORY OF SHABAKA

Piankhy's decision to reign from Napata would prove to be a critical mistake. The Egyptian princes in northern Egypt would take full advantage of his absence and revolt. Shabaka, his brother and successor, would be forced to reinvade Egypt because of the insolence of his northern subjects. The Nubian Pharaohs would no longer be able to rule the unified territories from their Nubian homeland. Instead, Shabaka's unified empire would have Memphis as its capital. After his victory over Bakenrenef (a brief king of the 24th dynasty), Shabaka would appoint a Nubian as the governor over Sais. Shabaka would then order Bakenrenef to be burned alive. He would demand oaths of loyalty from all of his other opponents. According to Herodotus (the famous Greek historian) Shabaka was a just ruler. Kush, it seems was more modern than most Kingdoms, in terms of its attitudes toward female leadership, and in its treatment of prisoners. Despite the gruesome death of the sedition prone Bakenrenef, Shabaka apparently ended capital punishment, preferring to sentence prisoners to public service (dyke construction for irrigation) instead. Shabaka would also establish diplomatic relations with the Assyrian Kings (in modern day northern Iraq). The Nubian Pharaohs were renowned for their religious piety. The strength of their faith, and the reverence with which they approached religious matters is heavily documented. They were also meticulous in their attempts to legitimize their reign through religious imagery, and substantial construction projects. An example is the Shabaka Stone Basalt Stela, which is a Nubian document, designed to seem older then it is. The stone slab, is written in the style that was common during the Old Kingdom Pyramid Texts (from the comparatively ancient 5th and 6th Egyptian dynasty, Nubia was the 25th dynasty). Objects like the Stela were pivotal in promoting the acceptance of Nubian rule among native Egyptians, and in merging Egyptian and Nubian cultures. The Nubians would depict themselves in traditional Egyptian motifs, but they would insist on emphasizing Nubian garb, Nubian clothing, the Nubian crown, and their Nubian physical features. They would make it very clear, that they were not simply another dynasty of Egyptians; they were Nubians, and they would emphasize this fact in religious art. Their statues would dawn the unique Kushite crown, which consisted of two cobras, representing their two domains. The metal cobras were placed over a Nubian head cap, to make the complete Nubian crown. Generally, the culturally similar Kushites were enthusiastically accepted as rulers, in contrast to groups like the Hyksos who were always viewed as foreign occupiers (They ruled Egypt during the 15-17th dynasties, in another period of disunity). The Nubian conquest of Egypt gave Shabaka a monopoly over luxury goods (although many of them passed through Nubian hands prior to the conquest). Prior to the conquest, Kush and Egypt were involved in a robust regional trading system, which involved products (such as gold, ivory, obsidian, etc.) from Africa's interior that passed through Kush and into Egypt. Finished products were then produced in Egypt. After the Kushite conquest, the whole system of trade was under Nubian management. The princes of the Syrian and Palestinian regions received numerous gifts from the Nubian Pharaoh. Papyrus scrolls, and Egyptian linen textiles were among the gifts shipped to the region. It is believed by some scholars that Kush's influence spread into Palestine. The presence of Egyptian/Kushite weights found in Jerusalem attest to (at least) a strong presence or awareness of Kush. Timber continued to be imported from Lebanon, in exchange for luxury products from Kush. Developing a complete understanding of Kush is difficult to ascertain directly because of a variety of reasons which include, the inability to translate Nubian script, and the loss of archeological opportunities. The gaps in information can however, be filled by studying Kush's relationship to more clearly understood civilizations, with remains that are more plentiful. Kush's relationship with Assyria offers us this opportunity.

Shabaka, the Nubian Pharaoh and Sargon the King of Assyria corresponded consistently. We learned of this robust communication from seals discovered at the Assyrian site of Kuyunjik. In Shabaka's reign we see the typical features of an empire and its sovereign. Shabaka used his diplomacy with Assyria to his advantage. He attempted to establish a foothold in Syria and Palestine, when Sargon sent his military on campaigns outside of his domain. The action probably harmed diplomatic relations between the two, but for our purposes it displays that Nubia was just as ambitious as any other administration. We have learned from the Great Inscription of Tang-I Var, which Assyria's Sargon II created, that their enemy- King Iamani (King of Ashdod) wanted refuge in Kush (which the Assyrians called Meluhha). Instead of granting the request, Shabaka's successor Shebitku would return the enemy king to the Assyrians. The correspondence of Shabaka and the denial of amnesty to the King of Ashadod, shows the maturity of diplomacy between the two states. Shabaka emphasized diplomacy in his relationship with the Assyrians, and was successful in preventing the encroachments of Sargon II, but after Sargon died (in 704 B.C) Shabaka would use the opportunity to support anti-Assyrian rebellions in Syria and amongst the Phoenicians. Shabaka was best known for his restoration of the gate at Karnak. Shabaka was buried at el-Kurru, in an opulent tomb, taking his horses and prized possessions into the after life (such as beaded blankets and silver trappings).

TAHARQA: The Greatest Nubian Pharaoh

Sargon II's successor, was Sennacherib, and he claimed the Assyrian throne in 705 B.C. He was successful in crushing several rebellions, and re-acquiring the territories lost after his father's death. Shabaka's Nubian successor, Shebitku would continue supporting anti-Assyrian movements, and would continue his opposition to the oppression of various groups throughout the region. This may have been out of self-interest as opposed to altruism. Assyria made no secret of its militant tendencies, or its hostile intentions towards any power that could threaten its dominance. Kush's propensity for supporting the weak and oppressed, may have been little more than a desire to undermine a competitive power in the region. Setting aside suspicions regarding the Nubian's motivations, Sennacherib's vicious reign would provide an opportunity for biblical fame for the young prince of Kush. Taharqa, the great warrior of Kushite civilization is recorded in The Bible's Book of Kings, and The Book of Isaiah, as having come to the aid of Hezekiah, King of Judah (Israel). In the 7ᵗʰ century B.C. the Assyrian army infiltrated the Gaza-strip, and the mainland of Israel. They captured all the large cities of Judah except for Jerusalem. When the Assyrians lay siege to the city, King Hezekiah, under the instruction of the Prophet Isaiah refused to submit to the Assyrian King. He cut off the water supply coming from the Gihon Spring, which was the only source of water outside of the walls of Jerusalem. The Nubians saw Sennacherib's actions as an incredible opportunity for the would be Nubian successor of the Pharaoh Shabitqo. At the age of 16 (or 20), Taharqa would move his army toward the city of Jerusalem. The Bible mentions this fact in Isaiah 37:9;

"Now Sennacherib received a report that Tirhakah, the Cushite, a king of Egypt , was marching out to fight against him. When he heard it, he sent messengers to Hezekiah with this word: "Say to Hezekiah king of Judah: Do not let the god you depend on deceive you when he says, 'Jerusalem will not be handed over to the king of Assyria.' Surely you have heard what the kings of Assyria have done to all the countries, destroying them completely. And will you be delivered? Did the gods of the nations that were destroyed by my forefathers deliver them—the gods of Gozan, Haran, Rezeph and the people of Eden who were in Tel Assar? Where is the king of Hamath, the king of Arpad, the king of the city of Sepharvaim, or of Hena or Ivvah?"

Nubian historical sources state that Taharqa distinguished himself in battle in defense of his ally, Israel. The Bible recounts King Hezekiah's prayer, and then the Prophet Isaiah responds with a word from the Lord, condemning the Assyrian hoards. After the exchange The Book of Isaiah concludes with verses 36,37;

Then the angel of the Lord went out and put to death a

hundred and eighty-five thousand men in the Assyrian camp.
When the people got up the next morning—there were all
the dead bodies! So Sennacherib king of Assyria broke
camp and withdrew. He returned to Nineveh and stayed
there

In Isaiah, we observe the Bible as both a historical
document and a document of faith. In between Hezekiah's
prayer, and the Prophet Isaiah's revelation from God, only
two events take place; the movement of Taharqa's troops
toward battle, and the sudden death of Sennacherib's forces.
Whether Taharqa utilized a tried and true Nubian military
strategy of ambush, or he engaged a dehydrated Assyrian
force directly, or he made use of Nubia's famous archers by
raining arrows down on the enemy from the mountains of
east Jerusalem, we may never know. The Bible simply states
that in the morning, 185,000 men were dead (this number,
may be inflated). The Battle, known to history as the Battle
of Eltekh, ended in defeat for the Assyrians. It should be
noted that although the bible and Kushite sources confirm
this event, we have yet to find archeological confirmation for
the Nubian assault. We have not uncovered the Nubian
camp, for instance. What we do know, is that the Assyrian
warriors died, and The Assyrian King, Sennacherib
withdrew to his capital in shame. Sennacherib's sources
claim victory in the engagement but he never returned to the
region. After returning to Ninveh, two of his sons
assassinated Sennacherib reportedly for his embarrassing
failure (however, it was 20 years later). He would be
succeeded by Esarhaddon, his only loyal remaining son. The
humiliating defeat of his father, and the persistent
interference of Kush in Assyrian affairs, inspired
tremendous animosity. Esarhaddon would meet Taharqa on
the battle field and Taharqa would be victorious in their first
engagement. We can learn volumes about the strength of
Kush from Taharqa's willingness to engage and even defeat a

monarch like Esarhaddon, who once declared "*I am powerful, I am ALL powerful. I am without equal among kings*". We may garner from the wars between Kush and Assyria, the prominent role Kush played in the international affairs of its time, and its influence on important turning points in world history. Without speculating, we can say that Judaism, which was the world's inspiration for monotheism was in a delicate stage of its development. We do not need to wildly prognosticate on how Assyrian victory over Judah would have affected the development of monotheism in general and Judaism, Christianity, and Islam specifically. It is enough to say, that Kush played an important role when the foundations of the world's great faiths were being laid. As allies with the Phoenicians, the Kush Empire helped secure international trade for the Mediterranean. To ensure his succession, Shabitqo named Taharqa as co-regent. Taharqa would become the fourth Nubian Phraraoh of the 25th dynasty. Crowned in Memphis, he would rule for 36 years, from 690 -664 B.C (more specifically 688 B.C). In 679 Esarhaddon, would subdue Palestine and Judea. In 677 the Assyrians (led by King Esarhaddon) would also attempt to persecute Arab tribes around the Dead Sea. Taharqa, would deliver a clear defeat, in defense of the tribes, to the army of the Assyrians. In 674 Esharddon would lead a massive army to the borders of Egypt. The battle would be a bloody lesson for the Assyrian King, as the newly crowned Pharaoh Taharqa would once again claim victory in the war. The defeat would be a resounding humiliation that would feed the fire of hatred between the two states. In 671, after a sincere prayer to the sun-god Shamesh, which was left for posterity on a Stele at Phoenicia, Esharddon would launch another campaign to take Palestine back from the Kushite-Egyptians. Later that year, the Assyrian King would cross the Sinai Desert and attempt another invasion of Egypt. This time his prayers were answered and fate would favor the Assyrian. He would drive the Kushites to Memphis, where he would capture Taharqa's royal harem, his wife and his son. Esarhaddon would find victory in this second battle with Taharqa. The Assyrian lord would mock Taharqa stating that he took "*His queen, his harem, Prince Ushankhuru his heir, and the rest of his sons and daughters, his property and his goods, his horses, his cattle, his sheep in countless numbers, I carried off to Assyria. The root of Kush I tore up out of Egypt*". Esarhaddon would construct a stele that depicts himself prominently holding two chains that pierce the tongues of his two most bothersome enemies; Taharqa, the Kushite military commander, and Abdi Milkuti, King of Sidon. Some sources insist that the Kushite character in the stele is Prince Ushankhuru the son of Taharqa and not Taharqa himself. The stele communicates as clearly as possible that Kush had become a meddlesome road block to Assyrian aspirations. An equally important conclusion that can be drawn from the stele is the strength of the Kushite relationship with the Phoenicians. The Phoenicians were based in modern Lebanon but they were a civilization of "mariners". The marvelous merchants of the Mediterranean Sea were the masters of international trade at the time. The relationship between Kush and Phoenicia was enduring and intimate. When the Assyrians eventually conquered Egypt, they would attempt to destroy every trace, and image of the Nubian Pharaoh's that had plagued them for so long. Documents that could have illuminated the Nubian perspective on a multitude of historical events, were destroyed. Monuments to their greatness were defaced, or torn down all together. The kingdom that Taharqa labored to protect and resurrect would be scrubbed of every hint of Nubian leadership. The Pharaoh's son, and heir (it is believed) was taken back to Nineveh. Esarhaddon would boast in a cuneiform inscription: "**I fought daily, very bloody battles against Taharka, king of Egypt and Nubia, the one accursed by all the great gods. Five times I hit him with the point of my arrows, inflicting wounds, and then I laid siege** to Memphis, his royal residence. I destroyed it, tore down its walls, and burnt it down. All Nubians I deported from Egypt, leaving not even one to do homage to me." The last point is particularly important. Esarhaddon boasts that he kills or deports every Nubian remaining after Taharka's defeat. Kush would maintain its territories south of Memphis, but the cost for Taharqa was high. Taharqa escaped to Upper Egypt, while Esarhaddon set up garrisons, and made tax collectors of local chiefs, beginning the establishment of his administration. Esarhaddon would make a king of Necho 1, and install this "sovereign" as his proxy in Sais. In 670 B.C. Taharqa would take advantage of Essarhaddon's absence, and re-establish control of Lower Egypt by defeating the Assyrian garrisons. The son of Esarhaddon, Ashurbanipal would return and defeat Taharqa. This time he would take Memphis and Thebes. The Pharaoh would return to Nubia, and despite pleas from the local princes, would never return to Egypt. In the last 8 years of his life, he would continue exercising his love of architectural projects, in Nubia. He would die (possibly of illness), and be buried at Nuri, in the largest Nubian pyramid ever constructed (150 ft tall=14 stories). He was succeeded by his nephew Tanutanami, whom he named co-regent. Tanwetamani would reinvade Egypt with an all Kushite force. He would capture Memphis, and attack the Delta. After killing Necho 1 in battle, he was recognized as the King of Egypt. Tanutanami's success may have been due, in part to the fierce hatred Egyptian citizens held for the Assyrians. Necho 1, was never able to convince the Egyptian people to cling to their Assyrian overlords. The Egyptians were significantly more sympathetic to Nubian rule, and preferred Nubian domination to the culturally unfamiliar Assyrians. Psammetichus, the son of Necho 1 would flee to Assyria, after his father's death at the hands of Tanutanami. When the Assyrians returned with a new army, they defeated Tanutamani. He would ultimately find sanctuary in

Napata. For his loyalty Psammetichus 1, was named king. The 54 years of Psamtik's rule would be followed by four kings from 610-526 B.C. Shortly after, the Persians would move against Psamtik III. The Persian King Cambyses would assume the title of Pharaoh. The Persians would attempt to extend their dominion into Nubia, but the Nubians defeated Cambyses, ejecting him from their region. The defeat of the Persians, who boasted one of the most remarkable militaries in history, also says volumes about the military prowess of the Kushites. It is easy to mistake the seemingly endless eruptions of conflict between the Nubians, Assyrians, and Persians as a meaningless catalog of miscellaneous historical battles. But they are much more than that. If we understand the greatness of Assyria, its nearly unparalleled military might, and its incredible cultural achievements, then we can understand how formidable Kush must have been to stand against them.

By understanding its relationship with Assyria, we can conclude that Kush held sway over much of Palestine, was a valuable ally for the Phoenicians, came to the defense of Israel, united Egypt, and possibly held territory in Arabia. The armies of Kush must have been among the finest in the world, to achieve numerous victories against the armies of Egypt, Rome, Assyria, and Persia, which were the world's most formidable fighting forces. Our study of Kush and its interactions with numerous foreign powers highlights the dramatically different relationship that the world once had with Africa and its mightiest empires. There was a time when African Empires and African figures captured the imagination of Europe. Herodutus the famous Greek historian wrote that Aethiopians (the name Greeks gave to Kushites) *"are said to be the tallest and handsomest men in the whole world"*. The power of African Kings would inspire the authors of Greek epics to include African characters in the mythology of the Greeks. In the epic Trojan War, the

Kushite King Memnon would earn a notable mention from Homer. In the battle for Troy, Memnon was implored to bring his massive army to aide the City of Troy. According to Greek mythology Memnon was nearly as skilled a warrior as Achilles (the son of an immortal). And like the central figure Hector, Achilles would kill Memnon. Memnon would be expounded upon as a character in greek mythology. In the epic poem, the Prose Edda, written by the Icelandic poet Snorri Sturluson Memnon is listed as the father of the Germanic God Thor.

THE QUEEN OF KUSH & WAR with ROME

In 31 B.C Augustus Ceasar became the emperor of Rome, and with it he also gained control of the recently acquired territory of Egypt. South of Egypt was the Empire of Kush which was established in 1050 B.C. Shortly after Ceasar came to power, he would find himself in conflict with his empire's southern neighbor. Whereas Egypt would ridicule its female rulers like Hatshepsut, and female leadership was rare in other countries, Queens in Kush were equal to Kings. Decisions regarding the administration of their kingdom and the weighty decisions of war, were considered by both rulers. In some instances, the Queens, who bore the title Candace or Kandake (the basis for the usage of the modern name), served as the commander and chief for the military. The Candace's were robust women. They would lead their armies into battle, often issuing battle field commands from atop war elephants. One fantastic tale, recorded in both Roman and Nubian sources, recounts the five-year struggle of The Candace Amanirenes. In 24 B.C. Cornellius Gallus, the First Chief Magistrate of Roman Egypt, would commit suicide. He would be succeeded by

Aelius Gallus Petronius, whom Caesar Augustus would order to conquer Arabia and Ethiopia. In western historical documents, especially Greek and Roman sources, Ethiopia is the general name given to all of Black Africa, south of Egypt. The details of what would follow are still a contentious issue, but the basic outlines are not at issue. All-out war, for five years would consume both the Nubian and Roman parties. According to Roman accounts, The Candace, Amanirenas and the Crown Prince, Akinidad would launch an unprovoked attack on Rome, while the Chief Magistrate Petronius was absent leading the assault against Arabia. It is unusual for one-sided sources to be entirely truthful, so we may doubt the validity of the claim that the attack was unprovoked. We should consider the possibility that the Candace became aware of Rome's intentions to attack her kingdom (when they were finished ravaging Arabia) and decided to out-flank the hostile power to the north (Rome). Some scholars argue that revolts erupted over the taxes and tributes demanded by Rome of its citizens, and that the Candance supported or even provoked rebellions in the Egyptian cities bordering Kush. Whatever the cause, the Candace would launch her attack on Rome and claim several victories. According to Strabo, the Candace was "***brave, strong, and blind in one eye***". As the conflict escalated the Queen lead her army, decimating the Roman forces at Syene (Aswan), Elephantine and Philae. Ancient artistic reliefs depict the Candace with twin swords, riding in the bed of her chariot. She drove her army straight into the heart of Roman controlled Egypt, and proceed straightaway to the city of Thebes (the Egyptian Capital). There, she would literally decapitate the Roman garrison with a tremendous defeat. Ever mindful of the symbolism of her actions, the Queen would seek to undermine the image of Roman authority in territories throughout the Nile Region by severing the heads of Statues of Augustus. She would bury the heads beneath Nubian temples and palaces. In

Kushite culture, trampling over the image of an enemy was a declaration of victory that symbolically reduced their dominance. In the entrance of her temples, the citizens of Kush would forever trample the head of the Roman Emperor. She even ordered the dedication of a temple to the victory in Meroe. European civilization has reclaimed the heads of the Roman Emperor which now sit in the British Museum of London. The heads of Augustus were not the only war trophies the Candace claimed. She also captured a great deal of "booty". Roman accounts alledge that she enslaved the population, and captured many prisoners. Objectively, we should note that enslaving, and liberating are often terms of perspective. A wall painting however does confirm the claim, at least in part, as it depicts several prisoners, including a Roman citizen. After the Romans experienced several stunning defeats, the Queen's victories would end when Rome's Gaius Petronius returned from Arabia. He assembled an army of 10,000 Roman soldiers, and the military genius drove the Nubians out of Aswan. Now that he could give the matter his full attention, Petronius forced the Kushites from Thebes, to Pselchis (a Kushite city named Maharraqa). Tempering his response, it seems Petronius then sent deputies to the Nubians to negotiate a peace, and demand that the Nubians acquiesce to Roman requests. The Kushites requested three days to consider the Roman offer. However, after three days, the Nubians didn't reply. The Roman advanced south to the Kushite city of Premnis (modern Karanog), which was south of Maharraqa. Next, he marched toward Napata, which was believed to be the Nubian capital. In Napata, Petronius forced Prince Akinidad to flee from the holy city, as he destroyed the hilltop capital city. However, questions must be raised about the nature of this victory. Recent research has suggested that Napata was never the capital city of the Nubians. Some researchers believe that Napata was used primarily for religious worship. It contained a palace for royal ceremonies, a temple, and a burial site, but was never a fortified city. Strabo records that the Queen returned with an army of "many thousands of men", but was unsuccessful in retaking Napata. The conclusion of this engagement is a confused bit of history. At the end of the war, The Romans withdrew again to the north, leaving behind the garrison, Qasr Ibrim (Primis), which represented the southern border of the Roman Empire. The Nubians made another attempt to take Qasr Ibrim, according to Roman sources, but Petronius was able to stop them. But here, we find a contradiction between the two sources. In the Stele erected at Fort Qasr Ibrim the Nubians claim military victory. After the battle the Queen then sent messengers to speak directly with the "King" of Rome. Both sides affirm the validity of this event. Petronius sent the messengers to Caesar in Syria, where they negotiated a successful peace. In the year 21/20 B.C. a peace treaty was signed, but the terms are strangely favorable to the Nubians. The treaty signed by the Romans, relinquishes their control of Qasr Ibrim, and the Romans extricated themselves from the region entirely (militarily) and removed themselves from their own southern border. The Southern Part of the Thirty Mile Strip, including Primis was evacuated by Rome. And the Nubians were exempted of having to pay any tribute. The agreement seems to alter the boundaries of the Roman Empire, in terms that would have been favorable to the Nubians. The Romans continued to occupy Dodekashoinos as a military border zone, but the new frontier of the Nubian Empire, was near Hiere Sycaminos (Maharraqa). After this violent back and forth, the relationship between the two titans became cordial. Following the treaty, technology is also transferred to the Nubians, in the form of the water wheel or sakia. Prior to the water wheel, Nubian agriculture was limited to areas surrounding the Nile (although this idea is being reconsidered). Water could not reach the rocky highlands away from the Nile which is why the highlands were not suitable for farming. But facilitating the irrigation of the higher fields, increased the population potential in places that were inhospitable before. After the treaty, there is an increase in the settlement of lower Nubia, and there is a noticeable rise in the economic prosperity of the region. Numerous villages with well furnished houses were established for populations living in relative opulence. There is even evidence of Roman merchants moving into Nubian cities, and living peacefully among the Nubians. The events are even more confusing when we consider that, both of Rome's Emperors, Nero and Augustus though separated in time, were both clear about their desire to conquer the Nubian kingdom, which served as a bottle neck for trade. (We know from the historical record that several decades prior to the incident with Candace, in 66-64 B.C. The Emperor Nero began drafting plans to conquer Kush). Augustus complicates our understanding of the event, even further by ordering his administrators to collaborate with the priesthood of Kush in the construction of the Temple at Dendur (15 B.C). In the Temple, Augustus is depicted as celebrating the local Nubian gods. The deities are two youths, Pahor and Pedese who were the sons of an elite local Nubian ruler. The two drowned in the Nile River, but were reimagined as divine heralds. A cult formed around worshiping the two youths. The temple also served as the cenotaph (an empty tomb, built when remains are unrecoverable). We must ask why a purportedly unprovoked attack, produced such respect for local customs and the state religion. Why would the Emperor of Rome, depict himself joyously celebrating the foreign gods of a hostile power? The most likely explanation, for these contradictions, seems to be that the Romans and Nubians found peace to be mutually beneficial. Some sources report that Amanirenas may have lost her son Akinidad in the war with Rome. The Candace, having tasted Roman might, was probably convinced that an all-out conquest of Egypt, was impossible (if it was even her desire in the first place). Rome, having experienced the Kushite appetite for war, may have been dissuaded by the back and forth, and was probably convinced that Kush was also an unlikely, albeit desirable acquisition. The truth of victory, probably lies in between the Nubian account, and the Roman perspective, both of which claim victory. We cannot be sure of which account to believe, but we do know that after the conflict, the relationship between the two regional giants was friendly, and despite its earlier desire, Rome would never again attempt to conquer Kush (Ethiopia).

THE FALL OF KUSH

Theories abound, regarding the fall of Kush. Some scholars blame incompetent leadership, which was exemplified by the reign of Sect Lie. In the Kushite culture, the morality of the leader was paramount. As the head of state, and a crucial pillar in the faith of the people, leaders were to be admired for their piety. The final king of Kush, Sect Lie was known for his insatiable lust for women and wealth. His behavior was so contemptible that historians believe that he was removed from the throne. This political instability may have contributed to the decline in Meroitic civilization. The historical record also includes a report from Rome. It indicates that after extricating itself from the northern most positions in Nubia, in 272 A.D., a mysterious group known as the Blemmyes began to pressure the Roman border, with raids and costly assaults. We know very little about the Blemmye, although Roman accounts vacillate between describing them as monstrous and begrudgingly recognizing them as formidable. In Roman legends, they are described as a tribe of monsters. The illborn beasts were rumored to have eyes and mouths that were in their chests. Pliny the Elder wrote that "the Blemmyes have no heads", and their "mouth and eyes are put in their chests". However, this is probably an example of how a capable foe is maligned in the historical records of those with whom they contend. The Blemmyes were a Nubian tribe, who may have also had Arab origins. They lived in the regions between the Nubian city of Meroe and Aswan, and by 197 A.D, they became so formidable that Pescennius Niger would court them (a Roman who coveted the throne). They would continue to threaten to invade the empire, at times forcing the roman army to withdraw from entire regions. The remnants of their culture contradict the Roman reports of a naked, and primitive people, as Meroitic culture heavily influenced them. The Blemmyes lived in fortified cities, with walls, towers, and architecture that displayed Egyptian, Helenisitic, Roman, and Nubian accents. However they began, the cities they built were dramatic demonstrations of progress (Faras, Balana, Kalabasha, and Aniba). Despite the claims of their warlike status, and the monstrous mythologies propagated by scholars like Pliny the Elder, other scholars like Strabo described the Blemmyes as a peaceful group, in the Eastern Desert. Whatever the truth may be, in 297, the Roman Emperor Diocletian would seek the help of another group called the Noba in fighting the Blemmyes. He invited the Noba, into the region with an offer to build cities for them that would vastly improve their lives, if they would fight off the Blemmyes for him. We learn from an inscription by Silko, The Prince of the Nobatae (the Noba) that they fought off the Blemmyes and forced them into the eastern deserts. The Noba effectively complied with the emperor's request, but the promised cities never came. The Emperor did allow the Noba to worship their Gods at Philae, but the Romans would do little else to support the new immigrants. In fact, the Emperor Justinian would eventually tear down Philae. If we believe the Roman accounts, this is how the Noba; the group that would become the descendants of the Kushite culture, came into the region. Scholars suggest that the nomadic Noba settled right in the cities of the Kushites. This influx, may have overburdened a politically unstable Kushite culture, and caused its collapse. The Noba, would benefit greatly from living amongst the urbane culture of the Nubians. They would learn skilled crafts, construction, and an appreciation for a settled existence which would compel them to give up their nomadic ways. In time this culture would evolve further, into a form called the Ballana Culture by historians. Scholars call this society "a culture in transition". It was growing in its complexity. It clearly demonstrates that skills the Noba acquired from the Kushites were being put into practice. And most importantly, as it only lasts from 350-600 **A.D.**, the culture was temporary. The Noba would transcend this state of evolution, and the culture in-flux, would emerge, as the descendants of Meroitic Kush, in a civilization known to history as Christian Nubia.

CHRISTIAN NUBIA: Indomitable Heirs of Kush

" It is a large city in the banks of the blessed Nile, and contains many churches and large houses and wide streets"

Ibn Salim Al- Aswani
10th Century Egyptian Diplomat to Nubia

The Noba descendants of Nubian Kush would not fade into the backdrop of history. They would carry the considerable accomplishments of their forebearers into the future by building another great civilization. Byzantine styled architecture, with grand houses of worship are a testimony to the civilization. Remnants of their libraries, rich jewelry, clothing, and weapons are all that remain of Christian Nubia. Archeologists have demonstrated that the inhabitants of the Christian kingdoms lived a high quality of life, in the three Kingdoms that make up Christian Nubia (Makuria, Nobatia and Alwa). Intricate crowns of gold and silver, were studded with jewels by artisans that endeavored to blend the artistic conventions of Nubian Meroe, with a new Byzantine styled

Nubian culture, joined through faith, to the larger Christian world. This generation of Nubians built large fortified cities, and small towns, many of which possessed column filled Christian cathedrals. The Byzantines facilitated the conversion of the Nubians to Christianity, and influenced the style of architecture and art in Christian Nubia. The Nubians built numerous monasteries of tremendous size, engaged in ample trade, and enjoyed a fully civilized and often wealthy existence. They built a Romanesque Nubian kingdom with learned bishops and libraries that challenge our preconceived notions about African civilization. We should understand that Christian Nubia was intimately engaged with the larger world. As a trading kingdom, Nubians received goods from all over the world. They were allied through faith with the Christian powers of their day, although in time they became far removed from them. There were Nubian participants in the crusades, and by all accounts Christian Nubia possessed an admirable military. The union of African nations with the broader world of Christendom resulted in black Africans living in Europe and European civilizations. Some black Africans even attained fame and renown in Europe. Saint Maurice is often reported to be an Egyptian but in virtually every physical depiction of the knight, he is unmistakably depicted as a black African. St. Maurice led the 6,600 soldiers of the Roman Theban Legion. He was martyred and elevated to the status of a saint, celebrated by the Coptic Orthodoxy, professional guilds and particularly in Germany. He represents the movement of Africans outside of Africa through its affiliations with the Christian world. There were three separate Christian kingdoms in classical Nubia. The kingdoms were called Nobatia, which was the northern most Nubian kingdom; Makuria which was south of Nobatia; and south of Nobatia, in the center of the old Meroitic kingdom was Alodia, the wealthiest of the Nubian kingdoms (Alwa in some sources).

CHRISTIAN NUBIA IN HISTORY

Christian Nubia, was contemporary with the Byzantine Empire (a continuation of the Roman Empire), and was also contemporary with the Sassanid Persian Empire. Since the days of Alexander- the Great, Persia had been one of the world's most advanced civilizations. Its grand cities, and sumptuous palaces were legendary in the west, and its military prowess was equally astounding. Christian Nubia existed in a power packed timeframe of major empires. And yet the collection of Nubian kingdoms accomplished a feat that seemed to be beyond the capabilities of both the Byzantines, and Persians. The Nubians would stand in the face of one of the mightiest armies in history, and would score a stunning victory against the Rashidun army of Islam. Historically, the Muslim army would dominate the middle east, and smash through the mighty Persian Empire. The Muslims would push back the Roman Byzantine Empire, conquer much of North Africa, and take Egypt as well. Their incredible series of conquests was called by convert and infidel alike, the Muslim Miracle. The Muslims, having vested the mightiest armies of their time, seemed poised to conquer much of the world. They were nearly undefeated when they arrived in Nubian Territory, and they believed that they were heading towards another fated victory. But the Muslim Miracle would come to a dramatic end, in Nubia. When the battles ended, the Muslims would find their forces severely battered, and they would be forced to sign an agreement for peace that still stands as one of the world's longest lasting treaties of peace.

THE BATTLE FOR DONGOLA

In 632 A.D., following the death of their Prophet Muhammad, the Armies of Islam would erupt out of the Arabian Peninsula undertaking a 24-year conquest, that would build one of the largest empires the world had ever witnessed. The wars would begin under the Rashidun Caliphs, as an effort to put down apostasy. The Rashidun Caliphs were the first four consecutive leaders of the Muslim Community, after the death of Muhammad. The humble kings of early Islam, lived in modest homes, met with their Muslim brothers in humble surroundings, and for these reasons were called the "rightly guided" caliphs. But after the death of the Prophet, the rightly guided leaders would be forced to contend with Muslims that were quickly going astray. New prophets were cropping up, with new revelations, and laying claim to authority over the Islamic community. Some Arabs, whose capitulation to Islam was made for political expedience would renounce their faith, and some were now refusing to pay the Jizya-or mandatory tribute payments. These new prophets, and the string of Arab renunciations, threatened to destroy the unity of the Muslim community. The first wars were intended to bring Muslims back into alignment with the original intent of Muhammad's message, but they would not stop there. The Muslims would spread their message of Islam to Syria, Persia, Europe and Roman controlled Byzantium by force. The fame of their conquests would abound as word of their strength spread. They endeavored to communicate to the whole world that victory for the Muslims was swift, decisive and guaranteed by god. The victories themselves, over the world's most powerful armies, were looked upon by the Muslims and the targets of their aggression, as miraculous. Many would convert to the religion based on the decisiveness of the Muslim victories. Many potential converts reasoned that if no one could stand against them, god must be with the Muslims. The Islamic Rashidun Army would communicate to much of the world that resistance meant certain destruction, whereas capitulation meant mercy and tolerance. In this era, Islam was known as a tolerant faith that permitted those living under its dominion, greater freedom than most other regimes. Having witnessed the military might of the Muslims, the Egyptians would offer very little resistance. In fact, the Coptic Christians believed that they would fare better under the rule of Muslims, then they had under the less tolerant Chalcedonian Christians of Roman Byzantium (633 A.D). Despite, the impression given by a doctrine of conquest, early Islam was regarded as a progressive faith, even by those they conquered. In 642, after receiving very little resistance in the conquest of Egypt, the Muslims believed conquest of Christian Nubia would be an easy affair. They proceeded south with an army of 20,000 cavalry-a tremendous force for the time, under the direction of Uqba bin Nafe, a great Muslim general. The first wave of attacks was meant to test the defensive capacity of the Nubians. Quick sporadic raiding parties would pester towns. This commonly used opening salvo however, was a mistake. The Nubian kingdoms had already been receiving refugees from the Muslim conquest of Egypt. The raids simply served as additional warning, and an increased opportunity to prepare for the impending battle. When the full forces of Uqba entered the region, they found that the Nubians were fierce warriors. Uqba himself, mentions that when he came upon an assemblage of Nubian Warriors, they engaged immediately and shot the Muslims directly in their eyes, with superb archery from their bow and arrows. In this one rapid attack, Uqba would lose 250 men. The Nubians, it would seem, were excellent horseman, and (like their Kushite predecessors) were exceptionally accurate archers. The Muslims, were fond of leather armor, and were protected from head to toe, with only their eyes, susceptible to penetration. The Nubians would seize on this single vulnerability in the Muslim armor, and target the eyes of the Islamic invaders with marksman like precision, in each of their confrontations with the Arabs. The Muslims would refer to the Nubians as the "Pupil Smiters". The Nubians would avoid prolonged battles, preferring instead to target the eyes of their enemies during rapid exchanges, and quick moving assaults. The Nubians would abandon entire towns, fill them with mud and flammable materials, and when the Arabs arrived, the Nubians would launch flaming arrows trapping the Muslim army. The Arabs would complain that the Nubians were using ambush tactics, which ironically had been the hallmark of the Muslim military. The Arabs would penetrate all the way up to the Nubian capital at Dongola before being forced out of the region entirely, through bloody attacks. The Muslim general Uqba would write back to his cousin Amr, and confess his losses to the "pupil smiters". He would leave Nubia in shame and defeat. It should be noted that Uqba would go on to claim that the land of the Nubians was not worth conquering, after his defeat. This event is known in history as the First Battle of Dongola, and despite the somewhat suspicious claim about the quality of Nubian lands, it would not be the only assault attempted by the Muslim army. At the Second Battle of Dongola, the Arabs would again launch a campaign to take possession of the "poor" quality land of the Nubians. This time, in 652, they would bring a catapult, and 5000 more men. The general this time, was Abdullah ibn Sa'ad and he would face a newly United Kingdom of Nobatia and Makuria, under King Qalidurat. Once again, the Muslims would drive right to the seat of the Nubian capital, at Dongola. They would even damage the Nubian cathedral. But, they would again, suffer a devastating loss. An Arab poet who witnessed the battle wrote that:

"My eyes ne'er saw another fight like Damqula, With rushing horses loaded down with coats of mail."

According to additional sources, the armies of Islam had never suffered such a catastrophic loss. It seems that the Nobatian archers were now supplemented with cavalry from the south, in Makuria (or Alwa). And the result of the cumulative effort was tragic for the Muslims. They would be forced to withdraw, and offer the Baqt treaty. The treaty establishes an agreement that the Muslims, would never again attempt to conquer Nubian lands by force. In the doctrine of early Muslims, there was a compulsion to bring all land under the submission of Islam. The Baqt treaty was unlike any other document of its time, because it acknowledges a non-Muslim power's right to exist, and establishes trade, on equal terms among a Christian nation and the Muslims, for the first time in history. The Nubian Kingdoms, unlike all other previously encountered lands and people, would be off limits for conquest. The treaty would also normalize free trade between the two nations of opposing faiths. They would trade as equals, and offer mutual tributes. This mutual exchange, between former enemies was a common African custom, used after wars as a demonstration of mutual respect. The Nubians would send a set number of slaves, and the Muslims would return wine, and an array of goods. For the first time in Islamic history, there was a middle ground, between the compulsion to spread Islam, and the reality that not all lands could be easily conquered. A precedent was set for trade as equals as opposed to trade as subordinates between Christians and Muslims. Our minds can race considering the effect this had on the world, and how it may have inspired other Christian Nations. May it have altered the mindset of the Muslim conquerors? How this treaty may have changed the world, can only be speculated. The Baqt treaty resides in history, as one of the longest lasting peace treaties in human history, as it lasted 600 years. The Muslims would choose to live in peace with their formidable Christian neighbors, and despite the claims about the quality of Nubian land, Muslims merchants would migrate into the area, and move into Nubian cities. And as opposed to utilizing conquest, Arabs would marry into Nubian families, and slowly convert the region through more passive means.

CHRISTIANITY COMES TO THE NUBIANS

All faiths must contend with divisions in doctrine, as differences in opinions and heresies will inevitably arise. Just as the early Muslims, were forced to curb the growth of apostasy, early Christians also found it necessary to correct the tendency for error in the far-flung churches of Christendom. The mechanism for their correction were Ecumenical Councils, in which the church bishops of the entire Christian world would meet to settle matters of doctrine. Those who could not accept the "infallible" ruling of the Council, and ultimately of the Pope, were deemed heretics, and would usually break off from the "one true church" and establish their own separate sect of Christianity. The remaining bishops and their followers would work to spread the authoritative rulings of the councils as apostles of the Christian faith. In 451 (October 8-November 1), the fourth of these ecumenical councils, known as the Council of Chalcedon would meet to reconcile a variety of doctrines regarding the nature of Jesus Christ. Ultimately the council would issue its "infallible" decree regarding the "full humanity and full divinity" of Jesus. Those who accepted the ruling were called Chalcedonians or Melkites and would work to bring all believers in Christ in line with the church's ruling. Those who rejected the Council were called Monophysite or Non-Chalcedonians, as they believed that

Jesus was purely divine, and possessed only a single nature. It seems that the distinction was not as significant as the passionate advocates may have believed at the time. Today, the two camps are in regular communion with one another, and have resolved that the issue that caused the initial schism, may have largely resulted from misunderstandings of language and translation. The two sides may have even been answering different questions. It may have been that the schism resulted over the translation of the words "nature" versus "person". Whereas one side felt it was asking if Christ is one person, the other felt that it was asking if he had one nature. The issue, to modern eyes seems purely academic, especially because most scholars believe that the two creeds have the same meaning. Irrespective of how small their differences may have been, the sects would energetically compete for adherents. The battle for souls, which divided even the Byzantine Emperors at times, was fierce and would head south, into Nubian lands. Per some sources, the Byzantine Empress Theodora delayed the departure of the Chalcedonian monks heading toward Nubia, to give the Monophysite priests a head start. If this happened, it worked. The record of John of Ephesus is often sighted, with some controversy, that in 545 A.D., under the influence of a priest called Julian, the Kingdom of Nobatia, would lean towards the Non-Chalcedonian belief. He similarly states that the southernmost kingdom of Alodia would also adopt the Monophysite belief system. The delay in travel, did not win the entire day for the Empress, as it seems that Makuria, had accepted the Chalcedonian doctrine of the Byzantine Empire, and was already (according to John of Ephesus) quite hostile to the monophysites. This account is not entirely accepted, as some documents suggest that Makurian conversion to the Monophysite faith of the Coptics came later (in 719 A.D). The importance of this, is that we see that Nubia factored in the major decisions and movements of their day. We see that the known-civilized world, was not simply aware of the Nubian kingdoms, but competed fiercely for their support.

THE ORIGIN OF CHRISTIAN NUBIA

While the minutia of faith and religion may seem like small matters, when studying an African Civilization, they were truly consequential for the kingdoms of Christian Nubia. Faith gave form to the Nubian kingdoms. After the fall of Kush, the Nubians continued many of the habits of their Kushite predecessors, and formed (what researchers called) the Ballana Culture. The Ballana culture was a temporary transitional culture, between Nubian Kush and Christian Nubia. It was essentially a phase that maintained many of the cultural habits and skills of Nubian Kush, but altered their form. Once the Nubians were converted to Christianity, the form of Nubian culture changed again. They continued to build cities and settlements, and develop their civilization, but as Christians, the Nubians would now reflect the influence of their new religion. They would now build churches instead of temples in nearly every town. The new houses of worship would reflect the influence of the Byzantines, whose ministry they accepted. Byzantine style churches would spring up in every town of Nubia. The result, is a civilization that obviously accepted cues from the Christian World around it. Roman style frescoes would adorn the homes of citizens. Some scholars have used these cultural accents to deride the civilization, and have questioned its African authenticity. Some have again attempted to bestow credit for the civilization to the priests that ministered in the area. We must acknowledge the strong influence of Byzantine Culture on the architecture, and artistic norms the Nubians adopted. However, the acceptance of the Christian faith cannot be used to deny the

Nubians credit for the development of their own civilization. The priests that entered the region were converting Kings, and nobles in the Nubian court. The subjects of their ministry were the descendants of one of the world's great empires. As the descendants of Nubian Kush, they learned the skills of their ancestors, built cities of stone, and even during the Ballana Culture's timeframe were a developing and sophisticated people. As a testament to the continuity of the Ballana Culture, with Nubian Kush, the Ballana crown would continue the motif of the cobra on the Nubian crown. It is true that the Nubians were influenced by the adoption of the Christian faith, and built architecture and art within the norms of their adopted religion, but it should not raise doubts about the indigenous impulse for civilization. Instead of building Nubian style temples, or Ballana structures, the Nubians began to build Byzantine style churches. Instead of viewing this as mimicry, we should acknowledge that they simply built houses of worship, in the "proper" way, according to their faith. In some cases, they simply converted old Nubian temples into new churches. The Nubians were not xenophobes, and readily accepted the input of outsiders. They were not divorced from the world around them, and the art and architecture they produced reflect these facts. The demand that the Nubians maintain architecture, art, language, and culture that is totally uninformed by the foreign faith they adopted is a standard that is not applied to other civilizations. To ignore the influence of the outside world, while intimately engaging with the world's other cultures, Africans would have literally had to stick their heads in the sands of the Nubian desert.

THE GOLDEN AGE OF CHRISTIAN NUBIA

While the Nubians were Christians, the Golden Age of their Christian civilization would coincide with the prominence of Islamic Civilization. After the Muslim conquest of Egypt, the Nubians would be cut off from the rest of Christendom. The Nubians were converted to Christianity in 545 A.D., and they would continue to prosper as the ties to their Christian brethren grew. After the Muslim conquest of Egypt, and the subsequent crushing defeat of the Muslims at the hands of the African Christians, the Muslims would sign a peace and trade treaty with the Nubians that would usher in an unprecedented, 500-year Golden Age that would see Nubia rise as a regional power. Nubian painting, architecture and pottery evolves significantly during this period. Nubia would grow exponentially between 750 A.D.- 1150 A.D. Prosperity however, would come at a cost. Segregated by distance from the rest of Christendom, Nubia, and its religion (along with the similarly Christian Abyssinia) would drift apart from the rest of the Christian world. They would develop ideas and religious practices that would have seemed strange and foreign to other Christians. However divergent their practices became, the Nubian adherence to Christianity would remain sincere. It is important to understand how Africa, and its empires factored into the complex politics and international affairs of the ancient world. During the Golden Age of Nobatia and Makuria, a Muslim Caliphate called the Fatimids ruled Egypt. They came to power by deposing the previous Islamic Dynasty. The Fatimids were Shia Muslims, while most of the world's Muslims were Sunni. The difference between the two sects lies in who the appropriate successor to the Prophet Muhammad should have been after his death. As Shi'ites, they had few allies in the Muslim world, and would forge ties with Christian Nubia

to create alliances that would protect them. At some time
between 969-973 A.D. The Fatimids, would send the
renowned historian, Ibn Salim Al-Aswani on a diplomatic
mission to Nubia. He would travel specifically to Makuria.
His mission began almost as soon as the Fatimids came to
power in 969 A.D. He was chosen because he was a native
to the Aswan and consequently, he was familiar with the land
and the Nubians. He travelled with a large accompaniment
of Muslim followers and was apparently charged with the
task of encouraging the Nubians to convert to Islam. When
he arrived in Nubian territory, King George II of Makuria
received him in his capital, Dongola. The intrepid diplomat
read a letter from Jawhar, the Fatimad Governor which
invited the Nubian king to embrace Islam. The letter also
strongly suggested that King George forward the required
payment of slaves in accordance with the Baqt treaty. In his
response, the King did not accept Islam, but instead he
invited Jawhar to embrace Christianity. He also stated his
intention to honor the Baqt as his ancestors had, but the
King conveyed that Nubia was also quite prepared to stand
against a military assault from Egypt. The defiance of the
Nubian King and his willingness to state plainly his
confidence in the military capacity of his army, is telling. The
friendly relationship of cooperation that followed is also
compelling. While in Makuria, Ibn Salim, recorded his
observations about Nubia. His first-hand account was
recorded in the Kitab Akhbar al Nubah wa- al Murqurrah
wa Alwa-al-Burjah wa-al-Nil, or the "Reports on Nubia,
Makuria, and Alwa". The text itself has disappeared from
history, however you can still read portions of it, in the "
Kitab al-Muqaffa, translated The Great Chronicle of Egypt,
and in "Kitab al-Mawa'iz, The Book of Wisdom written by
al-Maqrizi. Readers can also look to the Kitab al Fayad, or
The Book of Greatness by Minufi. The account is also
preserved by a Swiss traveler named Johann Ludwig
Burckhardt who immortalized Ibn Salim's observations.

Despite Burckhardt's Swiss origins, he was a faithful Muslim who travelled extensively throughout the Islamic world. He even traveled to Mecca because attending the Hajj enhanced his credibility as a Muslim and made a future trip to Africa's Timbuktu possible. Burckhardt is the explorer responsible for discovering the famed ruins of Petra (one of the 7 wonders of the world). We learn from the accounts of Ibn Salim and the sources that record his journey that Dongola, *"was a large city on the banks of the blessed Nile, and contains many churches and large houses and wide streets. The king's house is lofty, with several domes built of red brick, and resembles the buildings in Al-Irak (Iraq)"*. There were of course also modest accommodations with houses made of mud, reeds, or straw (a very common use for materials and in keeping with the rest of the ancient world. Medieval Europe referred to the same building materials as "wattle and daub". Today these materials are enjoying a resurgence as a sustainable building material). Ibn Salim remained in Dongola for an extended period. The diplomat also describes Alwa but most historians don't consider his observations to be a firsthand account. It is more likely to be a compilation of accounts from other travelers. The result of Salim's mission was cooperation, economically prosperous trade, and friendship between the Nubians and the Fatimad's. The Nubians would provide the Fatimad's with much of the manpower that made up much of their military and administration. The Nubians would also export ivory, cattle, ostrich feathers and other valuable products. The Fatimads would reciprocate the trade, sending wheat, wine, and linens. The relationship was mutually beneficial, and grew to be quite intimate. When the Fatimad Caliphate was deposed in 1169 by the Turks and the Turkish Ayyubid Dynasty, the Nubians would invade Egypt in support of their allies. This action would bring the Nubians face to face with one of history's most phenomenal generals; Saladin the founder of the Ayyubid Dynasty and eventual Sultan of

Egypt. Saladin began his career in Egypt as a general, primarily responsible for the defeat of the Crusader armies. The events that led to his clash with Christian Nubia and the black soldiers protecting the Fatimad Caliphate make an epic tale. Saladin came to Egypt to serve the Fatimad Caliph as an advisor. Despite his religious affiliation as a Sunni Muslim, Saladin was so skillful as a general that the Caliph selected him to be the Vizier (chief advisor) of his Shia government. Saladin would cultivate a deep friendship with the Caliph-al-Adid. Once he earned the Caliphs trust and was appointed as vizier, he conspired to destroy the Fatimad dynasty. The Fatimad dynasty maintained a strong contingent of black Africans in their military and black eunuchs as administrators in their government. One of the most trusted black eunuchs in the Fatimad government was Mu'tamin al-Khalifa. In some sources, he is reported to have held command over the Caliph's entire court. He learned of Saladin's plot to undermine the Fatimad Caliph and took steps to stop the traitorous vizier. He was determined to remove Saladin from his post, in service to his Caliph. There is some confusion in the history between sources but in The Chronicle of Ibn-al-Athir, we find the most compelling narrative. Mu'tamin conspired with native Egyptians and a Jewish scribe to send letters to the Crusader armies, soliciting an alliance which would invite the Crusader army into the country to counter Saladin and his forces. Saladin intercepted the letters, tortured a confession out of the scribe and sent assassins to execute the eunuch. The assassins tracked Mu'tamin to the village of al-Kharqaniyya. Outside of the protection of the palace, the eunuch was easily captured. Saladin's men severed his head and sent it to Saladin. Saladin promptly replaced Mu'tamin with a "white eunuch" and purged the court of all the black eunuchs who managed the affairs of the kingdom. When the black infantry that served as the backbone of the Fatimad army learned of the execution, they marched against Saladin in a rare act of racial solidarity (jinsiyya which means nationality). The two armies met in Old Cairo. In between the two grand palaces of the Fatimad Caliph and his Vizier, 50,000 black soldiers would engage Saladin's army. The battle raged in the streets as the Caliph al-Adid watched from the roof top. Victory in this urban setting was uncertain for both sides. But instead of reinforcing his troops on the street, Saladin, the supreme strategist, sent troops to al-Mansura which was the separate housing district of the black soldiers and their families. When Saladin's men arrived in the black quarter of town, they set fire to the entire neighborhood and slaughtered the wives and children of the black soldiers, in the middle of the fight in Cairo. When intelligence sources reported the news of the massacre to the black soldiers, they were distracted from the battle. Despite learning of the demise of their families, the warriors persisted in their fight. The fearless black regiments fought valiantly, while the Caliph al-Adid himself watched the fight from above, still unaware of Saladin's plot. He is recorded by Arab historians to have looked on saying: "Beware of the Black Slave Dogs! Drive them from the country!" When word of the Caliph's feelings reached the black soldiers, this final betrayal was sufficient to sap their strength. The two sides convened and terms were set for a withdrawl. Once the black soldiers departed from Cairo and dispersed to recover the remnants of their children and families, Saladin broke his vow and sent his brother to attack the disbanded army. He boasted of killing all the black soldiers but a handful of "fugitives". In history, Saladin is known primarily for the mercy he showed the Crusaders and his refusal to punish them after defeating their armies. Saladin did not show the Nubians the same kind of mercy. He purged the kingdom of blacks (much like Esarhaddon purged Nubians after his defeat of Taharqa) and removed them from any posts in government. Saladin would wait until the death of the Caliph to take over Egypt and force its conversion from Shia Islam to Sunni Islam.

This conflict is known to historians as The Battle of The Blacks (also The Battle of the Slaves and The Battle of Cairo). It is important to pause and note that the compelling narrative we have just conveyed is not entirely settled as historical fact. While the Battle of the Blacks is completely established as a fact of history and the execution of Mu'tamin which caused it is also accepted as fact, the events that preceeded it are questioned. We must always remember that history is written by the victors and in this case, the winners were the Sunni Muslims and Saladin's dynasty. We have absolutely no verification of the excuses the Sunni historians have left for posterity. The infamous letters courting an alliance with the Crusaders were torn up by Saladin. The narrative that Saladin reported to Sunni historians seems to foment long held bigotries. The idea of an evil black eunuch courting the reviled crusaders with the assistance of a Jewish co-conspirator seems to play into the commonly held racial and religious hatreds of Saladin's time. The entire narrative could very easily be an after-the fact justification for Saladin's desire to purge blacks from the royal Fatimad court. It is entirely plausible that Saladin simply assassinated the black chief eunuch, purged the other black administrators of the Fatimad court and was forced to battle the black army of 50,000 soldiers in the streets of Cairo because of his personal war on blacks. It is also possible that this was not the racial drama that a name like the "Battle of the Blacks" might suggest. The Nubians were the Fatimad's most loyal allies. Saladin may have simply been pre-emptively eliminating the most loyal members of the opposition and race may have been irrelevant. When the kingdoms of Christian Nubia learned of the attack on the Fatimad Dynasty, they would support resistance movements and send troops to attack. Some of the black Fatimad soldiers that escaped the carnage found refuge and support in Christian Nubia. The Ayyubid leader, Saladin would rush to suppress Fatimad loyalists and re-establish order from an emerging chaos. He would then push the Christian Nubians back by sending his brother Turan Shah, to invade Nubia. He would hold an area called Qasr Ibrim for several years. Qasr Ibrim was a major city and excavation of the site revealed the largest collection of Nubian documents ever discovered. The city possessed the famed Castle of Ibrim, which was built on the ruins of an earlier Egytian-Kushite temple. It is imperative that we continue to recognize the continuity and evolution of Nubian civilizations, recognizing that one built upon the development of another. In the Castle of Ibrim, a stele has been uncovered which is believed to have been a temple structure depicting Taharqa the Nubian Pharaoh, making an offering to a god (it is now in the British Museum). This point is important because it again highlights the continuity between the Kushites and Christian Nubia. It puts to rest any claim or temptation we might have to argue that the Christian kingdoms developed because of their interaction with the European Christian world. These claims of European inspiration have often been used to deny Africans proper attribution for the creation of their own civilizations. Readers will find that later historians would make such claims a consistent theme when explaining away the former glory of African civilizations. In returning to the subject of the Castle of Ibrim, we can again observe the continuity in culture maintained by Christian Nubia that evolved from Nubian Kushite culture. Near the fortress are "rock-cut memorial" churches dedicated to the Viceroys of Kush. After several years, Turan Shah would retreat north, leaving Qasr Ibrim and claim once again that Nubian land was not worth conquering. The Nubians would remain the most faithful supporters of the Fatimads and their memory. In 1174, when Kanz al-Dawla (a title which means Treasure of the State) attempted a re-invasion of Cairo in the name of the Fatimads, the Nubians would still support the doomed effort. Ironically when this effort failed, the Nubian's embrace of the Fatimad loyalists would usher in the downfall of Christian Nubia. The Muslims would move into the Christian Nubian communities and usher in its conversion to Islam.

THE DOWNFALL OF CHRISTIAN NUBIA

The decline of Christian Nubia may have been a result of a confluence of causes. After the rise of the Ayyubids, the competing Muslim dynasty that displaced the Fatimad's, traffic to Christian Nubia seems to have slowed. We have very few accounts of travel. Trade continued in some form, and Muslim merchants continued to move into the area, even settling in the Nubian capital of Dongola. But according to the Muslim scholar Ibn Khaldun, Arabization from invading Bedouin Arab tribes, and intermarriage with them destroyed the nations of Nubia. The Ayyubids were troubled by Bedouin Arabs and would forcefully pressure them to move southward into Nubian territory. When the Bedouins came, the Nubians would fortify their cities to defend themselves. They would move their cities to higher elevation positions, and build their homes to be stronger structures, equipped with hiding places for the storage of valuable personal items. But these precautions could not stop the influx of tribes, and the Arabization that would follow. Ibn Khaldun is not a historian that lacks bias and we should consider his propensity for race based analysis in accepting this assessment. It borders on bigoted to declare inter-marriage with another group as the cause of the decline of Nubian civilization, but we must consider that the collision of lifestyles, mores, and religion caused a fatal fracturing of culture. In Arab Bedouin culture, the emphasis on the lineage of the father, could cause Nubians that married into Arab families to abandon their Nubian heritage and the way of life associated with it, in favor of their newly acquired Arab familial status. As Islam, and Arabism grew in the area, the prestige associated with being Nubian declined. Those with, or even those without, Arab heritage began to feel pressured to deny their Nubian heritage, or fabricate an Arab lineage. In this way, the Muslim scholar Ibn Khaldun is credible when he blames inter-marriage for the decline in Nubian culture and civilization. What the armies of Islam could not accomplish, peaceful and passive intermarriage achieved. Over time, the Nubian states would lose prominence and power. They would become increasingly subject to the Muslim regimes in Egypt, which would continue to make demands of the Nubians. The Baqt treaty would now become a burden instead of a benefit, and the responsibilities enumerated within it grew beyond the capacity of the Nubians to fulfill. The Muslim dynasties in the north would punish the unwillingness to abide by the terms in the Baqt treaty, and would attempt to place friendly rulers, still of the Christian persuasion, on the Makurian throne. Those rulers would not be well received and yet despite the rejection of these handpicked Christian leaders, the external puppeteers would go a step further and audaciously place a Muslim leader named Sayf al-Din Abdullah Barshambu on the throne. He attempted to convert the nation to Islam, and turned the Dongola Cathedral into a mosque. His actions provoked a civil war which was the end of Nubia until the Ottoman Empire consumed it.

ALWA

Deep in the heart of old Kushite territory, the Kingdom of Alwa would rise. We know very little about its origins, or the Noba who settled there. We do know, from Ibn Hawqal, that Alodia (Alwa) was the largest and wealthiest of the Nubian Kingdoms. Their territory was vast, and covered the distance from Ethiopia to the area of central Sudan formerly known as Kordofan. The nation would also convert to Monophysite Christianity when missionaries from the Byzantine Empire entered the region in the 6th century. Its prominence would last for 700 years, from approximately 500 A.D.-1200 A.D. Their decline would begin in the 13th century. The Nubians would try to stave off the death of their civilization, and according to al-Harrani, they would move their capital to Wayula. The sparse remainder of knowledge we have concerning Alwa is owed to the Mamluks, whose emissaries would visit the area, are report that the region was divided into nine rulers. In the 16th century, another African ethnic group called the Funj conquered the area. Soceity would churn further when Alwa would be incorporated into another African Kingdom called Sennar. The decline of the most remote kingdom in Christian Nubia was long, and would end with Alodia attempting to establish an independent Kingdom called Dongola.

AXUM
The Divine
Empire

Ethiopia is the home of one of the world's oldest continuous civilizations. It was once the home of one of the most powerful empires on earth. As one of Africa's great Christian nations, Axum once thrived as a cosmopolitan metropolis. Its navy allowed the empire to be immersed in trade throughout India and the Mediterranean. A visitor to Axum, at the height of its power would have found, Christians, Muslims, Buddhists, and Hindu's, living and working in its capital, which boasted a population of 60,000 people. The ruins which include tremendous monolithic towers and monumental architecture are scattered throughout Ethiopia as reminders of its glorious past. Axum and its fantastic royal courts were exposed to Christianity in approximately 42 A.D., but the kingdom did not officially convert until approximately 325-328 A.D. The kingdom abandoned its former Sun worshiping faith during the reign of a King called Ezana. This conversion is relatively early in the development of Christianity and it allowed Axum to become the first state in the world to affirm its faith on the face of its minted coins. Numerous versions of silver, gold, and bronze Axumite coins bear the cross upon which their Christian faith was based. King Ezana is also credited with officially destroying the Nubian Kingdom of Kush. The Axumite Empire is officially recognized as beginning in 400 B.C. and it achieves true prominence by at-least 100 A.D. But the history of civilization and of admirable kingdoms in Ethiopia is much older. The oldest evidence of high cultural achievement exceeds 5000 years. However, the Pre-Christian Era of Axum is not very well understood. Scholars and governments of the time recognized Axum as one of the most powerful kingdoms on earth. The Persian scholar Mani, listed Axum as among the world's four most powerful empires, in the company of Rome, China, and Persia. At one time, it was one of the world's largest and most prosperous trading empires. Its strong navy gave it dominance over the Red Sea's extensive trade routes. Spanning nearly 1.25 million square kilometers, the empire would cover most of modern Eritrea in Africa, southern Egypt, the north of Sudan, Ethiopia and Djibouti (on the Horn of Africa). It also possessed overseas territories in Yemen, and Saudi Arabia (southern regions). Its major cities were called Yeha, Hawulti, Matara, and Oohaito. Axum's city of Adulis, was world famous as the port from which its navy shipped goods throughout the ancient world. The empire would go through several iterations, assuming the names Axum, Abyssinia, and Ethiopia (by 400 A.D.). The Ethiopians recorded their history in a widely-translated text, called The Kebra Negast or The Glory of Kings. While the text does record the history of Axum, it blends, mythology and fact. One of the most popular fact based myths in the Glory of Kings, is the reign of Queen Makeda. The Kebra Negast goes to great lengths to identify Queen Makeda as the Biblical Queen of Sheba. The Axumites have based many of their beliefs on their connection to the Dynasty of Solomon. Their King Menelik I, the first born of Makeda, is believed by Ethiopians, to have been the son of Solomon. The Axumites also believe themselves to be in possession of the lost Ark of the Covenant. These beliefs are almost certainly false because the Queen of Makeda, lived 1500 years after the real Queen of Sheba. However, Makeda's status as the Queen of Sheba, while important to Ethiopians, is less important than the fact that she was a wealthy and powerful Queen in Ethiopia. The remains of her palace, and a fantastic bath are inspiring displays of grandeur, located in a city called Dungar. The Axumites, have left a wealth of evidence, that proves beyond all doubt their former status. Unfortunately, 97% of the former empire remains untouched by archeologists. One of the most distinctive remnants of the empire are its monumental obelisks or stele. An obelisk is a very tall, four-sided monument, capped with a pyramid. A modern example of an obelisk would be the Washington Monument, on the west end of the National Mall in Washington D.C. In the ancient culture of Ethiopia, the obelisks are rounded on the ends and not capped by pyramid shapes. The monumental structures, which date as far back as 5000 B.C are tremendous monoliths that endeavor to touch the sky as markers for the graves of Axum's extensive monarchy. We should pause and take notice of the fact that the most ancient of these structures (as previously stated, have been dated to 5000 B.C) may have been constructed almost 1800 years before the first Pharaoh unified ancient Egypt (3150 B.C). They are among the ancient world's most impressive structures. They are carved from pure granite, shaped and decorated -quite possibly by obsidian blades (which we use in modern surgery). They weigh up to 500 tons, and once erected, they are affixed atop a platform of stairs. Carving, erecting and stabilizing these massive monoliths is an engineering miracle that would challenge us today. The platforms lead to underground tombs, in which the bodies and extensive treasures of kings and royals were kept. Once again, we see monarchs that carry their wealth with them into the afterlife. The tombs consist of multiple rooms, built without mortar. The superbly laid slabs of stone which make up the tombs are tightly fit-seamless displays of Axumite masonry. One of the Axumite obelisks stretched 33 meters or 100 ft (9 stories) into the air. Another obelisk, stolen by the Italian government and erected in Rome, was 1700 years in age and reached a height of 24 meters or 72 feet (6 stories). The obelisks are intricately carved, with features that resemble doors and windows. It is believed by most scholars that the obelisks are abstract representations of Axumite palaces, which make them sky-scraping castles, allowing the dead to continue ruling into the afterlife.

THE ROCK HEWN CHURCHES OF LALIBELA

"I weary of writing more about these buildings, because it seems to me that I shall not be believed if I write more ... I swear by God, in whose power I am, that all I have written is the truth."
Francisco Alvares
Portuguese Priest -1520

Between the 12th and 14th Century, the Axumite King Lalibela would cement his place in history, and astonish the world, with a completely innovative method of construction. Lalibela was deeply spiritual, and at the time of the crusades, he endeavored to create an alternative destination for Christian pilgrims that were anxious to avoid the battle zone of the Middle East. He would dedicate himself to the creation of a new holy land or (as it came to be called) a "New Jerusalem" for Christians. To draw the pilgrims of the

Christian world, Lalibela endeavored to create astonishing monuments that would strike the Christian soul as inspired by God. Lalibela would construct grand cathedrals from solid stone, carving them right out of the volcanic rock of the Ethiopian highlands. No one understands precisely how the churches were constructed. Lalibela claimed that the angels carved the churches for him but it seems that Ethiopian artisans chiseled the external shape of the churches, right down to their platform bases first. Then the artisans would hollow out the interior, carving purely decorative support structures like columns, arches, and windows. The churches seem to be based on earlier Axumite buildings and previously existing constructions, as they possess all the necessary support and buttress features of real structures. The cathedrals even reflect the international posture of the empire, with eastern inspired window features, Hebrew Stars, Byzantine Eagles, and architectural elements that reflect the intimate interactions of Axum with numerous cultures. One of Lalibela's churches was built on top of an artificial lake, carved into a mountain side, with trap doors leading to the water below for baptisms. All of the churches are linked by subterranean tunnels for clergy to travel from one place of worship to another in perfect security and without detection, in case of attack. But the churches and the miles of tunnels that join them were not Lalibela's only achievement. Lalibela was sincere in his desire to create a literal New Jerusalem. He would copy the topography of the holy land, and transpose it onto the Ethiopian highlands. Entire rivers were carved into the Ethiopian landscape. Every measure was taken to make an exact copy of the holy land's natural features. Lalibela's blessed churches would serve as sanctified sights for the new worshippers. For a time, his plan would work. Christians longing to be buried on holy ground, or in need of miraculous healing, or those seeking absolution from sin, would pilgrimage to Ethiopia. It's important to note that in studying the rock cathedrals, we encounter a conflict between history and myth. Although Axumite written history credits the ruler Lalibela with the construction of the churches, it is unlikely that a single ruler was responsible for their construction. Archeology indicates that several rulers would have had to support the painstaking process of carving these structures from solid volcanic rock. The churches of Lalibela are all relatively close to one another. The most famous or perhaps the most striking of the churches, is The Church of St. George which is also called Bete Giyorgis. It is carved directly downward into a volcanic hill. From above, it becomes clear that the church is carved in the shape of the Axumite cross. We should consider the flawless precision required to shape this structure. In this method of construction, there are no second chances. Once material is removed, it cannot be placed back. The cross even follows the natural slope of the mountain. The church rests on a bed of massive stairs, with ramps for parishioners and clergy to walk down. The inside flaunts the cosmetic brilliance of the structure, as columns, arches, reliefs and frescos delight the eyes of visitors. Outside of the church is a trench designed for baptisms. The site of the church is stunning and still in use by beautifully costumed clergy, during carefully coordinated festivals and thousands of worshippers. In the north, is the largest monolithic church in the world. It is called Bete Medhane Alem. Pictures cannot do justice to the sheer mass of these structures, or the effort required to construct them. The churches are massive monuments to African creativity and skill. Also in the north is Bete Maryam, or The Church of St. Mary. It is ornately decorated, with stone cut roses, frescoes and Ethiopian styled scenes from the Old Testament. The Bete Golgatha is a church that is said to hold the tomb of Lalibela. The Salasee Chapel and the Tomb of Adam round out the northern churches. In the east are the Bete Abba Libanos, Bete Amanuek, Bete Gabriel- Rufael and Bete Merkorios. The churches are all meticulous in their construction and artistry. Among the first European visitors to these churches was the Portuguese priest Francisco Alvares. He concluded his writings on the churches with, "*I weary of writing more about these buildings, because it seems to me that I shall not be believed if I write more. I swear by God, in whose power I am, that all I have written is the truth.*" Today these churches are given an unofficial title as The Eighth Wonder of The World (an umbrella term that is used to describe buildings as impressive as the official 7 Wonders of the World). They still amaze travelers that can brave the journey to the remote highlands of Ethiopia. Tourists that make the journey confirm that the beauty of the churches compliments the colorful spirituality of the Ethiopian people and clergy. The town of Lalibela, which houses the churches, is the home of numerous festivals celebrating the Christian faith of the Ethiopian Church. Dramatic processions fill the streets, in the carefully coordinated activities that fill the calendar year. The traditional garb and robes of the priests are accented by dramatic, powerful crosses that are used to bless onlookers. The power of the Ethiopian kingdom may have waned, but the power of their religion is alive and well.

GONDAR: THE AFRICAN CAMELOT

Beautiful from its beginnings, Gondar, hope of the wretched, and hope of the Great! Gondar without measure or bounds! O dove of John; Gondar, generous-hearted, mother! Gondar, never bowed by affliction! Gondar with its merry name! Gondar, seat of prosperity and of savory food! Gondar, dwelling of King Iyasu and of mighty Bakaffa! Gondar, which emulated the City of David, the land of Salem! She will be a myth unto eternity!
Unknown Poet

In the wake of devastating attacks from the conquering armies of an Islamic warlord named Ahmed Gragn, the Ethiopian king Fasilides would build a picturesque capital that he and his successors would fill with romantic castles. Long before the advent of Islam, Axum/Abyssinia was a major power, immersed in trade, and exercising its influence in Arabia and throughout the region. Even, as the Muslim Empire became the dominant power in the region (and the world) Abyssinia remained a stronghold of Christianity, and a stubborn obstacle to Muslim dominance. Ahmed Gragn was a Somali General, intent on ending Abyssinian prominence. When he successfully attacked the nation, he displaced its rulers, and temporarily crippled the kingdom. Fascilides would restore what Gragn had hoped to destroy, when he established a new capital in the Ethiopian city of Gondar. The Castles of Gondar are an orgy of medieval beauty, set in a seemingly perfect Ethiopian countryside. They celebrate loudly the incredible accomplishments of Abyssinian culture. The city of Gondar, was founded by the Emperor Fasilidas, who, according to legend was lead to the site, by an angel of God. In other narratives, a mysterious buffalo, lead him to the site, while on a hunting trip. Fasilidas, was also influenced by an ancient prophecy, which said that the next capital would be founded in a city, whose name began with the letter G. The miraculous founding of Gondar is fitting for a city, whose surroundings are almost heavenly. Established between the lush hills of Ethiopia, Gondar rests at an altitude of 2300 meters, providing breathtaking views of much of the surrounding farmland, and the beautiful Lake Tana. Between 1635 and the 1640's, Fascilides would embark on an ambitious building campaign. The Castle of Fasilidas, is a striking architectural achievement. He would build seven churches, which included the famed St. mary's, as well as a 3-story stone pavilion, overlooking a sunken bath, in addition to several bridges. The grandeur of the capital would continue to grow under, Emperor Iyasu, the grandson of Fasilidas. Emperor Iyasu would continue to add stunning architectural achievements to Africa's Camelot. He would build a palace that his chronicler (in true Abyssinian fashion) would call "finer than the House of Solomon". While the chronicler was clearly making a comparison that he could never verify, or justify, it is true that Iyasu's Palace was remarkable for its beauty. The inner walls of the palace were layered with ivory, loaded with mirrored adornments, and painted with palm tree murals. The ceiling of the palace was covered in gold leaf and precious stones. Iyasu also built the Church of Debra Berhan Selassie, the Light of the Trinity. The exterior of the church, is deceptively modest, but it is on the interior that the source of the acclaim of the church becomes apparent. The Debra Berhan, is covered in religious murals of overwhelming intensity. Each wall of the building is dedicated to a different religious scene or historical event. On the ceiling are eighty angels, miraculously detailed and each with a different facial expression. They peer down on worshippers to provide a sense of infinite security and protection. On the southern wall are scenes of St. Mary; On the eastern wall is the life of Jesus; the western wall depicts important saints, like Saint George-who is depicted in red and gold, on a prancing white horse. Gondar, like Camelot, would be a seemingly picture perfect kingdom. The similarities continue and just as Camelot would suffer from scandal and intrigue, Gondar would also be threatened by treachery. The Emperor Iyasu would fall into a deep depression, because of the loss of his favorite concubine. His son would seize the opportunity to take the throne and assassinate his father. The son would in turn be murdered, and the future of Gondar would seem to be in peril. The tradition of glorious construction would continue however, under the Emperor Bakaffa, who would build a fine castle. His wife would add her own creation to the legacy of incredible constructions, when The Empress Bakaffa would also build a grand castle. Bakaffa would be succeeded by Iyasu II, who would attempt to live up to his namesake, by building a wide range of buildings and developing Ethiopia's northern and western hills. The city of Gondar would eventually reach a population of 60,000 people. In time, the prominence of the city would fall, as the glory of Abyssinia became an increasingly distant memory.

THE ORIGIN OF AXUM

The Origin of the Axumite Kingdom has always been mysterious and confused. The incredibly long, and well documented history of Ethiopian prominence and prosperity caused early scholars to argue that the Ethiopians were not an entirely African race. In fact, many scholars attempted to argue that Ethiopians, were black Caucasians! They found support for their theories in the language of the Ethiopians. Geez, the language of Ethiopia was thought to have been a Semitic language. Early scholars would argue that the Ethiopians and their long history of empire was the result of Semitic speaking immigrants that colonized Ethiopia. Scholars would repeat the familiar theme of denying Africans credit for their own achievements by arguing that Ethiopia was the result of colonization, and not indigenous genius. Early scholars chose the Sabaeans as the source of Ethiopian civilization. The Sabaeans came from a southern Arabian Kingdom in Yemen. Recent scholars have reconciled and removed old prejudices from our assessments of Axumite civilization. They have determined that the language of Geez is not a foreign language. It is entirely indigenous. They have also learned that the Sabaean root for Ethiopian civilization was not as deep as it once seemed. There may have been Sabaeans that lived-in

Ethiopia, but their presence would have been brief and would have been in the form of a small military encampment. We have come to realize that the Sabaeans had very little impact on Ethiopia. The true roots of Axum, are in civilizations like D'mt, which was an extremely sophisticated African Kingdom that predated the arrival of any Sabaeans. D'mt was a well-built necropolis or ritual center, surrounded by complex irrigation systems that fed extensive agricultural schemes. D'mt, which existed from 700-400 BC, was one of numerous pre-cursors to the Axumite kingdom that would eventually be unified under a single authority.

MIGHTY AXUM: THE DESTROYER OF KUSH

The presence of Rome was a boon for Axum's shipping industry, because the Roman Empire was a veracious consumer of African products, and Indian goods, both of which were transported through Axumite portals. The port city of Adulis placed Axum directly in between the markets for products and the supply of raw materials. Prior to the sea-trade, overland trade routes brought materials from the in-land regions of Africa, moved along the coast, and fed the appetites of Kush and Egypt. As a competing supplier of gold, ivory, and exotic animals, Axum would become an early rival to Kush. As the two powers struggled for economic dominance, they would become locked into a conflict that would lead Axum to bring about the end of the Empire of Kush. By 100 A.D., Axum had displaced the Kushites in trade and acquired land previously occupied by the Nubians. The Axumites would establish caravans to Egypt to bypass trade on the Nile corridor. A Roman document called the Periplus of the Erythraean Sea discusses the shift in Ivory consumption and export from the Kushite controlled Meroe, in favor of Axumite controlled Adulis. Axum's influence would continue to grow, and dominate trade on the Red Sea by 300 A.D. Eventually Axum would focus its military might on Kush, bring an end to its existence, and cause Kush to fade into obscurity. A stele records the deeds of King Ezana, who lead the military assault that silenced Kush forever. From the Inscription of Ezana, written in 325 A.D. we read:

"*Through the might of the Lord of All I took the field against the Noba (Nubians) when the people of Noba revolted, when they boasted and "He will not cross over the Takkaze," said the Noba, when they did violence to the peoples Mangurto and Hasa and Barya, and the Black Noba waged war on the Red Noba and a second and a third time broke their oath and without consideration slew their neighbors and plundered our envoys and messengers whom I had sent to interrogate them, robbing them of their possessions and seizing their lances. When I sent again and they did not hear me, and reviled me, and made off, I took the field against them. And I armed myself with the power of the Lord of the Land and fought on the Takkaze at the ford of Kemalke. And thereupon they fled and stood not still, and I pursued the fugitives twenty-three days slaying them and capturing others and taking plunder from them, where I came; while prisoners and plunder were brought back by my own people who marched out; while I burnt their towns, those of masonry and those of straw, and seized their corn and their bronze and the dried meat and the images in their temples and destroyed the stocks of corn and cotton; and the enemy plunged into the river Seda, and many perished in the water, the number I know not, and as their vessels foundered a multitude of people, men and women were drowned. . .And I arrived at the Kasu [Kush], slaying them and taking others prisoner at the junction of the rivers Seda and Takkaze. And on the day after my arrival I dispatched into the field the troop of Mahaza and the Damawa and Falha and Sera up the Seda against the towns of masonry and of straw; their towns of masonry are called >Alwa, Daro. And they slew and took prisoners and threw them into the water and they returned safe and sound, after they had terrified their enemies and had conquered through the power of the Lord of the Land. And I sent the troop Halen and the troop Laken and the troop Sabarat and Falha and Sera down the Seda against the towns of straw of the Noba and Negues; the towns of masonry of the Kasu which the Noba had taken were Tabito, Fertoti; and they arrived at the territory of the Red Noba, and my people returned safe and sound after they had taken prisoners and slain others and had seized their plunder through the power of the Lord of Heaven. And I erected a throne at the junction of the rivers Seda and Takkaze, opposite the town of masonry which is on this peninsula"*.

Many scholars consider this moment to be the end of the Kushite Kingdom, but if we read this document carefully we see that Kush was already significantly degraded as a culture and empire. It seems that Ezana is responding to a revolt among the Noba, who were an ethnic group that settled among the Kushites, and in the eyes of many scholars were so disruptive and taxing on Kushite culture that they destroyed the nation long before Ezana acted. It seems that the Noba were so firmly subject to Ezana's authority that the King resented their disobedience. Ezana's inscription sounds more like a police action to restore order, than a military assault on a rival empire. The status of Kush aside, this event seals the fate of Kush, and signals the absolute regional dominance of Axum. King Ezana cemented the fate of Kush through his use of force, but he also set the course of his own nation through his use of faith. In approximately 325 - 328 A.D. Ezana made Christianity the official religion of the state. The King was educated as a child by his slave Frumentius, a Greek Phoenician who ministered to the monarch, and ultimately led him to a sincere Christian faith. In the earliest days of its conversion, the union of faith would produce bonds between Rome and Axum that were more lasting than their economic interactions. The bonds of faith would produce an intimate relationship and numerous cooperative interactions between the two world powers. One such interaction tells the story of Axum's expansion of its influence into Arabia, with the cooperation of Rome.

AXUM'S CONQUEST OF ARABIA

In the year 550 A.D. a group of pagans in Arabia called the Omeritae began persecuting Christians on the Arabian coast, in Yemen. Located across the Red Sea, on the Arabian Peninsula near the East Coast of Africa, the Omeritae, were Hellenistic pagans, which meant that their gods were derived or influenced by the historic Greek deities. When news of the persecution reached Rome, the Emperor Justinian immediately sought the assistance of his ally, the Negus (King) of Axum. Rome and Axum were not merely intertwined through trade, a common faith joined them. The two rulers could not abide the slaughter of their fellow brothers in Christ. The two defenders of Christendom resolved that military action was necessary and beneficial. Rome donated ships, and the Negus ordered the construction of a new fleet as well. He also assembled an army that set sail for the journey which was approximately five days and five nights, across the Red Sea. The army which scholars suggest numbered over 100,000 men and included war elephants, wasted no time cutting down the villains, and killing the Omeritae king. The Axumites were already the dominant power in Red Sea trade, and were in effect one of the world's wealthiest and most powerful trading empires. Their relationship to Rome however, is often misunderstood. From the Roman perspective, Axum was considered an ally, and perhaps through the union of faith a proxy. The historical record confirms a strong bond, and instances of cooperation. However, from the Axumite perspective, as well as the perspective of Arab scholars both contemporary and those of the relevant time, Axum was a competing power to Rome. While, there were instances of cooperation, the Axumite state would strive for dominance, and independence not subservience. It maintained a strategic and economic relationship with Rome, but never accepted any semblance of subjugation. To the contrary, Axum was Rome's equal, and in many cases a rival, economically and in terms of military might. According to the Persian scholar, Mani, who lived during this time, four great empires dominated the world; Persia, China, Rome, and Axum. After the conquest of the Omeritae lands in Yemen, the Negus Ellestheaus of Axum, would install a Christian convert of Omeritae birth, by the name of Esimiphaeus, as the new King of the Omeritae. During his reign, the Emperor Justinian would again appeal to their common Christianity in his cause against the Persian Empire. He would ask the Axumites to leverage their control over the Red Sea silk trade (of which Rome was a major consumer) to squeeze the Persians out of the network. Realizing that the Romans purchased Indian silk through the Axumites, who obtained it from the Persians, Justinian was no longer interested in filling Persian coffers with Roman coinage, however indirectly it may have been. The Roman Emperor suggested that the Axumites should remove the Persians from the equation by obtaining silk directly from India. For Esimiphaeus, the proxy of the Axumite state, the Roman Emperor suggested a more direct course of action. He asked the newly crowned king to launch a full-scale invasion of the Persian Empire. Justinian even suggested a commander for the mission (Caisus, an exile responsible for the death of a relative of King Esimiphaeus). In the end, both requests were rebuffed, for logistical reasons and a lack of benefit for the Axumites. In the case of the invasion, Persia was covered by a great deal of desert, and they saw no benefit in conquering such inhospitable lands. This incident reveals the strategic nature of the Axumite relationship with Rome. When cooperation was mutually beneficial then partnerships were forth coming. However, when Rome's interests and Axum's interests were in conflict, not even the bonds of faith could compel acquiescence. Esimiphaeus would not reign for very long on the Arabian coast. The very army assembled by the Negus to install him, would remove the Omeritae, in favor of one of their own. They would choose a former Roman slave, named Abramus (also referred to as Abraha). Abramus (a.ka. Abraha) was an Abyssinian, who had shaken off the bonds of Roman slavery, to become involved in trade at the Axumite port city of Adulis. He would now be chosen as King, ruling over much of present day Yemen, while Esimiphaeus was imprisoned. The act of treachery would inspire the Negus to send two additional armies to Arabia to rescue Esimiphaeus. The first would kill its own commander and join Abramus in his mutiny. The second would be soundly defeated. The upheaval would strain the relationship between Axum and its newly acquired territory. King Abramus would not reinstate his payment of tribute to Axum until after the death of Negus Ellesthaeus. Abramus, the Axumite King of (part of) Arabia, would go on to become an important and infamous figure in the history of the Arabs, and memorable in the formation of Islam.

THE YEAR OF THE ELEPHANT

Like the Bible, the Koran serves a dual role, as a record of history, and an article of faith. If we study the document, with an eye towards its factual recollections, then like the Bible, it refers to events for which we can find more concrete sources that yield reliable descriptions of historical events. In the Koran, the central figure of importance is known to adherents of the Islamic faith as the Prophet Muhammad. If we treat him as a historical figure, it will become apparent that the events surrounding his life and the growth of his faith, were significantly impacted by black Africans generally and specifically by the African Empire of Axum. The great trading empire, with its territories on the Arabian Peninsula played a pivotal role in safeguarding the religion of Islam from persecution when the faith was in its infancy. In the Koran's Surat (chapter) 105, the circumstances surrounding the Prophet Muhammad's birth are retold. In these events, the Axumite Empire, plays a crucial, yet antagonistic role. The year of the Prophet Muhammad's birth is remembered as The Year of the Elephant in Islamic history. His birth coincided with an Ethiopian (or Axumite) invasion, so memorable that his birth is associated with the outcome of the battle. Abramus is referred to, in Arab sources as Abraha. He is often referred to as a viceroy of Axum, but he apparently took steps to elevate his status and re-brand himself as the historical King of Saba in Yemen (Saba-refers to an ancient and advanced civilization known as the Sabaeans who ruled the Arabian Coast). Abramus was sincere in his loyalty to his Christian faith. He ordered the construction of a church so fine that, according to legend, even the Roman Byzantine's admired it. The Cathedral at Sanaa was known as Al-Qulais to the Arabs in Sinai, and was a source of great pride for Abraha. It was designed to be so beautiful that it's majesty would woo non-believers and encourage conversions. During this time, the Arabs were still pagans, and were accustomed to making a spiritual pilgrimage to worship their idols in Mecca at the Kaaba (a habit they would continue after the advent of Islam). Today the Kaaba is the most sacred site in Islam. It is a complex of structures, but appears as a cube shaped, granite building. According to Islamic tradition, Abraham the father of Judaism, constructed the original building. In pre-Islamic Arabia, the site was so holy, that all feuds and outbursts of violence were suspended in proximity to the Kaaba. King Abraha was so proud of his new church that he offered it as an alternative to the Kaaba, for the Arab pilgrimage. Abraha sent an Arab named Muhammad Khuza'I to Mecca and to the Hijaz (a region in Western Saudi Arabia, which consists of Mecca, Medina, and other holy sites in Islam) to suggest that Abraha's church would be a better site for worship, because it would be pure from the worship and housing of idols. The events that followed were recorded in the Sirah Rasul Allah, which literally means the Life of the Apostle of God. A "Sirah" records the life of an individual; their birth, and their death. In the Sirah Rasul Allah, the life of the Prophet Muhammad is recorded. It records the occasion of the Axumite Abraha offering the pre-Islamic Arabs his grand cathedral as a destination for their pilgrimage (which it seems incited them to violence)

"With Abraha there were some Arabs who had come to seek his bounty, among them Muhammad ibn Khuza'I ibn Khuzaba al-Dhakwani, al-Sulami, with a number of his tribesmen including a brother of his called Qays. While they were with him a feast of Abraha occurred and he sent to invite them to the feast. Now he used to eat an animal's testicles, so when the invitation was brought they said, "By God, if we eat this the Arabs will hold it against us as long as

we live". Thereupon Muhammad ibn Khuza'I got up and went to Abraha and said, "O King, this is a festival of ours in which we eat only the loins and shoulders." Abraha replied that he would send them what they liked, because his sole purpose in inviting them was to show that he honored them. Then he crowned Muhammad ibn Khuza'I and made him Emir of Mudar, and ordered him to go among the people to invite them to pilgrimage at his cathedral which he had built. When Muhammad ibn Khuza'I got as far as the land of Kinana, the people of the lowland, knowing what he had come for, sent a man of Hudhayl called Urwa bin Hayyad al-Milasi, who shot him with an arrow, killing him. His brother Qays who was with him fled to Abraha and told him the news, which increased his rage and fury and he swore to raid the Kinana tribe and destroy the temple."

It is important to take note of the accurate information that can be garnered from this religious text. Abraha is clearly defined as a ruler with at-least limited influence deep into Arabia. He not only maintains the company of influential Arabs, but exercises the ability (and what he believes to be his right) to crown or appoint leaders among the Arab population. We also learn from this text that what may have begun as an act of benevolence and generosity, was interpreted as an insult, resulting in a member of the Quraysh, a tribe of the Arabs (possibly) taking violent action. In other documents, it is believed that one of the Quraysh also defiled or destroyed Abraha's church. This act set off a chain of events that set both parties on a course towards war. Abraha ordered an army of 40,000 Ethiopian warriors to march on Mecca and destroy the Arab Kabba. From the Arab perspective Abraha was simply attempting to eliminate competition for his religion. The battle which followed left an indelible imprint in the minds of the Arabs because of the visual spectacle of a tremendous white war elephant leading the army. Historians have allowed for the possibility that an entire heard of eight war elephants, transported from the mainland of Ethiopian Axum, was used in this battle. The unique and terrible sight of war elephants was a flagrant display of military might. The army, with its elephants trampled through several attempts by the Arabs to stop them. The army and its elephants stood poised for victory, when they neared the boundary of Mecca. At this point, the records insert mythology. According to the Koran, in Surat 105, upon arriving at the holy site, the white elephant refused to cross the boundary of Mecca, and began kneeling and ultimately sat down. The Axumites tried to encourage the elephant, and even resorted to beating it, but the elephant would go no further. According to the legend, the elephant could be turned towards Syria, or Yemen, and would progress in those directions, but when turned towards the Kaaba the animal would kneel, in adoration to the city. During this confusion, the Arab tribes united to defend the Kaaba. Abraha sent an Arab from northern Arabia, called a Himyar to assure the Arabs that Abraha simply wished to destroy the Kaaba, and not the people. Abdu'l-Muttalib, a leader among the Arabs, sent the Meccans into the hills, while he and the Quraish stayed near the Kaaba to defend it. Abraha, offered to meet with them to discuss the matter, and when Abdu'l left the meeting he said "*The Owner of this House is its Defender, and I am sure He will save it from the attack of the adversaries and will not dishonor the servants of His House*." According to the text, the next day, Abraha and his army were prepared to assault the city when dark clouds of small birds filled the sky. They carried rocks in their beaks, and battered the Ethiopian forces, until the 40,000-strong army fled the scene. Abraha was wounded and died during his retreat to Yemen. The animals in the conflict were spared, as a sign which marked the event as holy, and it came to be known as the Year of the White Elephant. We must look beyond the clear mythology in the story to segregate accurate history from religious doctrine.

The miraculous ending of the battle is immaterial when compared to the information that is conveyed about the nature of Axum, and its reach into Arabia. The battle's conclusion maybe a myth, but the battle itself is not. Abraha and his awe-inspiring cathedral were real as was his attack on the Kaaba. While Abraha played an inglorious role in this adventure, the event itself testifies to the strength of the Axumite Kingdom. The Axumites boasted an ability to amass a substantial army, and reach deeply into Arabia to exercise its prominence as a regional power. This event is of seminal importance in the formation of one of the world's largest religions.

AXUM: A REFUGE FROM OPPRESSION

According to historical sources, the religious figure known as Muhammad was never fond of the popular idol worship of Mecca. The injustices of Arab society disturbed him. The victimization of the poor, the abuse of women, and the slaughter of the weak were a heavy weight on his soul. He spent much of his time outside of the city contemplating these injustices, in caves on the superbly named Mountain of Light (Jabal al-Nur). According to the Koran, when he received his first revelations, his beloved wife Khadija was the first to comfort him, and her cousin was the first to warn him about the persecutions that would come from within their own tribe. Muhammad's cousin is believed to have been a Christian, familiar with the stories and sacrifices of Christian saints. Muhammad himself, was also familiar with Christian and Jewish dogma, because of his occupation in trade. As the conductor of a thriving trade caravan, Muhammad interacted extensively with Jewish and Christian merchants. In time, he would find that the warning of his wife's cousin, regarding the persecution that generally welcomes prophets with new messages, would prove to be dangerously accurate. When Muhammad told the members of his tribe (the Quraish) about his " revelations" of one true God, they rejected him. In fact, most of the prominent members of Arab society rejected his message, and with few exceptions the first Muslims were composed of the poor, women, and slaves. In time, some prominent members of Meccan society began to join the "Prophet" which meant that his influence was beginning to threaten the most important members of the Quraish tribe. The tribe soon dedicated itself to the persecution of Muhammad's first Muslim followers. Muhammad and his converts were banished to a dry valley and trade with them was forbidden. Muhammad's uncle Abu Talib, and his beloved wife would die during this time because of the hardship. Although the persecution became severe, Muhammad was nominally protected from violence by the status of his family but new converts like Abu Jahl (the 7th convert) were tortured. In one of the most egregious examples of persecution, an Ethiopian slave, named Bilal Ibn Rabah, was taken out into the desert, at the height of the midday sun, when the sands temperature can boil exposed flesh. His master would pin him onto the scorching sand with the weight of large boulders, placed on his chest. His master would demand that he pray to the pagan gods for reprieve. Another famous Muslim, called Abu Bakr would buy the slave and free him, to end his torment. This scene would repeat itself, on multiple occasions and Abu Bakr would feel compelled to free several other slaves. The rampant persecution of his followers would lead a desperate Muhammad to send his first companions to Axum, or Abyssinia, (modern day Ethiopia), where Muhammad told them "a king rules without injustice, a land of truthfulness-until God leads us to a way out of our difficulty". Under the cover of night, the first Muslims would leave Mecca in two boats, which set sail from the Shuaibah Port, for the Ethiopian state of Axum. This event is known as The First Hijra, or The First Pilgrimage.

THE FIRST HIJRA AND THE WISE NEGUS

After the treachery of Abraha, the devoutly Christian Emperor of Axum may seem like an unlikely defender for the early Muslim converts. However, the Ethiopian King Ashama Ibn Abjar, was as Muhammad declared, wise and uncommonly tolerant of different faiths. The persecuted companions of Muhammad would find refuge in the King's court, while the Quraish would pursue the fugitives right to the throne of the Negus (the Royal Title for Emperor). In the Kingdom of the Negus, the Muslims were free to worship as they pleased, unhindered and unmolested. The decision to send his companions into the arms of the Negus is interesting not only because of the Axumite assault on the Kaaba before Muhammad's birth, but also because the Emperor of Axum was a friend of Amr ibn al-Aas, who would be sent by the Quraish, to Axum to retrieve the heretic Muslims. Compounding the risk was the Emperor's close relationship with Abu Sufyan, the leader of the Queraish. When the refugees came to his court, the Negus was not harsh, or brash, and he didn't base his decision on his friendships with the Quraish establishment. Although the Queraish came bearing gifts, the Negus was not swayed prematurely. He patiently asked that the holy scriptures of the Muslims be read aloud, in his presence, to evaluate the new faith. Ja'far Ibn Abu Talib, Muhammad's cousin, recited verses from the Koran's, Chapter of Maryam which is the 19th sura or chapter in the Koran. The chapter is the story of the miraculous birth of John the Baptist and the miraculous virgin birth of Jesus. The sura essentially highlights commonalities between the two faiths of Christianity and Islam. It is said that upon hearing the poetic verses, the Negus began to weep, and refused to turn the Muslims over to the Queraish. The following day Amr, hoping to make the Muslims less palatable to the Negus, demanded that the Mohammedans' disclose their creed regarding Jesus in the presence of the Emperor. Ja'far declared that in Islam Jesus is *"a messenger of God, the word of God, and the miraculously born son of the virgin Mary"*. To this, King Ashama drew a line on the ground with his mace, and stated that the distance between his faith and the Muslims was no greater than the width of the line. He looked on at the members of this new-competitive faith and said, *"By God, Jesus is not more than what you have described him. By God I will not give you up to anyone"*. It is obvious that both sides were attempting to manipulate the sympathies of the Emperor. The Queraish were hoping to cleave the Muslims from the Negus by emphasizing that they do not revere Jesus, in the same way that Christians do. Amr was hoping that the perception of offense would compel the King to discard the Muslim fugitives. The Muslims were obviously hoping to graft themselves to the King, by emphasizing their shared beliefs and avoiding differences between the two faiths. In the end the Negus would side with the Muslims. A second wave of Muslims, numbering over 100 came to Axum and were given amnesty. He gave the Muslims permission to stay in Axum, for as long as they desired. The first Muslims would practice their faith openly and freely, for the first time, under the protection of an African Emperor. By protecting these first Muslims, and not turning them over to the Queraish, the Axumite Negus, was making a decision that would alter the course of world history. We can only speculate on the consequences to history, if his decision had been different. Islamic scholars would like to believe that Negus Ashama converted to Islam but there is very little in the historical record to substantiate this claim. In fact, the fate of Axum may have been very different, if King Ashama had converted, but it seems that he did not. He held fast to his beloved Christian doctrines, and his kingdom remained a Christian nation that was tolerant of other faiths. Observing African history from above the arch of time, a pattern becomes visible. In its early development, the Kushites came to the aid of Judaism in its infancy. The first Christians also found refuge in the lands of Kush, and the early Palestinians were also given aid by the Nubians. Adding to this legacy of tolerance, Ashama would forge a relationship with the early Muslims that would serve his empire throughout the distant future. We cannot overstate the importance of this event in world history, and its significance to one of the world's largest faiths. Muslims, appreciating his wisdom and tolerance would avoid the temptation to attack Axum on most occasions, but once Islam became a global powerhouse there would be a significant lapse in gratitude to the nation that offered refuge to the first Muslims. The second Rashidun Caliph, Umar ibn Al-Khattab who came to power two years after Muhammad's death, would launch his navy against the Axumite state but would be defeated by the mighty empire. The Axumites would defeat one of the greatest conquerers in Islamic history, who conquered much of Persia (Sassanid Empire), Iraq, Iran, Jordan, Georgia, Armenia, and the Roman Byzantines. After failing to conquer the land militarily, the global Islamic system of trade would apply severe economic pressures that would end Axum's dominance in trade (by assuming control of Axumite trade routes). Native Muslim warlords and Pagen enemies would even harass the state, destroying state capitals and forcing migrations of the administrative state. The great deed of Axum was never rewarded and their sacrifice was never truly honored. The decline of the Axumite state is a sad and ironic end for a nation led by an Emperor that Islamic liturgy portrays as an intimate affiliate of Muhammad. In some sources the two men were described as having a near psychic connection. It is said in Muslim apocrypha (Hadith), that when the Negus died, no messenger carried the news and yet inexplicably, the Prophet Muhammad knew the Negus was dead. He proclaimed his death and mourned Negus Ashama; Muhammad reportedly instructed his followers to "Leave the Abyssinians in peace, as long as they do not take the offensive".

THE LEGEND OF PRESTER JOHN

In the Middle Ages, Europe was largely ignorant of Africa's interior. Rumors and legends captivated the minds of early Europeans that heard about mysterious African Kings, with immense wealth and power. The legends began with the Empire of Ghana, and its immensely wealthy monarch. However, new tales would feed the appetites of Europeans hungry for information about the Dark Continent. The Legend of Prester John was one of the most famous stories told among Europeans. Prestor John was rumored to be a fantastically powerful, and wealthy king, deep in the heart of Africa. He was the Christian lord of a Christian Kingdom, surrounded by, and constantly at war with Muslims.

Europeans imagined that Prester John possessed the mythological Fountain of Youth, and a mysterious mirror that allowed him to monitor events in any province in his kingdom. It may have been comforting for early Europeans to imagine an African King, with whom they could identify. Prester John's location in Africa however, remained a mystery. Europeans would long to contact this King, and some even hoped that he would become an ally in their struggle with the Islamic powers of their day. Europeans would clamor for any detail that might reveal his whereabouts, in the hopes of contacting the black Crusader-King. When the Portuguese penetrated Africa, they felt certain that they had found the legendary Prestor John, in Ethiopia. Despite the lack of a fountain of youth, Europeans largely accepted Ethiopia as the home of the noble king, whose struggle had captivated their imaginations. In many ways, their assumption was reasonable. Ethiopia was a Christian kingdom, surrounded by Muslim powers and pagan tribes. The Ethiopian Kings did wage war against the surrounding powers, and were constantly locked in tense struggles with the Ottoman Empire and their Muslim allies. A famous text called The Conquest of Abyssinia recalls the siege of Abyssinia by the Adel Sultanate (an Islamic State governing the Horn of Africa) which was allied with the Ottomans. Ethiopia, more than other proposed locations (like India) fit the legendary description of Prester John's kingdom. Several delegations of diplomats were sent from Ethiopia to Europe. The relationship with Europe and especially Portugal grew because of the pressure from Muslim powers on Ethiopia. The Ethiopians sought allies against the Ottomans, and Muslim aggression in general. The bonds of the Christian faith, facilitated those interactions. There were even discussions of unifying the Ethiopian church with European Christianity. An Ethiopian delegation joined the bishops of the Roman Catholic Church during the ecumenical Council of Florence, in 1441.

Despite the Ethiopian delegation's constant attempts to correct them, Europeans continued to call the Emperor of Ethiopia, Prester John. The value of the Prester John mythology is that it helps us understand that there was once a time, before the full swing of the slave trade, when the nations of Africa were still strong, and when Europe saw Africa and Africans in a very different light. The relationship was not always contentious. There were moments of cooperation, alliances, and instances of mutual respect. In the end, Axum or Abyssinia would fall from prominence for a confluence of causes that spread over a span of several centuries. Despite saving the First Muslims from extinction, Islamic states would actively work to undermine the Axumite state. The growth of Islam globally resulted in a passive pressure that economically squeezed Abyssinia. The Christian nation would lose its dominance in sea trade and its overland trade routes. Hostile Muslim powers and pagen tribes would tax the state's military and result in a long decline for Ethiopia. The nation would maintain its prominence admirably for centuries but the combination of economic isolation, constant military struggles and internal dynastic struggles would be fatal to its status as a true empire. However destructive the cabal of pressures may have been, Ethiopia would still be strong enough to repel the European powers that were dividing Africa into colonies for exploitation. Ethiopia and Liberia would be the only two African states that successfully resisted Europe's imperial conquest. Ethiopia would admirably defeat the Italian, Arab powers and Turkish armies conspiring to end the prominence of the former empire.

THE SWAHILI

MANSIONS, MERCHANTS & SAILING SHIPS

On the East Coast of Africa, a fabulously wealthy, mercantile civilization would flaunt its cosmopolitan lifestyle for all to see. The Swahili (also referred to as The Zanj) would take the wild landscapes of the East African coast, and transform mangrove swamps, and creeks, into a lush tropical paradise. From the shoreline, their large stone mansions could be seen, as accents to the fantastic coral stone mosques which served as the spiritual centers for their urban civilization. Elaborate multi-story buildings, lined their narrow streets. Grand palaces and monumental tombs were the byproducts of this entrepreneurial culture, obsessed with trade. Trade was much more than an occupation for the merchants of the East Coast, it was at the heart of every aspect of their lives. Trade defined the placement of their settlements. Trade and the equitable distribution of it among merchants, was the primary responsibility of their Kings and governing councils. Trade influenced their customs, their dress, and their beliefs. In fact, the Swahili did not compete through muscular demonstrations of military prowess, as many of the world's other civilizations were prone. Instead, the Swahili preferred to compete with one another in trade. They separated themselves into independent city's or states that were governed more like sovereign commercial entities. The Swahili would ride the monsoon winds across the Indian

Ocean, and sail the Red Sea to carry their wares into Southern Arabia, Madagascar, the Malabar Coast of India and Sumatra. They would supply most of the Arab World, Europe, and even China with an astonishing array of African commodities and a wide variety of finished products. The entrepreneurs of the east African coast, in partnership with (and sometimes at the expense of) their inland neighbors would export gold, ivory, perfumes, sandalwood, timber, dyes, and slaves while importing fine china, iron, and fabrics. The markets on the East Coast would have rivaled any in the ancient world, as the sailing Dhows (rigged boats) of the Swahili and the foreign ships at port brought many of the world's greatest luxuries back to their cities. The Swahili would adorn their homes with Chinese Porcelain, rare manuscripts, and magnificent luxuries from all over the ancient world, all of which were displayed as proof of their status and wealth as patricians. The wealth of a Swahili defined his status. The standing of a merchant in Swahili culture was dependent on a uniquely symbiotic relationship between wealth and Islamic piety. In patrician eyes, wealth and morality were intertwined. One could not exist without the other. As a merchant society, trustworthiness in trade, and the importance of honoring an agreement, were of paramount importance. However, it was the urban lifestyle of the patricians, with their magnificent mansions, which distinguished them from the other occupants of the East Coast. The nobility would endeavor to construct rigorous divisions between themselves and their associates on the interior of Africa. Their urban lifestyle, magnificent mansions, and Islamic values were conceptually joined to create a complex web of hierarchy and differentiation. In some sense, a Patrician's mansion was a testament to his morality. How they lived, how they dressed, and how they behaved were all indicative of piety. Morality and urbanity were one in the same, and both were jealously guarded as markers which distinguished them from their rustic inland neighbors. Despite their strenuous efforts to differentiate themselves, the Swahili interacted extensively with the communities around them. They established partnerships, at times through ties of kinship, with societies of "hunters and gatherers, fisherman, pastoralists, agriculturalists", mineral suppliers, "seasonal laborers," and others that were used for military defense. Swahili society, is an excellent microcosm of African civilization. Within the same geographic region, the urban, educated, cosmopolitan and wealthy could co-exist with, and depend upon various gradations of the tribal. As much as they attempted to differentiate themselves, the Swahili depended on the large agricultural farming societies that provided produce. Equally important in this cultural exchange were fishing villages, filled with large homes made from mud walls and palm leaf roofs (fine accommodations for much of the world then). Swahili urbanity was balanced in equilibrium with hut dwellers and nomads tracking wild game, and civilizations of miners that pried precious metals from the earth. These various societies thrived in the same vicinity as an urban, luxury based culture, enjoying its fine architecture and literature. The Swahili were only part of a greater African tale of strong organization and the growth of empires. They were merchant middle men that linked an industrious-well organized interior, which produced the African commodities coveted by the outside world, while the Swahili merely brokered the deals that shipped African goods to Arabia, China, Europe, India, Persia, and Yemen. Their ability to carry African wares to the farthest reaches of the commercially inclined world allowed the Swahili to bring home the influences of India, Arabia, Europe, and even China to their shores. In this international web of trade, the Swahili positioned themselves as the nexus of cultural exchange, enjoying the conventions of the world's most notable civilizations. They would merge these cultural conventions seamlessly with their own to create a refined culture that was uniquely African yet clearly influenced by outsiders. The Swahili would gladly incorporate a variety of styles into their already very well developed culture. The result would be nearly 40 towns and cities, as comfortable and artistic as any in the world. The wealthiest cities were Gedi, Pate, Malindi, Zanzibar, Mogadishu, Barawa, Mombasa (Kenya), and most especially, Kilwa. In total researchers have identified over 173 smaller Swahili settlements. The Urban towns built of stone, plaster, and earth, accented with wooden archways ornately carved, reminiscent of Indian fashions, defined the outlines of their towns which were known as Mji (or the plural Miji). The women of the towns were draped in fine silks and jewels by their husbands as another sign of their patrician status, in a manner that ironically seemed to contradict the Islamic demand for modesty. The men shunned trousers, which were the standard fashion elsewhere in the Islamic World, in favor of ornate African style wraps (often made of silk). They would hold concerts in private amphitheaters and courtyards. Wealthy men, and their guests would sit in comfort as male and female poets, would recite poems in Kiamu (indigenous language) to celebrate the creative accomplishments of this literate society. This display of progressivism on interactions between genders was rare throughout the ancient world, and yet strangely typical of many places in Africa. The reputation of the Swahili coast would bring visitors from all over the world. The City of Mogadishu, for instance, was internationally renowned for its commercial opportunities and the piety of its inhabitants. It was referred to throughout the ancient world as The City of Islam. Large vessels from all over the world would dock in the ports, or careen themselves on the beaches, while their crews would enjoy the hospitality and accommodations of the Swahili until the return of the monsoon winds. We can develop a better understanding of Swahili civilization through the testimony of one of the world's most famous ancient travelers. He was an Arab from Morocco, named

Ibn Battuta.

THE SWAHILI: THROUGH THE EYES OF A TRAVELER

In 1331 A.D. one of the world's most famous travelers would visit the Swahili territories. His name was Ibn Battuta and he came from the City of Tangier in Morocco. His trip to visit the Swahili states can give us a fantastic, first hand account of life in this African paradise. When Battuta completed his spiritual obligation to visit Mecca for the Hajj (in Saudi Arabia), he sailed to East Africa, propelled by the northeastern monsoon winds, where he landed in a region called the Land of the Berbers. The Berbers he noted, were "*a people of the blacks*", and were also Shafii Muslims (*Shafii is a fiqh or school of islamic thought which applies the Koran to interpret rules for daily life. Shafii fiqh is one of four schools-within Sunni Islam; the other three are Hanafi, Maliki, and Hanbali. The Shafii system of interpretation is currently the second largest school within the Sunni Branch. It is used predominantly in Brunei, Djibouti, Egypt, Eritrea, Ethiopia, India, Indonesia, Lebanon, Maldives, Malaysia, Myanmar, Palestine, the Philippines, Signapore, Somalia, and Thailand*). Ibn Battuta would arrive in the City of Zeila, which he described as a large city, with a "*great market*" but he also noted that the city was nauseating. In discussing the kingdoms and empires of Africa we should not attempt to create the impression that the cosmopolitan flare of any individual city in Africa was repeated everywhere. Stereotyping with the goal of aggrandizing is unfortunately common in our treatment of western cultures in history. When we study European history, we neglect the poverty and general living conditions and often portray Europeans as living uniformly in picturesque hamlets or grand houses. We should not repeat this error for the benefit of African culture. Pretending that the comfort of Swahili mansions was uniform throughout Africa, would be no more accurate than the tendency to imagine that all Europeans enjoyed life at court. In our attempt to have a balanced understanding of life in Africa, we must readily accept and report depictions of poverty, hunger, and the poor living conditions of the commoner. Ibn Battuta provides us an opportunity to develop a balanced impression of Africa from his first hand account. Despite the earlier description of Swahili villages and mansions, not everyone on the east coast enjoyed the same level of opulence. This point is made very clear by Ibn Battuta. He notes that the City of Zeila was large, and its market grand, but the city was also one of the "*dirtiest, most desolate and smelliest towns in the world*". In fact, the odors, which were the result of the massive quantities of fish and camel slaughtered in the alleys of this market town, caused Battuta to spend the night aboard his vessel being tossed by the rough ocean. He found it preferable to lose sleep aboard his ship than to rest with the stench of the city. He promptly left the City of Zeila for the great City of Mogadishu. The city he reported was "*endless in size*". The men that lived there were very powerful merchants. The city, he noted, manufactured cloths of unparalleled beauty, which he stated "*have no rival*" and were shipped as far as Egypt. He then provides us with a description of the local custom that would have greeted any visiting merchant or ship coming into port. He tells us that when ships arrived at port, a group of young people greeted them in small boats called Sunbuqs. The group of boys was sent to every ship in port, with a covered dish of food for the visitors. New visiting merchants were escorted to the house of a host represented by the young men. The merchant could not go anywhere else in the city before going to the house of his host. The visiting merchant was logged as the official guest of the host, and the merchant could not sell any of his goods without the host. Any sales that were made without the host, were void. Battuta himself was the guest of the Qadi or Islamic Judge, but he was taken to meet the Shaikh (or Sultan). The Shaikh awaiting Battuta's visit was Abu Bakr son of Shaikh Umar. He spoke in a Mogadishu language, but was also fluent in Arabic. While waiting to meet the Shaikh, Battuta was given a dish of areca nuts and betal leaves, which he ate with the Qadi (who was Egyptian in origin). He was given quarters in the Scholars House, which was reserved for students studying Islamic Law. He then met with the Wazir (advisors) in charge of guests, who greeted him with the customary- "*al salamu alaikum*". He was then given another meal, of rice and ghee. The rice was formed in a ball and served with sides of "kushan" which was a relish of chicken, meat, fish, and vegetables. He also enjoyed a dish of pre-ripened banana cooked in milk with pickled lemon, & pickled chillies, that was vinegared, and salted, with green ginger and mangoes. The travelers experience gives us an idea of the Swahili diet, and provides us with an understanding of African cuisine. Battuta also noted that "*One of the people of Mogadishu habitually eats as much as a group of us would. They are extremely large and fat of body*". He would stay in Mogadishu for three days, and he would be fed in similar fashion, three times a day-which he reported was customary for the Swahili. On the fourth day, Battuta experienced the spiritual life of the Swahili by attending Friday Mosque services, for which he was given a suit made of silk to wear. The clothes he was given provide a glimpse into African fashion at this time. The silk clothes consisted of a wrap which tied around his waist. The Swahili, he noted were not fond of trousers. He was given a shirt made of Egyptian Linen, a lined gown made from fabric from Jerusalem, and an embroidered Egyptian Turban. After the mosque's prayer service, he met again with the Shaikh. They walked out onto the mosque's courtyard together, where the Shaikh prayed at the grave of his father. The Shaikh was also accompanied by his Wazirs, Amirs, and the commanders of his army. Battuta noted that the Swahili custom of greeting was similar to the custom in Yemen. Coming out of the mosque, the Shaikh put on his sandals. His head was covered by four umbrella-like canopies made of colored silk and on top of each canopy was the figure of a golden bird. The Shaikh wore a green robe made of fabric from Jerusalem, and underneath it was a loose collection of robes from Egypt. He was also wrapped in silk and wore a long turban. As the Shaikh walked, drummers, trumpeters, and pipe players proceeded in front of him. He went into his council room with the officers of his government, who sat in the audience chamber. The Qadi (Judge) sat on a special mat, reserved for him alone. The men prayed their afternoon prayer, (the Asr), and the drums, pipes, trumpets and flutes resumed. On Saturday, Battuta witnessed the practice of adjudication in Swahili society (this custom of public courts was very common throughout Africa). On Saturday, the Qadi, faqihs, sharifs, and men of standing gathered in a second council room. They sat on a series of platforms, one of which was for the Qadi himself, and separate platforms for each group. An audience of honored Muslims that performed the pilgrimage to Mecca, observed the proceedings. During Battuta's visit this group consisted of the Wazirs, Amirs and battalion heads. Food was brought in and the Shaikh ate with everyone that gathered. The rest of the people ate in a dining hall, and the Shaikh returned to his home. The Qadi, Wazirs, private secretary, and four of the leading Amirs heard litigation between members of the public. The Qadi made his judgements in accordance with sharia laws on religious matters. In other issues the council of ministers and Amirs rendered judgement. If they needed to consult with the Shaikh, a note was sent to the Shaikh and he replied on the back of the same note. After witnessing the administration of justice in Swahili lands, Battuta left Mogadishu and sailed for Kilwa. He arrived in first in Mombasa. There were banana, lemon and citron trees, and a fruit called jammun-which was like an extremely sweet olive. The people of the island, didn't grow grain and were dependent on the food they received from the Swahili coast. Their diet was primarily of bananas and fish. Battuta noted that they were "*trustworthy and righteous*". Their mosques he noted were built of wood, but were "*expertly built*". The people of Mombasa he noted don't wear shoes, and at the door of their mosques were wells with wooden containers. Before entering the mosque, it was mandatory to wash one's feet and rub your feet on a thick mat. He then left for Kilwa, which he claimed was "*amongst the most beautiful of cities and most elegantly built. All of it is wood, and the ceiling of its houses are of al-dis (reeds)*". The inhabitants of Kilwa were extremely black Zanj, with cuts on their faces. They were considered virtuous and righteous by Battuta, and were also Shafii muslims by affiliation. In Kilwa he met with the Sultan of Kilwa, Abu al-Muzaffar who was often called the Father of Gifts. He had a reputation for generosity. His generosity however, was at the expense of other non-Muslim Zanj which he raided for slaves and wealth. But as a "good Muslim", he set aside a fifth of the loot for the Sharifs or descendents of the prophet-Arabs traditionally from Iraq, and Hijaz. And when they came to Kilwa it was given to them. This system of Arab supremacy purchased esteem for those willing to honor it. The Sultan, Battuta noted was a very honorable man that sat and ate with the poor and gave respect to men of faith and of "*prophetic descent*". We are given an anecdote by Battuta, who tells of a Yemeni beggar (he was called a "fakir"- which could be a religious man forsaking possessions or just a poor man) who confronted the Sultan leaving the mosque. He begged him for clothes and the Sultan gladly gave him what he was wearing. The Sultan entered the mosque, went to the home of the preacher, and put on different clothes, and returned to give the beggar his own clothes. The Sultan's son, also bought the clothes back from the fakir, by giving him ten slaves to which the Sultan added another ten more slaves and two loads of ivory. In early Islamic culture, these extravagant displays of charity were proof of a person's moral character.

THE MYTH OF THE SWAHILI ORIGINS

Early scholars once belittled the phenomenon of Swahili culture as an Arab Civilization, established as a colony by entrepreneurial Arabs and Persians from the City of Shiraz. Some scholars, considered themselves to be generous by describing the Swahili as an Afro-Arab culture. This deeply engrained misconception was the legacy of research conducted by early scholars whose minds were still firmly rooted in the prevailing wisdom of their day. Their theories gained acceptance among archeologists and anthropologists that struggled to reconcile the opulence of Swahili life, with the racial dogmas that limited their perspective. They believed that blacks were incapable of creating a culture so clearly on par with their own, and they searched feverishly for an explanation that could fit within the racist framework that dominated their intellectual landscape. The theory that the Swahili were a mixed race, whose culture was birthed by refined Arabs and Persians forced by the paucity of options, to intermarry with indigenous Africans, fit well within their predetermined framework. The Black Zanj (an alternative reference to the Swahili), were presumed to have been inactive bystanders, benefiting from the bounty brought to the shores of their coast, and blessed by intermarriage with more civilized Persians and Arabs. In this fictional narrative, the indigenous Africans were slaves, commoners, concubines, and nothing more. The story line here is the same as Kush, Christian Nubia, and Axum, and was found to be equally false. Early researchers were biased, and clearly ignored the obvious evidence that contradicted their conclusions, but they were also provided evidence for their theories, by the Swahili themselves. The Swahili Chronicles were the written histories of the east Africans. They were the compilations of indigenous written records of the Swahili but they made proclamations of notable and possibly Royal Persian and Arab ancestry. These claims, written by the Swahili themselves, were sufficient evidence for biased scholars desperately seeking explanations that affirmed their preconceived notions about race and black civilization. Swahili society, by the late 19th and early 20th centuries, was clearly Islamic, and the African Bantu Language spoken by its members clearly borrowed many words from Arabic. Swahili architecture was dramatic, beautiful, and clearly Islamic. The style of dress, the customs, and habits were well within the norms of Arabized populations throughout the world. And there were numerous settlements of Persians and Arabs, many of which claimed credit for Swahili civilization. Early researchers, working with Swahili documents and sources, were supplied with all the evidence they required to pronounce Swahili Culture as a non-African construct. But these scholars ignored a great deal of exculpatory evidence as well. The Swahili recorded their history in Chronicles which were believed to represent the origins of their cities and settlements. Multiple Chronicles supported the belief that Shirazi Persians colonized the Swahili coast and its islands, and these documents were sighted as sources for early scholars and their theories. Swahili settlements often had separate documents, such as the Kilwa Chronicle, which scholars used to deny the African origin of Swahili civilization. The evidence compiled consisted of Swahili documents, Arabic Documents and still others like the summary of the Kilwa Chronicle written by Europeans like Joao De Barros (a famous Portuguese sailor and historian). While the details of the origin myths change from one document to the next, the basic outline of the story remained the same. They tell the tale of six Persian sons that arrive off the East Coast of Africa in seven ships. They are presumed to be wealthy merchants or (in some Chronicles) Princes, sent by the Sultan. The ships stopped at various locations, and, in the case of Kilwa purchased the land from the local inhabitants. A famous central figure, in this story is the merchant prince Ali-whose name and identity are not always consistent in various chronicles. The noble Persian gives the local king payment in a hefty sum of dyed cloths (enough cloth to surround the island) and the Prince agrees to marry the daughter of the indigenous king. For his part, the King agrees to retire to the mainland. In some Chronicles the king attempts to sneak back onto the island, with the intention of killing the Persian Prince, but he is prevented by Islamic Magic, wielded by the noble Muslim. In some versions, the Prince uses the powerful magic of Islam to carve a channel that forever separates Kilwa from the mainland, while in others the Prince reads from the Koran and ends the treachery of the King. In Swahili versions of the story, the local inhabitants were already Muslims prior to the arrival of the Shirazi Persians. The indigenous African Muslims show their fellow Muslims to a mosque which has already been built on the island. The Chronicles were for early scholars' confirmation of their own daily observations of Swahili life, which was deeply Islamic. For these early scholars, an Islamic Civilization was indicative of a civilization built by Arabs. Another unlikely union of common interest would form over time, as these early Eurocentric Scholars and Afro Centric Scholars would both come to see the Islamic nature of Swahili life, as a threat to the notion that Swahili culture could be indigenous. Traditional academics would continue to rely on their selective reading of Swahili sources, and Africanists would remain on the fringe in denial of the foreign input clear in Swahili culture in a cooperative effort to avoid the truth. Both camps would refuse to acknowledge the obvious middle ground. In our quest to develop a complete understanding of Swahili history, we can turn to several original first hand testimonies from early visitors to the coast. We can attempt to reconcile their observations with archeology, and then attempt to discover the true nature and meaning of the Swahili Chronicles. We must also attempt to uncover the process by which Islam spread throughout the coast. The history of Islam, is inextricably linked to the history of the Swahili people, and they cannot be studied as separate issues.

THE TRUTH OF THE SWAHILI ORIGINS

One of the earliest descriptions of the Swahili Coast, was recorded by the Romans. The document is called the Pleripus of the Erythraean Sea. It was written in the year 40 A.D., by an anonymous trader. It provides a detailed account of his voyage to the East Coast of Africa along the Red Sea. The author describes islands near the mainland, which he gives names like Menouthias, and Pemba. He mentions the inhabitants and their use of sewn boats, dugout canoes and basket traps for fish. The Pleripus, and another Greek Document called Geography-written by Ptolemy, were meant to inform their readers about opportunities for trade that were available to those able to make the voyage. At the time that these documents were written the trade off the Swahili coast was not robust. Trading opportunities would improve as the inhabitants grew in sophistication, and sailing, and as the broader world improved its ability to access these sites. By the third century (200 A.D) the East Coast may have already been trading directly with the Persian Gulf. Our interest in the document is in the anonymous description of the local Africans. They are clearly depicted as rudimentary sailors, with sewn boats, and dugout canoes. *(Sewn boats is a reference to a construction method that was common in Africa and elsewhere in the world. A boat is literally sewn together by reads, planks and flexible materials. The chosen building material is essentially interwoven until they are locked together to form a sea-worthy structure. It may sound like creating a large wicker basket, but this method results in very capable crafts. Natural adhesives seal the structure to create a durable craft. The technology can be expanded, and become very sophisticated as increasingly complex structures become possible. Large vessels that are very sea worthy can be created by seasoned builders. The term can also apply to vessels that are constructed without nails, which would apply to Egyptian vessels, whose wooden planks were literally fastened together by rope. The method seems odd to modern minds, but sewing boats has been a mainstay in nautical technology. The Ethiopian Axumite Empire was said to have ruled the seas as one of the world's greatest trading empires, carrying its wares throughout the orient on its sewn ships. They also defeated the navy of the second Rashidun Caliph Umar. Vessels for this technology can be as large as later developed Portuguese Vessels. One researcher duplicated this technology and found that the ships can indeed cross rough and turbulent seas. He created his own sewn vessel and sailed across the Red Sea, and found that the ships can last for weeks before needing maintenance or replacement).* The sewn boats of this early African society were probably very basic, as were their dugout canoes, but they enabled them to colonize offshore islands and master the rudiments of sailing. These early societies were fisherman, importing iron spears, axes, knives, and awls. Glass beads, wine and grain were luxuries imported with trade. This is our first glimpse of early life on the East Coast, which was later confirmed with archeology. We learned from archeology that the early Bantu-speaking groups on the East Coast were hunter gatherers, agro-pastoralists that maintained large herds of cattle, sheep and goats while farming grasses like sorghum and millet and small farmers in permanent villages. According to scholars like Mike Horton and John Middleton, the Swahili, arose out of "one or more" of the early inhabitant groups. According to Horton and Middleton, recent discoveries have proven that "these early farmers had a maritime technology". This ocean culture would spread out along the coast, and begin trade by entering the Indian Ocean trading network. The Roman account is not our only depiction of early Zanj life. A somewhat fantastic folk tale was recorded from an early 10th century, Persian captain, by the famed collector, Buzurg Ibn Shah-riyar. The captain's account was recorded in The Book of the Marvels of India. This text records a folk story which cannot be relied upon for accuracy of events but again gives us an idea of the evolution of early Bantu culture and Pre-Swahili society. According to the Arab legend, the vessel of an Arab captain encountered a terrible storm which caused his vessel to become shipwrecked on the East Coast of Africa. His sailors were filled with terror because they heard rumors that the inhabitants of the coast were savage cannibals. The Zanj (The Blacks) reputation inspired fear in the Muslim travelers and when they encountered the locals, they fully expected to meet the savage monsters popularized by Arab myths. The journeymen were immediately taken to the King of the Zanj, whom to their surprise, displayed no interest in eating them. The King was interested only in trade with the Muslims. The two sides enjoyed the company of one another, and after the visit the King accompanied his visitors back to their ship. After enjoying the hospitality of the Zanj, the ship's captain decided that the strapping king would fetch a substantial profit in the slave markets of the Islamic world. He kidnapped the King, who foolishly boarded their vessel. He was taken to the middle east, where he was sold as a slave. During his years in captivity, the King studied the Koran and became a Muslim. In time, he escaped enslavement, and traveled back to his kingdom on the East Coast. Several years later, the same Arab captain became shipwrecked on the same African shore. He was once again brought to the Zanj King, who immediately recognized the captain. But instead of rewarding the captain's dishonesty with vengeance or even a similar captivity, the King forgave the Arab sailor. The King informed the captain that, because of his treachery, he was converted to Islam. The King warned the sailor that his behavior should not be repeated with any other Zanj, because he had now converted his fellow countrymen to Islam. He warned the sailor that he, and all other Arabs should now treat the Muslims there, as brothers. This is an Arab folktale and it gives us an account of the beginning of probable Arab interactions with the Zanj. The tale of the sailor and the kidnapped King is almost certainly false, however the story allows us to understand how the spread of Islam on the East Coast was affected. It seems that many of the Zanj, converted to Islam, as a means of protecting themselves from Arab slave raiders. While many scholars argued that Islam and its Arab missionaries gave birth to Swahili civilization, archeology has proven that Islam was merely one of its influences. Africans were among the world's earliest converts to Islam., as inhabitants in Arabia, West Africans, and the Swahili lands. All throughout Africa, blacks converted to the new faith enthusiastically. Excavation of sites like Shanga show that mosques were being built by the early date of 780 and possibly 720 A.D. This conversion has often been mistaken to mean that Arab missionaries, and thus conquerors brought the religion to the Africans, while colonizing the coast. But we now know that Africans traveling as merchants or slaves likely converted because of their travels. "African merchants could well have sailed to the Gulf Ports on a regular basis", and facilitated the conversion of the Swahili coast themselves. The story recorded in The Book of the Marvels of India, may be fantastic, but elements of it reveal a larger truth about the process of the spread of Islam. In the story the King returns from the Middle East and converts his brethren to protect them from enslavement and this is an accurate depiction of how the Bantu spread Islam amongst themselves. We can say that Islam influenced the form of Swahili civilization, just as trade and the numerous cultural encounters also influenced Swahili culture, but it did not give birth to the Swahili. As the earlier story demonstrates, the Swahili were in their earliest state, Bantu speaking, Zanj farmers, living in settled communities. They began to master the sea at an early date, and entered the wide network of trade along the Indian Ocean. They converted to Islam, as previously stated as a means of protecting themselves against slave raids, and as a means of gaining greater access in the Islamic trading community, in addition to genuine convictions of faith. Scholars that attempted to find proof for their racial theories in the Swahili Chronicles, were failing to consider the purpose for which the Swahili compiled these chronicles. The Swahili were an intricate part of a larger Islamic Brotherhood that stretched across oceans and continents. The Swahili would gain legitimacy and access in this trading community through the manipulation of their lineage and portraying themselves as having Persian and Arab heritage. Trade within the Islamic world, was often mediated through perceived ties of kinship, and the Swahili would strive to foster these ties. Swahili civilization reflected the Muslim world. As the Islamic World would divide doctrinally into Shia, Sunni, Kharijite, and Sufi forms of Islam, the Swahili culture would likewise reflect these divisions. As the Umma or Islamic Community further branched off into sects within those larger divisions, they too would be mirrored along the Swahili Coast. There would be Shia Muslims-of the Shafi rite, and Sunni-Ibadi Muslims among the Swahili. All the various branches within these divisions of Islam would also be reflected in Swahili Culture. The desire of the Swahili to reflect the larger Islamic World, was not an attempt to mimic the rest of the Muslim community, rather it seems that the Swahili would allow their religious loyalties to be informed by the identity of their trading partners. As previously stated, kinship and religious ties facilitated trade! As Horton and Middleton, state "there is a clear relationship between the progress of East African Islam and the patterns of overseas trade". The Swahili, **"often changed their affiliations and were fairly tolerant of differences within clans or even family groups"**. Within clans or families, the affiliations could be varied, and were also a reflection of the trading partners of the individual or the clan. The Swahili then, associated themselves with Islam, and with various branches of Islam, as a means of acquiring greater social, economic, and religious standing to gain access to trading networks. They maintained a level of tolerance and flexibility within their own faith practices, in part to allow for necessary shifts in allegiance for economic reasons. Early scholars that read the Kilwa Chronicles, and other Swahili documents misunderstood their purpose. The emphasis on Shirazi Persian origin, was not an accurate declaration of heritage, instead it was a reflection of the political order with which a particular group of Swahilis wanted to align themselves. In the Middle East, between 945-1055 A.D, the Persian City of Shiraz gained prominence as a group of mercenary troops called the Buyids. They would take control of the Caliphate and would establish an opulent new order. They were Shi'ites (of the Zaidite branch), and their newfound wealth and power would reverberate throughout the Islamic Empire. The Swahili would, in their day, reflect the prominence of this new political order. They would align themselves with this dynasty and its economic prominence by grafting the City of Shiraz into their origin story. The Buyids were prestigious and wealthy and the Swahili would trade with this new political order. They would essentially take sides (with the winner of course) in the religious and political dispute, of their day. The Chronicles, we now know, were effectively falsified family trees designed to align Swahili merchants with trading partners. The Swahili used religion and politics to their advantage. They could never have suspected that future generations of foreign researchers would use the Chronicles to give Persians and Arabs credit for the civilization built by black Zanj. There is a tendency in acknowledging that the Swahili were creating ultimately fallacious family ties in their Chronicles, to see the Swahili in cold, clinical or calculating terms. It is easy to mistake their faith as insincere and their histories as subterfuge but this is also incorrect. The histories are versions of a truth. The Shirazi origin myth is widespread in the south, but much weaker in the northern ports. The "arrival" of the Shirzi Persions should be interpreted as the recollection of migration patterns among the Swahili themselves, and not of a foreign power. Thus, African Muslims, from islands like the Lamu Archipelago moved south, in 1000 A.D., carrying with them their coins, and a distinct brand of Islam. As Horton and Middleton state, "the Shirazi traditions represent the arrival of Islam into many of these areas". The Kilwa story (and those like it) is in its own way true, however the characters are not who they seem to be. The arriving Persians are in fact the Swahili themselves, and they are the bearers of the magical form of Islam that they use to distinguish themselves and separate themselves from the natives. The Swahili would use Islamic practice to differentiate themselves from the other groups living in the region. The Shirazi myth is a tale of immigration, in which the Swahili recast themselves as Shirazi Persians to fit themselves into the political and religious fluctuations of the larger Muslim world. According to Middleton and Horton, the Shirazi in the Swahili tales were **"indigenous African Muslims who played the politics of the Middle East to their advantage, and still used a foundation myth a millennium later to assert their authority". "African Islam"** was **"diverse and fluid, and the particular communities held no particular** loyalty to one sect or another but were content to change their religious orientation as part of their wider political action". It was only in the eyes of scholars interested in undermining indigenous claims to the creation of Swahili culture that the Chronicles were used to affect this result. None of the Arab accents in Swahili culture, pointed to by researchers can be taken to discredit the African ownership of Swahili society. The universally praised architecture of the Swahili states which many noted incorporated middle eastern styles, was the result of a long history of indigenous architectural development. The Zanj it seems, moved from the interior of Africa to the coast, and they developed norms for constructing their communities. The famed Swahili settlements, are built in the very same way as earlier Zanj communities. Archeologists have discovered that the Zanj, simply began with mud construction, graduated to wood, and eventually shifted their material choice to stone (which may have been an imported idea). They would often rebuild the same structure, in the same spot, but in the newer material. The cities, its buildings, and mosques are clear reflections of these early indigenous constructions. While the materials may have changed, and may have been influenced by the Zanj interactions with the outside world, the design, and construction of its beautiful buildings have been definitively proven to be an indigenous invention, by local African architects, following a well-established blueprint. The often touted, Arabic loan words in the Swahili language, are relatively few, and are most likely the result of the proliferation of Koranic scholarship and Islamic worship in daily life. Virtually all cultures, even our own English language, eventually borrow words from cultures they interact with closely. Arabic in the Swahili dialect was the result of conversion. It did not alter the syntax or language structure. Its use is limited to commonly used words or phrases from the study of the Koran. It is much more a testament to the literacy of the civilization than it is proof of its inauthenticity. It did not give form to, or give rise to the Swahili language. The Arabs, and Persians that western scholars hoped were responsible for the construction of the Swahili states, did not arrive in mass, until the 18-19th century, well after the rise of the Swahili cities. We need not pretend though, as some Africanist scholars do, that Swahili civilization did not borrow heavily from, or incorporate the cultural influences they encountered through trade. But we should acknowledge that the Swahili would have had to assume a stupefying, stubborn, and xenophobic posture, to refuse any influence from its trading partners. Openness, we should acknowledge, is not dependence. In many ways, our misunderstanding about Swahili culture, is a misunderstanding about our own culture, and the multi-cultural influences that made our modern world possible. It is rare that we acknowledge the depths to which Arab/Islamic civilization was only possible as a result of the Greek, Indian, Persian and Byzantine Influence; Nor do we recognize the returned favor to western culture, for its renaissance in art, architecture, medicine, and textiles inspired by African and Islamic culture. When we depict European court life, or Renaissance architecture, rarely do we acknowledge the Eastern influence on its style and technology. And when we think of Islam, rarely do we note the African contribution to an institution that was, by design meant to be international. Influence within Swahili culture, or any other culture, should never be confused with the invention of that culture. Just as the Zanj would be influenced by the Islamic world, they and their descendants would influence the Muslim World.

THE ZANJ REBELLION

Scholars today disagree on whether the Zanj Rebellion was a result of weakness in the Islamic Caliphate, or the cause of weakness in the Caliphate. The Islamic Caliph was essentially the leader of the entire Muslim Community. Less familiar readers can think of a Caliph as a Pope with political authority and control over a government that in theory should command the obedience of all Muslims throughout the world. The concept of the Caliph has fallen away in the modern world-as Muslims split themselves into various governments and denominations. However, in the ancient world of early Islam, the Caliph and his Government was recognized as the rightful heir of the Prophet Muhammad's authority. Its government controlled the entire Middle East, much of India, and North Africa. In fact, the only regions of the trading world, outside of the Caliphate's authority was Muslim controlled Spain, Europe (which was in the full throws of the Dark Ages), Non-Muslim China, and parts of sub-Saharan Africa. The official government of the Caliphate, was ample, powerful, and nearly worldwide. But this empire would nearly fall, and would for a time, be crippled by East Coast Africans initially taken as slaves. As the religion of Islam continued to grow, and Arabs would continue to assert their right to privilege within the doctrines of the faith, evermore slaves would be required in the areas between Mesopotamia and Iraq to fill laborious jobs. Near the city of Basra, in southern Iraq, East African slaves, would form the backbone of the agricultural and plantation economy. They would be condemned to the tortuous occupation of harvesting Sugar Cane in the inhospitable marshes and flood zones of the region. Despite the Islamic prohibitions against the harsh treatment and abuse of slaves, the plight of black slaves in the marshlands would be severe. The slaves, which were generally called Zanj, a term that became a synonym for all blacks, were not all specifically the descendants of the Swahili, but most were indeed from East Africa. The slaves would clear the nitrous top soils, transforming harsh swamplands, into arable and livable land. Misery and suffering would provoke frustration, and on several occasions the Zanj would tire of the abuse and would revolt. Their uprisings however, were not well organized and met with limited success. However, in 869 A.D. their fates would change, when a young agitator claiming to be the descendent of the former Caliph Ali ibn Abu Talib would arrive in Basra. Prior to his arrival, Ali, lived in the Abbasid Capital where he grew very close with the slaves of Caliph al-Muntasir. He was intent on capitalizing on the divisions and economic disparities throughout the Caliphate, and he eventually provoked an uprising in Bahrain. When the uprising failed, Ali would come to Basrah and again seek out the black slaves suffering in the marshes. He would appeal to the slaves, and claim that God had sent him to liberate them. He would be known by the title, Sahib-al Zanj, Arabic for "Companion of the Blacks" or "Proprieter of the Blacks". Ali's claim of hereditary right to the Caliphate was not accepted by many outside of his movement, and he would adopt the Shi-ite Kharijite doctrine, which separated the right to lead from one's heritage, instead placing the emphasis on ability. The Kharijite doctrine read that "the most qualified man should reign, even if he was an Abyssinian slave". The Zanj movement was now in full swing, and the fight would turn very ugly. Zanj leaders like Yahya of Bahrain would be arrested. He was flogged two hundred times, in the presence of Caliph al Mu'tamid. His arms and legs would be amputated, while his body was slashed with swords. His throat was slit and his body mutilated as his remains were burned. In defiance, the Zanj would continue their assaults on Abbasid towns, and their movement would grow to include Bedouins. The black slaves joined with free blacks and serfs of all races to build an army that was reported to exceed 500,000 men. They conducted night raids and used gorilla tactics to decimate the towns and infrastructure of the old Caliphate. Scholars that dare to estimate, place the loss of life between hundreds of thousands to upward of a million deaths. The economic destruction to the Abbasid Caliphate was as incalculable as the death toll. Some regions never recovered from the decimation caused by the fighting. The Zanj would build their own Capital City called Moktara, or the City of the Elect, and stretch their influence to an area within 70 miles of the Abbasid Capital in Baghdad (The name "City of the Elect" emphasized their creed of choosing leaders based on their ability and not race or heritage aka. Al-Mukhtarah). They built six fortified cities, seized ports, and constructed a navy. The Zanj would maintain their territories for fifteen years, and with separatist movements in Iran, the Abbasid Caliphate would be brought to its knees. The Zanj revolt would alter the politics of the entire Caliphate by creating space for the formation of an independent state and dynasty in Egypt, founded by Ahmad ibn Tulun. The Tulunid Dynatsy relied heavily on black soldiers in its military. When its first Caliph, the aforementioned Ahmad ibn Tulun died, the soldiers in his possession consisted of 24,000 whites and 45,000 black soldiers. Upon his death, his son and successor was led in procession by a royal guard of 1000 black soldiers. The scene was described as follows: *"wearing black cloaks and black turbans, so that a watcher could fancy them to be a black sea spreading over the face of the earth because of the blackness of their color and of their garments. With the glitter of their shields, of the chasing on their swords and of the helmets under their turbans, they made a really splendid sight."* The Zanj rebellion made the Tulunid dynasty possible and altered the politics of the entire Islamic world by exposing the weaknesses of the Abbasid Caliphate. The rise of the new Sultanate in Egypt, the ascension of new authorities in the eastern provinces, and the prominence of the Saffarid Dynatsy which ruled Iran and parts of modern Afghanistan, were all made possible by the seismic tremors caused by the Zanj Revolt. But in time, the Zanj themselves would begin to take slaves, and the moral integrity of their community would degrade. The Abbasid Caliphate would collect itself, focus its efforts and rely on a steady supply of bribes and incentives for defectors to undermine the Zanj state. Many of the Zanj would now side with the Abbasid Caliph and fight under the governor-regent Al-Muwaffaq, the Caliphs brother. The disintegration of the Zanj would usher in the downfall of their new dominion. In the end, Ali would be captured and killed, but the treatment of slaves would forever change. The harsh conditions and outrageous workloads would be curbed. The Black Zanj would become peasants, serfs, or wage laborers, and Muslims would adhere more closely to the religious admonition that they should not abuse their slaves. The Abbasid Caliphate would now secure itself by incorporating black soldiers into their military. It is worth noting that when the Abbasid Caliphate eventually returned to Egypt to conquer the Tulunid Dynasty, they slaughtered all the black soldiers. And despite incorporating blacks into their own military, by 930 A.D., the white cavalry turned against the black infantryman, killing them in battle and ending the prominence of black soldiers in the eastern caliphate. Black soldiers would not see a return to prominence until the rise of a new dynasty called the Fatimad Caliphate in Egypt. The Fatimad Caliph-al Mustansir was the son of a Sudanese woman who ruled Egypt in his place and incorporated trusted Nubian soldiers and eunuchs with the administration and security of the kingdom. Today some scholars, refute the belief that the Zanj Revolt was a slave revolt. They instead believe that the movement was the result of discontent among East African merchants that had settled in the area. They argue that the Zanj slaves were slow to join the movement, and despite their numbering above 500,000 they claim that the Zanj were part of a greater movement of the lower classes and disenfranchised. This however, is a very new theory that breaks with the traditional understanding of the event known as the ZANJ REBELLION. Even in this new interpretation, the event is still interpreted as a black revolt of free and wealthy blacks joining forces with enslaved blacks (and later incorporating Arabs, Bedouins, and serfs). There was however, a long history of slave uprisings. Long before Ali, the Blacks were lead by Rabah Shir Zanji, The Lion of the Zanj. He led a large rebellion in Basra, in 694 A.D. Although, he was ultimately defeated, armed rebellions, continued until the 9th century. Even in Bahrain, Ali was working with discontented slaves, and when he came to Basra, he immediately sought out dissatisfied Zanj. The slaves of the Islamic world, had already staged revolts, and while Ali claimed religious authority through his proclaimed ancestry, he did not need to do much to insight their rebellion, or organize them towards action.

THE SWAHILI & CHINESE TREASURE SHIPS

The wealth of Swahili culture would attract the entire trading world to East Africa. In 1416, the Chinese sailing fleet of the famed Zheng He, would arrive on the coast. Zheng He was tasked by the Chinese Emperor with sailing the globe and spreading the glory of his royal influence throughout the world. Zheng He would honor his Emperor by building a fleet of fabulously opulent sailing ships, that were so large they dwarfed the vessels of the world's most powerful nations. There were four decks and 24 cast iron cannons on Zheng He's aptly named "Treasure Ships". They were 450 feet long and 180 feet wide which made them twice as big as the largest European vessels. The Treasure Ships were four to five times larger than the ships that carried Christopher Columbus to the New World. Hundreds of soldiers, translators, and holy-men would man each vessel. The ships were designed to embody the power and might of China's divine ruler. The hundreds of soldiers aboard each vessel left a clear impression of the Emperor's might with any land they encountered. Zheng He commanded a fleet of over 300 vessels and travelled so extensively that researchers have yet to truly reconcile the extent of his travels with the claims recorded in the annals of Chinese history. When his incredible fleet paused for a respite in Bengal India, the sight of an African Giraffe astonished them. The Giraffe was a gift from East African envoys from Malindi (located on the coast of modern day Kenya). The Chinese were so astonished by the animal that they implored the Bengali King to part with it so that they could transport the animal back to the court of their Emperor. The Malindi envoys returned to their homeland to acquire another Giraffe and rendezvous with the Chinese fleet. By October of the year 1415 Malindi Ambassadors arrived at the court of the Chinese Emperor. A year later envoys from Mogadishu and delegates from the Swahili state of Brava were also in attendance at Peking. In the same year, Zheng He and his fleet carried the dignitaries back to Mogadishu and Brava, marking the first formal visit of the Chinese Imperial Government to Africa. The Chinese would build relationships and exchange envoys with the East Africans, 450 years before the first Chinese delegations would go to Europe. The Chinese who produced the porcelain dishes that decorated countless Swahili mansions would visit Mogadishu, Brava and Zhubu. They would also solicit the aid of an African guide who traveled with them on their vessels and advised them on their journey. Readers can look toward the memoir of Fei Xin, a Chinese crew member in Zheng He's fleet, for an account of their African journey. Africa's renown was recognizable throughout the ancient world and Africans made contributions to the achievements of civilizations worldwide. We should pause to note that East African envoys were already at the court of the Bengali King as East Africans were already trading with India and influencing its culture. If readers want to further explore the history of East Africans in India, they should look for the name Habshi and the term Siddi which were the names used to refer to blacks in Indian history. It is worth noting that this variation in terms was one of the motivations for the book, Nubia. In studying the history of African Empires, the unfamiliarity of many of the places and actors create a challenge but further complicating our studies is the fact that these names often change depending on the source. The same person, place or even group of people, can be known by multiple names. And this makes developing connections or even a coherent story difficult. Nubia was written to make those connections a little easier to recognize. For instance, the Bantu of East Africa became the Swahili, who developed a global shipping industry and the Swahili were also the Zanj who built the infrastructure upon which the most cosmopolitan cities in the Islamic world were laid and for a time, hobbled one of the strongest global empires ever conceived with their revolt. The Zanj (whom future chapters will show), left East Africa as slaves and warriors forming the backbone of armies in India and were known as the Habshi or Siddi in India.

THE FANTASTIC CITIES OF THE SWAHILI:
Gedi, Pate, Malindi, Mogadishu, Mombasa, & The Incomparable Kilwa

The Swahili Kingdoms left such an indelible footprint of palaces and grand housing that we can catalog the cities that made up their domains. There are over 116 archeological settlements and sites in former Swahili territories and we could never cover them all in this book. We can however, highlight a few notable sites that readers should become familiar with to fully appreciate the cultural achievements of the Swahili. We can begin with the City of Gedi, which was located on the coast of modern day Kenya. It was south of the Swahili City of Malindi, and to the north of the City of Watamu. Mosques, palaces, houses, tombs, and a fort, filled the city with Swhaili architecture. The buildings were made of coral stone, earth, and plaster. The city even possessed a port, in the 13th century. The details of the incredible settlement are covered in a text ignorantly titled "The Arab City of Gedi: Excavations at the Great Mosque: Architecture and Finds". The text was written by James Kirkman and it again represents the effort of early researchers to deny native Africans attribution for the incredibly luxurious Swahili culture. The City of Pate, was another notable Swahili settlement. It's remains are located on Pate Island, which is near the northern coast of Kenya, in the Lamu Archipelago. Pate is on the south-western coast of the Island. The history of the city, suffers from the same self-inflicted confusion that plagues much of Swahili history. Its chronicles claim that the city was established by the Nabahani family of immigrants from Oman, in the 8th century. The Nabahani were the ruling dynasty governing Oman and the Swahili of Pate were clearly attempting to link themselves to this dynasty for trade. Archeology has proven that the city is significantly older-and much of the chronicle's claims about its origins have been disproven. During the 18th century, Pate was in its Golden Age. Its architects erected some of the finest homes on the East African coast. Swahili culture in Pate failed the test of Islamic humility as it's jewelry makers maximized their potential as artisans of gold. Pate's skilled weavers would flaunt their expertise, by creating fine fabrics made with luxury materials like silk. The comfortable furniture that adorned Swahili homes was made by carpenters designing exquisite decor. Musicians and poets enjoyed a liberal Swahili culture that permitted the artistry of men and women equally. Musicians expressed themselves through an instrument called the Siwa, while male and female poets (poetess) authored compositions in the language of Kiamu-a dialect of the Swahili. One such poetess, Mwana Kupona lives on through her work. Her most famous creation is called Utendi wa Mwana Kupona or The Book of Mwana Kupona. This book is a variant of the biblical Book of Proverbs but in this African text Mwana is a mother and wife giving advice to her daughter about marriage and motherhood. Another famous Swahili text is The Utendi wa Tambuka. It is an early document that was written in the Yunga royal palace. It is effectively an epic poem that follows the heroics of the first followers of the Islamic Prophet Muhammad. In English, the title of the poem is The Story of Heraclius or The Book of the Battle of Tambuka. It recounts the unending wars between the Byzantines and Arabs during the earliest days of the invention of Islam. It begins with the Battle of Mu'tah which was an early clash between the first Muslims and the Byzantine Roman empire. The battle creates an incredible intersection as the Muslim armies were led by Zayd ibn Harithah, aka Zayd the adopted son of the Prophet Muhammad (he is generally identified as being black and future chapters will discuss him in depth). The epic poem continues up until the fall of Constantinople. This sample of literature gives us an idea of the deep involvement of African states in the global community as the focus of the story is on the memorable history that shaped the part of the world that was relevant to the Swahili. Pate, like many other African polities would fall due to conflict with its neighbors. Pate unified with the Mazuri clan of Mombasa/Oman, and led an assault on the sovereign city of Lamu. The losses Pate suffered in the attack on Lamu were irreparable. By 1892 the population had fallen from 7000 to

300, signaling the end for the city. The City of Malindi, was once one of the most powerful Swahili cities. Its nearest rival, was the great Swahili City of Mombasa. Malindi, was a port city for foreign visitors, which was exemplified by the envoys the city sent to the Chinese Emperor, and the same envoys that escorted Zheng He back to Africa. In 1498, the Portuguese explorer, Vasco da Gama, signed a trade pact, with Malindi. He also acquired a guide for his trip to India. It is worth pausing to acknowledge that Vasco da Gama, the famed navigator, known primarily for his "discovery" of a route to India made the journey utilizing the expertise of a guide he secured in Malindi. A year later, in 1499 the Portuguese built a trading post in Malindi, as a rest stop on the way to India. This post was a critical link in their trade network with India. The City of Mogadishu was the most prominent city in the so-called, Land of the Berbers (Bilad al Barbar), or Horn of Africa. Mogadishu came to be known internationally as The City of Islam. In 1331, Ibn Battuta visited the city and described it as "*an exceedingly large city*". He commented on the rich merchants, its famous fabrics (bound for Egypt), and its well educated Somali Sultan and his fluency in Arabic. Mogadishu came to control the gold trade of East Africa for several centuries. The City of Mombasa and its origins are nebulous. Mombasa was a nexus for the spice trade and for the exchange of gold and ivory. Its people had trade connections with India and China. The city was a crucial point in the Indian Ocean trade network, to which it exported sesamum (an African flower), ivory, millet, and coconut. How early this trade developed is a mystery. Al Idrisi, a famous Arab geographer, mentions the prosperity of the trade in 1151. In 1331, Ibn Battuta also visited the town, which was filled with Shafi'I Muslims, that he described as "*a religious people, trustworthy and righteous*". Their mosques he said, "*are made of wood, expertly built*". In the 15th century, Duarte Barbosa, a Portuguese voyager wrote that "*Mombasa is a place of great traffic and has a good harbor in which there are always moored small craft of many kinds and also great ships, both of which are bound from Sofola, others which sail to the island of Zanzibar"*. Mombasa was essentially the primary port city of Kenya in the Middle Ages and was used to trade with China, other African Port Cities, Persia, Arab networks, Yemen, and India. In 1415, the great Chinese fleet of Zheng He also visited Mombasa. The great Portuguese sailor Vasco da Gama also came to the city but the Swahili of this town showed little interest in the goods of the Portuguese, and early Europe in general. Two years later, after being rebuffed in trade, the Portuguese would sack the town. Hindsight allows us the benefit to second guess the political choices of the Swahili. After the assault of their town by the Portuguese, Mombasa became independent from Kilwa Kisiwani in 1502, and renamed itself, Myita (Swahili) or Manbasa (Arabic). The Swahili it seems never organized themselves into a united front against aggression. After two decades, The Portuguese would again attack in 1528 and generations later, they began building Fort Jesus in 1593 to colonize the area. The full expansion of Portuguese influence inspired the formal recognition of Mombasa as a colony in 1638. By the late 19th century, the horrors of subjugation were manifest and Mombasa epitomized the plantation state. There is still some controversy on the role of slavery in Mombasa. Some researchers believe that slavery may have never been an important component of its economy. The universally heralded City of Kilwa Kisiwani was built on an island off the East Coast of Africa, in present day Tanzania. By the 12th Century, Kilwa was the most powerful city on the East Coast. The reach of their influence spread beyond the southern regions of Mozambique. Ibn Battuta visited the city in 1330. He said the city, was among the most beautiful in the world. This was a considerable compliment coming from someone who nearly travelled the entire world. He noted the humility and piety of its ruler, Sultan al-Hasan ibn Sulaiman. The city's great Palace of Husuni Kubwa was built during this era, and the Great Mosque of Kilwa was expanded in the 14th century with new construction. We have learned a great deal about the scale of Swahili luxury from recent archeology. In 1961 Nevill Chitic excavated the mosque and the palace of the last Kilwa ruler (Husuni Kubwa). It was the largest domestic residence in East Africa. The palace had well over 100 rooms, with galleries, patios, residential halls, and octagonal swimming pools.

THE DECLINE OF THE SWAHILI

In 1498, Vasco Da Gama arrived on the Cape of Good Hope. Da Gama and his sailors were astonished by the larger ships on the coast. They saw the wealth and extent of trade and became determined to seize it. In 1500, the Portuguese formally sailed to East Africa for the first time. This expedition was under the command of Pedro Alvares Cabral. When the Portuguese saw the Swahili, they were astonished. One sailor on the ship wrote:

"In this land there are rich merchants and there is much gold and silver and amber and pearls. Those of the land wear clothes of fine cotton and of silk and many fine things, and they are blackmen"

Zanzibar was the first Swahili City to fall to the Portuguese. In 1503, the Portuguese captain Ruy Luourenco Ravasco fired cannons on the people of Zanzibar until the Sultan agreed to pay an annual tribute of 100 miticals. Ravasco would sail along the Swahili coast and seize ships, and ransom them for gold. In 1505, an official Portuguese fleet of 11 heavily armed ships, led by Francisco d'Almedia seized control of more towns. A Portuguese eye witness, said "*From our ships the fine houses, terraces, and minarets, with the palms and trees in the orchards, made the city look so beautiful that our men were eager to land and overcome the pride of this barbarian, who spent all that night in bringing into the island archers from the mainland.*" The Sultan fled, and the Portuguese took the town. The Vicar-General and Franciscan priests paraded through the town carrying crosses and singing the Te Deum (a Christian hymn). They went to the palace, where the captain prayed. After offering sincere prayers, they plundered the town stealing the merchandise of the Swahili and the storehouses of individual family provisions. They built a fortress, and appointed a puppet as sultan. The Portuguese sailed up the coast to Mombassa and the captains of the vessels colluded to burn the town to the ground that evening and storm the city by morning. Once the fire started, its flames burned all night long, collapsing houses and destroying the warehouses filled with Swahili goods. Each man stole whatever he found with the agreement that the pirates would divide the spoils with each man keeping a twentieth of what he found. They stole gold, silver, and pearls, looting the lifesavings of the Swahili patricians. They terrorized families by bashing doors open with axes and iron bars. Among the items, they seized were rich silks, gold embroidered cloths, and carpets, one of which was "without equal for beauty, was sent to the King of Portugal together with many other valuables (History of Africa by Shillington)". The Sultan of Mombasa refused to pay tribute to the Portuguese and maintained trading contacts with Arabia and the Persian Gulf. They therefore attacked his city twice more in 1528 and 1589. The Portuguese wanted to dominate Indian Ocean trade, or cripple it. They therefore built Fort Jesus at Mombasa. It was completed in 1599, and remained the center of Portuguese authority for 100 years (16th-17th century).

There is no simple way to categorize villains and victims in African history and depending on perspective the same characters change roles. In 1526, a muslim-Somali general named Ahmad ibn Ibrahim (whom we discussed in our review of Axum) saw Christian Ethiopia as a threat to Muslim security and he declared Jihad. He is a famed general, that is often identified as Arab, despite his clear African ancestry. His attack displaced the Abyssinian dynasty, forcing the displaced royals to found the City of Gondar. The Christian Ethiopian Kings were in touch with the Portuguese for years and ambassadors had been exchanged in 1520. The Portuguese sent a small but well equipped force in the north of the country, when Ahmad attacked. The combined Abyssinian and Portuguese force stopped the Muslim assault in 1543. This is a small example of the alliances that existed, and their consequences. The same Portuguese that decimated the prosperity of Swahili cities were also the allies of Christian Abyssinia. The ministry of Christianity to Africans by European powers was often a political move, meant to destabilize traditional governments, and to divide leaders from their subjects, and to forge economic alliances. Many kings, once converted, were encouraged to abandon their governing councils in favor of the consultation of European priests. The political instability this fostered resulted in civil and religious wars. Once African rulers recognized the danger of foreign interference, the missionaries were expelled or killed. Africans were interested in trade with Europe but the missionaries were promoting ideas that threatened traditional religions which were often the only basis for a ruler's authority. Slavery also began to erode entire communities, turning tribe against tribe and at times large empires against smaller communities near their domain. In the beginning, the Portuguese took only non-Christian slaves. This exemption from slavery through membership in the Body of Christ incentivized many Africans to convert to the religion much like the promised exemption from slavery through membership in the global Muslim brotherhood encouraged conversion to Islam. Neither promise was ever honored. With the growth of the slave trade, the Portuguese gave up the pretense that black Christian converts were fellow believers, and all blacks became eligible for slavery. Slavery and the political interference of European powers caused the unraveling of numerous African cultures. Even Christian Ethiopia would be forced to expel missionaries for political interference. Leo Africanus- a famed African geographer in the service of the Pope-mentions, in his "Geographical Historie of Africa", the existence of magnificent stately temples in various African countries. He was charged with compiling a description of Africa for the Vatican and Europe, which had not yet become fully aware of Africa's kingdoms. In his memoirs, he laments the destruction of ancient African texts by Europeans. His record gives us an understanding of the sinister destruction of African culture, governments, and monuments facilitated by the religious fanaticism of European ministry. After the period of Portuguese dominance over the Swahili, the Portuguese would be expelled in 1698 by the Imam of Oman. Whereas the Portuguese were in many ways a passing disturbance to Swahili civilization and culture, Omani influences would prove more enduring. They would introduce many Arabic words into the Swahili language, and they encouraged the belief that their practice of Islam and their social status should be viewed as superior. They authored the idea that Arab Ancestry was a mark of superiority. It is this philosophy and its propagation throughout Swahili society that continue to damage Swahili culture today. The class and status system introduced by the authority of Oman persists, leading some modern Swahili to identify themselves as "Arab" and civilized and their fellow Africans as "non-Arabs" and inferior.

GREAT ZIMBABWE

The Granite Cities of The Inland Empires

The great secret of the Swahili was the supply chain behind their commercial enterprise. Obscured from view by their beachside mansions, were the Inland trading kingdoms that fueled the furnace of their trade. Although these nations were hidden from the view of outsiders, their magnificent medieval cities ruled the deep interior of Africa. As merchants, the Swahili marketed a stunning array of African commodities. But the source of these products was an enduring and sophisticated network of inland kingdoms, that covered vast swaths of the African Continent. These kingdoms housed tremendously large populations in granite masterpieces known as The Venerated Houses, by the less sophisticated tribes living outside of their shimmering black citadels. Here, beyond the forests, nestled at the bottom of lush rolling hillside valleys were ancient networks of well-established nations that labored to meet the herculean task of harvesting, mining, and manufacturing the products demanded by the Indian ocean trade networks. These kingdoms would have direct and indirect ties with The Arab Middle East, India, China, and Europe. In many cases, they would interact with the external world through the Swahili, who as middle men, simply marketed and shipped the goods that they produced. Their reliance on Swahili connections inadvertently caused these medieval kingdoms to fade into the backdrop of history, but their massive cities have jutted out from the obscuring brush of Africa's forests, calling attention to the incredible achievement and legacy of these advanced cultures. The most famous of the interior kingdoms, was The Kingdom of Zimbabwe. Today, the kingdom is known for the round ruin, referred to as Great Zimbabwe. The iconic Great Zimbabwe that we visit as tourists, is a humble version of a once tremendous city, consisting of three sections. The Hill Complex, the Valley Complex, and the Great Enclosure were all separate sections of Great Zimbabwe. When the German explorer Karl Mauch discovered it, the Great Enclosure was so magnificent that he thought it was a Phoenician Palace, or possibly the operating capital of the Queen of Sheba. Mauch and other Europeans of the time, were consumed with Biblical archeology and obsessively sought the city of Ophir (the source of King Solomon's gold). Europeans were also obsessed with creating intersections that weaved their own ancestry into such biblical sites. Mauch did not find Great Zimbabwe through his own ingenuity. He was led to the site by a fellow German named Adam Render. Render, a progressive for his time, married into the tribe of Chief Pika and ultimately exploited this connection to lead Mauch to the site. When it was discovered, white settlers argued that they had finally found proof that whites settled the region before the indigenous Africans. In a rapacious search for proof of his theory, Mauch tore the city apart, discarding any evidence that pointed to an African origin for the city. But Mauch would not be the only reckless westerner. Another explorer named Willi Posselt hauled off a large monumental statue, known as the Soapstone Bird; and W.G. Neal lay waste to the site, robbing it of its gold and other valuables. James Theodore Bent, Richard Hall and Ian Smith would add their names to this legacy of madness, denying all evidence that insinuated an African origin for the city. The ruin today, is all that remains of these brutal surveys. But even in this age of darkness, there were some bright lights. David Randall MacIver, Gertrude Caton-Thompson, and J.F. Schofield all risked their reputations and professional careers to confirm that the incredible structures of Zimbabwe were indeed the result of African genius. We learned from their efforts that the famous tourist site was once the capital city of a kingdom that covered 100-200 miles, an area the size of the modern-day state of Maine. The construction of Great Zimbabwe began in the 11th century. For 300 years, the architects of this African civilization would expand upon the initial building phase. The walls which protected the inhabitants on the interior, would reach 36 feet high, or approximately 3.5 stories. Its massive walls were built of granite and would wind in circular fashion, at times for lengths of up to 820 feet (longer than two football fields). The capital city would cover 1,784 acres and serve as the seat of power for the throne of Zimbabwe's Monarch. A population that exceeded 18,000 people would live and work in The Great Enclosure, making the city as large as the London of its day. The Great Zimbabwe site consists of 12 groups of buildings that cover 3 square miles, innumerable passages, and enclosing walls. The outer wall was made from over 100,000 tons of granite blocks. Each block was meticulously shaped. A temple complex within the central enclosure was 35 ft high, and 830 ft in circumference. Its floor was made with a powdered granite cement, and the structure boasted a drainage system. The Great Western Enclosure covered 11,000 square feet. The

Western Wall was outfitted with 6 conical turrets, each spaced 12 feet apart. Guards patrolled the tops of the walls. In Great Zimbabwe, the King would live within the walls of his court and his 18,000 capital city subjects would enjoy this existence of comfort with him, in the same way that dependent populations lived within the protective walls of feudal land lords, and kings in medieval Europe. While the citizens inside of Great Zimbabwe, lived in round houses, these were not round homes of the primitive variety. These round homes were made from a substance called Daga, which is a mixture of clay and gravel. The walls were then finished to produce a polished glaze. The bungalows were built with wooden beams, and their painted walls displayed nature inspired murals of animals and people. Ornate wooden doors sealed their entryways. Daga was also used to make fireplaces, beds, and tables. Archeologists have found imported stoneware and glazed dishes from china, painted bowls from Persia, and colored glass from the Middle East. There were sophisticated metal working facilities, including a gold workshop, on the site. Before the period of pillage, there were many gold items, of a seemingly ceremonial nature. Gold battle-axes and relics represent the remains of Zimbabwe's material culture. The ruins in Great Zimbabwe are just one of hundreds of ruins, that stretch over 270,000 square miles (an area larger than the state of Texas). They spread out throughout Zimbabwe, Botswana, Mozambique, and the northern portion of South Africa. Outside of the King's court, at Great Zimbabwe, the monarch's authority expressed itself in the form of over 200 similar sites, which were miniature versions of the Great Zimbabwe city-complex. These much smaller cities were effectively the homes of the kingdom's substantial population of citizens; the effective nobles of medieval Africa. These areas are known as The Hill Complex and the Valley Complex. The

Hill Complex is the oldest of the three areas. It was occupied between the ninth and thirteenth century (800 A.D.- 1200 A.D.). Great Zimbabwe was occupied from the 13th century to the 15th century (1200- 1400 A.D). The Valley Complex would be occupied from the 14th to the 16th century (1300-1500 A.D.). When we consider the history of empires stretching back to mighty Kush and up until the time of the fabulously wealthy Swahili, we must recognize that inland Kingdoms like Zimbabwe and the hard-working tribes of the interior were a part of the economic infrastructure that made a robust and global trade of African commodities possible. These inland powers played their role in a system of supply and demand that made Africa a powerhouse in trade.

THE ORIGINS OF ZIMBABWE

The Kingdom of Zimbabwe, was not an isolated aberration, out of the norm in this part of Africa. The kingdom was the result of a long history of cultural evolution. The founding fathers of Zimbabwe entered the region as colonists, from an Empire called Mapungubwe. The former citizens of this kingdom brought with them the culture of stone construction that had been established in the old kingdom. Mapungubwe existed as an empire of the Shona-Bantu speaking people, from 1075-1250 A.D. The empire's citizens lived lives divided by class. Class and status determined, how and where a subject of Mapungubwe lived. The Capital City of the empire was named Mapungubwe, and the king's stone compound was built on the flat 300m plateau (900 ft) of a very steep hill. The stone residence of the king, was erected high above the base of the hill. The king's court would gather in the wooden palisade that surrounded the base of the hill, to bring complaints and concerns to the king, who addressed their needs from above. The base of the hill was a natural amphitheater, magnifying the Monarchs pronouncements. From his hilltop compound, the King would hear cases from his subjects, offering his rulings for all to hear. The cases would be organized for hearing, by the king's primary councilor. The councilor's residence was also built of stone, and was located at the base of the hill, adjacent to the court's location. Prominent citizens-or district leaders of Mapungubwe also lived in stone homes, atop hills similar to-but smaller than the kings hill. Commoners lived in low latitude sites, where life was centered around family and agriculture. This stone-built kingdom became a regional trading power, that stretched across modern day Botswana, Zimbabwe, and South Africa. They mined limited amounts of gold for shipment to their Swahili trading partners. Their primary export to the Swahili, was ivory, which they were well positioned to harvest from nearby elephant fields. African ivory was softer (easier to carve into sculptures) and thus superior to ivory from elsewhere in the world. When the Swahili demand for ivory was eclipsed by a rising international demand for gold, settlers from Mapungubwe would settle in between the gold rich hills of Zimbabwe. The new kingdom would soon eclipse Mapungubwe, while changes in climate would seal the old kingdom's fate. Zimbabwe would become larger, more powerful, and more prosperous than its predecessor. There would be 150 tribute paying rulers, living in smaller versions of the Great Zimbabwe Complex, throughout the kingdom's territory. Great Zimbabwe, like Mapungubwe, would be replaced by the rise of another Shona Kingdom and would be built on the commerce of new trading opportunities. When the demand for salt sent Prince Nyatsimba Mutota in search of new resources, he would find rich supplies in the lands of the Tavara people. They were a group of elephant hunters that were easily displaced by the Monarch and his army. This kingdom would grow during the 15th century, interacting with the Portuguese well after the fall of the Swahili. Ultimately, the residents of Great Zimbabwe and the inland empires, abandoned their cities for unknown reasons. We can surmise that these African empires seemed to follow the same trends of trade and market forces that governed the creation of all the world's greatest political powers.

THE EMPIRES OF GOLD

GHANA: The Empire of Gold

In the 11th century, faint whispers of a grand kingdom, and its noble king would trickle into Europe. Well-traveled and educated elites were told of a wise king called the Ghana, who possessed fantastic wealth and ruled an empire in Africa. It was said that the Ghana ruled a kingdom where the trade in books eclipsed all other commodities, and gold was in unbelievable abundance. With knowledge of little else about the African state, the kingdom of Wagadou would become known by the moniker of its king: "The Ghana". Ghana's wealth, army, and trade would become legendary throughout all of Europe, and merchants from all over the world would rush to the kingdom. The scholars of Europe would hurriedly scribble the tales of travelers and merchants. Al-Bakri, a scholar in the city of Cordoba, which is in modern day Spain, would collect the stories of travelers in 1067. He was told that the Ghana could assemble an army of 200,000 soldiers and cavalry, in a single day. Al-Bakri wrote that the king:

"Gives an audience to his people, in order to listen to their complaints and set them right...he sits in a pavilion around which stand 10 horses with gold embodied trappings. Behind the king stand 10 pages holding shields and gold mounted swords; on his right are the sons or princes of his empire, splendidly clad and with gold plaited in their hair. Before him sits the high priest, and behind the high priest sit the other priests...The door of the pavilion is guarded by dogs of an excellent breed who almost never leave the king's presence and who wear collars of gold and silver studded with bells of the same material"

Travelers reported that gold pulsed through the entire kingdom. The rumors were not far from the truth. The Ghana, and his kingdom were among the wealthiest nations on earth. Ghana, and The Sudan in general would be known as perhaps, the wealthiest place on earth. An incomprehensible network of obscure gold mines provided West Africa with natural wealth. Gold from the Sudan was prized as the purest gold on earth. In time, Ghana would provide the supply for the currencies of many of history's most powerful empires in Europe and the middle east. The wealth of Ghana, was also based on a trade, which traversed the Sahara Desert. The economy of West Africa exploded as merchants carried the gold, salt, and ivory of the kingdom to North Africa, the Middle East, and Europe. Gold and salt were once the world's most valuable commodities. Populations required salt as a seasoning and a preservative. No army on earth could be victorious in a prolonged battle without the use of salt. Salt was arguably more valuable then gold, and Ghana was in possession of vast reserves of both! The trade was made easier by the introduction of the camel, which came to Africa in the 1ˢᵗ century A.D. Their arrival to Ghana, in the late 8ᵗʰ century, allowed trade to expand as camel caravans carried African commodities across the sea of the desert. It is important to note that cities and a vast system of regional trade existed long before the arrival of Islam or Arabs. The correction is pivotal because early scholars made the trite and often used argument that the wealth and commercial strength of West African kingdoms like Ghana, were the result of Arab mercantilism and not the result of indigenous African efforts. These theories again cast Africans as innocent bystanders, benefiting from the bounty produced by Arab entrepreneurship and denied Africans authorship of their own civilizations. These early researchers argued that trade arrived with Islam, which was carried by Arabs. This was false. West Africa certainly benefitted from expanded opportunities in trade as new markets were created by the world-wide prominence of Islamic kingdoms, but trade and commerce were already prominent in West Africa. Islamic Arabs were joining in and contributing to the preexisting condition not inventing it. Well after the establishment of Wagadou, the Kingdom would grow and capitalize on these new opportunities in trade. This new economy necessitated expansions in the Ghana's territory and control of various trade routes. In the early 8ᵗʰ century, Sanhaja Berbers would be among the first traders to describe the kingdom. As time went on, more detailed accounts would emerge from the Sahara. The capital of Ghana was called Koumbi Saleh. It began as two separate cities, six miles apart. They were joined by a six-mile road, which eased travel for those needing to traverse the distance. However, as trade increased, merchants, scholars, Imams, and tradesmen, rushed into the Ghana's territories. Eventually, so many immigrants moved into the space between the two cities, that the two districts became one. Most homes were made of wood, and clay for commoners, while the wealthy lived in homes made of wood and stone. The metropolis, which housed approximately 30,000 people was divided into the merchant district and the royal capital which was surrounded by a wall. The interior was filled with the palace, which was the most magnificent structure in the city, and a sacred grove of trees, used for religious Soninke rituals. Prior to the advent of Islam in Ghana, the Soninke essentially worshiped the Emperor, and a mythological serpent in the Niger River. In the merchant district, a largely Arab and Berber populous enjoyed twelve mosques, and plenty of housing. The division between the Muslim quarter, and the indigenous population is telling. While the Ghana himself did convert to Islam, he did so reluctantly, and only to protect the integrity of his trade with Muslims. Desert dwelling Muslim's would often attack the Emperor's caravans. It was believed that conversion would prevent or discourage fellow Muslims from raiding. According to the Soninke legend, the King's conversion was halfhearted at best. Trade brought manufactured goods, such as textiles, European cloths, and ornaments into Ghana, which allowed its royals to experience the finest luxuries of the ancient world. The Ghana would tax exports and imports by demanding a percentage of the physical goods being exchanged, as opposed to demanding currencies.

THE ORIGIN OF GHANA

In approximately 1600 B.C. an African ethnic group called the Mande would build sophisticated settlements, 400 or more, expertly carved out of stone, with well-defined streets. Scholars refer to the settlement as the Tichitt Walata

Complex, and its inhabitants constructed the first stone settlements built in all of Africa, outside of the Nile River Region, and Ethiopia. This urban complex and culture, would find itself dispersed by incursions from primitive Berber tribes, from the North African desert region. The culture, with its four-tiered hierarchy, and tribute system, would collapse into small settlements, during the middle of the 4th century, in an area that would become known as Awkar. One of Africa's earliest cultural achievements would have its development severely interrupted, by outside interference. However, in 750-800 A.D., Majan Dyabe Cisse would ambitiously conquer the area, and would unify the Awkar region. The new kingdom, would be called Wagadou, which means Land of the Herds. It would build off the culture of the Tichitt-Walata Complex.

THE END OF GHANA

In the 11th century, by 1059 the Sahara Desert began to expand. The dense population of the empire was depleting the region, and food supplies began to diminish. Food was plentiful in good economic times, when it could be obtained through trade, but in less prosperous times, food supplies were wanting. Outside forces would pressure the empire as well. The Almoravids, were Bedouin Arabs who would ironically be lead, by a black African convert to Islam. His name was Abu-Bakr Ibn-Umar, and he would lead a jihad, aimed at capturing the trade routes of Ghana, and force the reluctant Soninke into conversion. He was successful by 1067. According to some scholars, the Almoravids, were never able to reestablish the system of production and trade built by the previous administration. This version of history is not entirely accepted. According to scholars like, Conrad and Fisher, this story is merely local folklore. Others believe that numerous factors contributed to the downfall of Ghana.

Scholars like Dierk Lange believe that the Almoravid interference was a minor contributor to the multitude of destructive causes. Competition and displacement were the likely culprit which resulted in the fall of Ghana as new kingdoms, led by different ethnic groups rose to assert themselves. While Ghana was the product of the Soninke, a subgroup of the Mande, another group called the Sosso would erect a kingdom called Kaniaga in 1140. The Sosso, led by Diara Kante would capture the capital of Ghana, Koumbi Saleh in 1180, establishing the Diarisso Dynasty. Under King Soumaoro Kante, they would attempt to extend their influence by conquering the kingdom of Kangaba which was the creation of the Mandinka. The Mandinka however, would tire of Sosso rule and would rebel under the leadership of the great Prince Sundiata Keita. Sundiata would forge a partnership with Soumaba Cisse, the King of Ghana which was now a mere vassal state. Sundiata and the Mandinka would lead Ghana and a loose federation of Mande states to defeat King Soumaoro Kante, the leader of the Sosso at the Battle of Kirina in 1235. The impetus for this revolt was excessive tribute payments or taxes. Ghana would cease to be an independent nation but would be folded into Sundiata's new Empire of Mali.

THE EMPIRE OF MALI

Where Ghana once stood, a new empire would rise and take its place. It extended the borders of the old kingdom all the way to the Atlantic Ocean. Its territory was as large as Western Europe and however wealthy Ghana may have been, the new kingdom of Mali would be even wealthier. Ghana's ostentatious displays of golden abundance would seem humble by comparison to its successor. In this new kingdom, trade would reach new heights, and Ghana's robust book trade continued to grow as scholarship and education became national hall marks. Art and architecture would abound, and the greatness of the nation would force the entire world to pause and take notice. The most famous ruler of Mali would be the Emperor Mansa Musa, who was quite possibly the wealthiest monarch on earth. The Kingdom of Mali would be among the largest empires on earth, second only to the Mongol Empire of Genghis Khan, which (despite the fame of conquerors like Alexander the Great, or renown of empires like Rome) was the largest empire in the history of the world. The kingdom of Mali would be governed by one of the few constitutions in the world. It granted rights and responsibilities to all the clans in the Mali empire, and established the equality of women and men before the law. Mali was also governed with one of the few deliberative bodies in the world. Officials in the Gbara were chosen, usually through election, to represent their faction (although the emperor maintained the final say). In Mali, scholarship would reach new heights as 3 Major Universities, and 180 Koranic Schools fed the scholastic appetites of the population. Sankore University at Timbuktu would amass over 700,000 manuscripts, and become one of the greatest institutes of learning in the Muslim world. The Emperor of the Mali Empire, maintained a standing professional army of 200,000 soldiers. The armor-clad warriors used sword and shield to maintain peace and prevent criminality in the kingdom. The lifeblood of the Mali Empire was its robust trade. Preserving the safety of transport caravans and traveling merchants was the Emperor's highest priority.

TIMBUKTU: THE CITY OF THE SCHOLARS

When we think of Africa historically, we often think of it as a dark continent, filled with illiteracy. The popular mythology has been that African cultures were oral cultures and reading and writing were concepts introduced by European colonists. Most people continue to believe that Africans failed to record their history in writing. These ideas developed for a wide variety of reasons. They were in part based on bias and prejudice, but they were also based on misunderstandings of events in Africa. African empires, and even many tribal communities have rich traditions of literacy. Village playrights, erudite philosophers and scientific scholars would fill African libraries with original manuscripts on a variety of topics. The famous City of Timbuktu was often referred to as "The City of Knowledge" because it epitomized this literary tradition. In the kingdom of Ghana, the production and reproduction of books was one of the largest industries. Scholars, merchants, and the nobility had an insatiable lust for learning, and the thirst for education continued to grow as the Mali Empire replaced the Ghana Empire. In West Africa, tremendous libraries were maintained as private and public collections for scholars and their students in several universities. Books in West Africa were literally a work of art unto themselves. The books were written in bold Arabic calligraphies, with gold infused inks. Bold decorative patterns were painted in sharp colors as ornamentation for the African texts. The manuscripts were carried in beautiful leather book coverings, but unlike books in the west, African texts were never bound to their covers. In a unique African custom, the leather covers simply contained the manuscripts which were neatly stacked in order, usually without page numberings or indications for order. The purpose for leaving African texts unbound, was generally academic. Scholars maintained large student followings to whom they often distributed sections of their books. The unbound books made instruction easier, because several students could borrow different sections of the same book for study. There were no page numbers or indicators of order because the erudite scholars were expected to be masters of every book in their collection. They were expected to be so familiar with their prized collections that they could maintain the order of books from memory. The libraries in Timbuktu were as up to date as any in the world. In the Islamic world education centered around the Islamic sciences of Quranic study and Rhetoric. Many of the texts in Timbuktu were religious in nature. There were numerous treaties on the various schools of Islamic thought. But there were also numerous writings on politics, biology, mathematics, medicine, and astronomy. Some of the books on astronomy seem to pre- date the works of Copernicus and Galileo. At Sankore Univesity 25,000 students would pass through a courtyard, built to the exact dimensions of the Kaaba in Mecca. The University at Jingaray Ber, and the University of Sidi Yahya, were also exceptionally challenging institutions in Timbuktu. The Universities in Timbuktu, were once considered to be among the greatest universities in the world. The reputation of these institutions and their scholars transcended the remoteness of their desert location and students came from as far as the Middle East, to study under some of the finest academic faculty in the world. The rulers of African empires, were so wealthy and so willing to support the acquisition of knowledge that scholars found West Africa to be a comfortable setting, in which to pursue their fields of study. An old anecdote that modern academics often site gives us an understanding of how the ancient African universities of Mali compared to universities outside of Africa and throughout the Muslim world. The anecdote is about the arrival of a visiting professor from outside of the black Islamic institutions. The Mali Emperor Mansa Musa returned from his Hajj with numerous Arab scholars, many of which were found to be severely undereducated by the standards of Timbuktu. The most egregious example was an Arab professor named Arahman Adimmi. He was invited to teach, but upon his arrival, despite his excellent credentials, he was found to be so lacking academically, that he was forced to complete pre-requisite courses in Marrakech before he could even sit with the students at Sankore. The story is used to suggest that the African universities were vastly superior to universities in Baghdad and elsewhere in the Islamic world. This is, of course, unnecessary hyperbole. It is enough to say that we have sufficient evidence to prudently state that the African institutes were certainly equal to universities throughout the Muslim world. We have learned through audits of the remnants of academic programs, and the selections present in the once incredible libraries of Timbuktu, that African graduates were atleast equal to the graduates of other universities in the Muslim world. Many non-African historical sources attest to the renown attained by African graduates. A famous proverb recalls the greatness of African education, in Timbuktu. It states that "***Salt comes from the north, Gold the south, and silver from the country of the white men, but the word of God and the treasures of wisdom are only to be found in Timbuktu***". Timbuktu itself was a brilliant and vibrant trading city, with a multi ethnic flare, filled with Mali natives, immigrants, and visitors. Blacks of all ethnic stripes, Arabs and Muslims from all over the Islamic world, and Jewish merchants enjoyed the cosmopolitan city and empire.

Despite its 14th century population of 115,000, which was five times larger than the population of medieval London, Timbuktu was one of the smaller cities within the Mali Empire. Researchers are learning that Mali, and West Africa in general, was filled with tremendously large cities, that rivaled the size of any, in the world. Mali is believed to have boasted over 400 cities, and a dense urban population. Many of them are barely recognizable anymore, as they have been remanded back into the desert sands from which they were built. But, where deserts now abound, populous cities once dominated. Intrepid archeologists are re-writing the history of West Africa, based on the remains of cities that once covered much of West Africa. From its earliest days, West African cities housed some of the largest urban populations in the world.

THE FOUNDING OF TIMBUKTU

The founding of Timbuktu is a confused bit of history. Modern ethnic strife has inspired various groups to claim Timbuktu as the exclusive creation of their ancestors. Additionally, the racially biased scholarship of early western researchers must also be screened out if we want to recover the origin of Timbuktu. The most famous and perhaps the most compelling of the origin myths is The Story of Buktu's Well. Buktu is believed to have been a Tuereg slave girl. According to the myth, the nomadic Tuereg, were accustomed to camping near the river during the dry seasons, but during the rainy season they established a small inland base as a refuge from water pests and diseases from the river. The base, which was centered around a well, was maintained by Buktu the slave girl. Timbuktu, literally means the well of Buktu. This story was recorded in the

Tarikh al-Sudan, published by Abd al-Sadi, in the 17th century. Yet as ethnic strife has increased over time, this version of history is not entirely accepted, by black Africans who argue that their ancestors were responsible for establishing Timbuktu. Their case is not frivolous. It seems that the wells that Buktu might have been guarding had been in use by black Africans for some time prior to the establishment of the Tuereg base. Modern scholars have determined that while we cannot pinpoint the precise date of it's founding, Timbuktu was established around the twelfth century because of trade by Saharan pastoralists with boatmen on the Niger River. Merchants from Djenne would soon come to set up markets and the urbane City of Knowledge would grow over time.

ARCHITECTURE IN THE MALI EMPIRE

The construction technology of early Mali enabled its experienced architects to erect large buildings on a tremendous scale. The Great Mosque of Djenne, in the city of Djenne, is the largest adobe construction in the world. The City of Djenne was once a tremendous locale for scholarship and commerce. It rivaled Timbuktu for its academic prowess. Another famed city in the empire was the ancient city of Gao. In Gao, archeologists have discovered remnants of early architecture that paint a vivid picture of the buildings that filled the cities of Mali. In Gao researchers found the remains of stained glass window panes of pink, blue-green and purple glass. Window frames in Gao, are believed to have been made of alabaster. The urban, populations of Africa lived in cities that were often unique, and beautiful, with their own aesthetic. Some of these West

African cities were situated along the banks of the Niger River. Visitors might sail down the tranquil waterway in locally built boats, entering the city through the African equivalent of gondolas. The homes and administrative buildings of Mali often had grand, unique entrances, and even today are still accented with the same Moroccan inspired doors, and gorgeous Islamic privacy windows that ancient residents enjoyed. In the city of Niani, the Mali Emperor Mansa Musa would build the Hall of Audience. The grand construction, was a domed building, entered from within the palace. It was adorned with colorful arabesques. The windows of the upper floor were framed with wood, and plated in silver. The windows of the lower floor were also framed in wood, but plated with gold. Most of the surviving information about Mali and its kings, was recorded by Arab historians. The primary contributors were the Arab scholars Abu sa'id, Al-Umari, Ibn Battuta, Ibn Khaldun, and Uthman ad-Dukkali. Battuta travelled through much of West Africa, and described the audience hall of The Mali Emperor Mansa Sulaiman. The Sultan, Battuta says, entered his cupola- domed roof, from inside of his palace. The audience side of the chamber had " *three wooden arches*" and woodwork "*covered with sheets of beaten silver and beneath these, three more covered with beaten gold, or rather, it is silver covered with gilt. The windows have woollen curtains which are raised on a day when the sultan will be in session*". Ibn Battuta was describing the habit of Mali emperors to hold an audience with common citizens, to hear and resolve civil disputes. On the day that the Musa held audience, over three hundred slaves would stand in front of the palace. Some of the slaves had bows, while others had spears and shields. A procession of commanders, Amirs or officers, and holy men would follow. The King's interpreter would stand at the door, "*wearing splendid robes*" and a turban, with a sword tucked in a golden sheath. Bugles made from elephant tusks and drummers completed the spectacle. The 14th century Arab scholar, Al- Umari wrote:

"*The capital extends in length and breadth to a distance of approximately, one barid (6-12 miles). It is not surrounded by a wall and most of it is scattered. The town is surrounded on four sides by the "Nile" (he was referring to the Niger River). The buildings of this town are made of iwad or clay like the walls of the gardens of Damascus. This consists of building two thirds of a cubit (approximately 30 cm) in clay, then leaving it to dry, then building above it in the same way, and so on until it is complete. The roofs are of wood and reeds and are generally domed or conical, in the form of cupolas of camel-backs, similar to the arch-shaped openings of vaults.*"

Ibn Khaldun wrote that the buildings of Mali were "*solidly built and faced with plaster*". The buildings that have survived into modernity match these early testimonials. The architecture of Mali was unique, innovative and inspired. In the absence of stone, the West African Empire would utilize earthen building materials which is colloquially called "Mud". It can be argued that many forms of architecture, in many cultures, scar the landscape; that their "beauty" is based on their contrast with the natural surroundings. Some forms of architecture fail to blend in with nature. They stick out, apart from the natural landscape, as the clear and unmistakable work of men. In Mali, architects take an entirely different approach. Inspired by naturally occurring mounds in the region, the Mali style of architecture, results in buildings that look as if they are a natural part of the environment. Buildings made of earth and clay in Mali, taper at the bottom like plants sprouting up out of the dry Mali soil. They appear as if the earth has grown a dwelling, mosque, or university from itself. It is shocking to realize that in Mali, buildings as large as palaces can be sculpted out of clay or mud.

THE MARVELOUS "MUD" OF MALI

The choice of mud as a building material is as complementary to the West African environment, as the organic shapes used in Mali design. In the modern west, the term mud conjures images of simple huts, poverty, and structures that barely qualify as habitable architecture. But this impression is the result of a lack of awareness about earthen architecture; it's history and strength. The " Mud" they use is effectively treated, and becomes as hard as cement. It breaths like a living part of the landscape, allowing for much needed transfers of heat which prevents cracking, and structural instability. During the day, the Mud, absorbs all the substantial heat that the desert environment musters. This absorption of heat, keeps the interior of Mali's buildings very cool. At night, the thick walls of the Mud buildings release the heat, absorbed during the day, effectively warming the interior during Mali's surprisingly cold desert nights. The Mali style of architecture is organic, and modern, lacking sharp edges. The buildings of Mali can be incredibly large, as the Mali Africans pushed this technology to the limit. It is on the interior of the Mali buildings that their genius and skill truly shines. Arches, columns, stairwells, and domes, fill the halls, mosques, and administrative buildings of Mali. Malians utilized sun baked bricks of earth in their constructions, just as numerous contemporary societies in the ancient world. In Yemen for instance, superb palaces, and -multi story buildings, are built entirely from Mud. The original great wall of China was built with earthen bricks. The familiar grey stone facades of the Great Wall were not added until after the construction of the original wall. Native American use of Adobe structures is the most familiar use of earthen architecture (adobe is simply another name for Mud). The use of Stone in Europe would not become common until later dates in European history. Stone castles would only begin to be built towards the end of the 13th century. Cities like London would be primarily constructed of wood and thatch or straw until The Great Fire of London, in 1666. In much of Europe wood would be the most common construction material and many homes were built from a substance called Cob. Cob is simply Mud, and straw or other course fiber materials. Mud or earth was a common building material, throughout the world, especially in places where stone was remote. It should be noted that Mud, Cob, Earth and Adobe are being revitalized as building materials by environmentalists and modern architects. The material is cheap, green and abundant. The ingenious artisans of the Mali culture would even find a place for Mud in their clothing. Mud was used as a dye-aid in the design of now world famous Mud Cloth, which is a popular fashion in Mali. The mud is painted on a locally manufactured white fabric. The mud holds its place, as it is submerged in dyes. The mud is then removed revealing intricate designs that often have significant meanings. Mud cloth has become recognizable from its aesthetic but not in name or proper attribution to the Africans that invented it. Mud cloth is often used by famous fashion designers without proper cultural attribution.

THE ORIGIN OF THE MALI EMPIRE

The rise of Mali as a new regional power, signaled the ascension of a new African ethnic group. In Africa, ethnic groups are cultures unto themselves. They are separated by language and practices that often make them very distinct from their neighbors. In the Kingdom of Ghana, the Soninke ethnic group would enjoy a status of privilege, as the descendants of the nation's founders. But in time, internal political discord, and external military and economic pressures, would bring the nation's existence to an end. No longer would the Soninke and their culture hold sway over the region. In their stead, a new ethnic group called the Manding would dominate the evolving cultures in the area, and become the driving force of cultural progress in West Africa. When Ghana fell, a former province, called Mali, would split into twelve kingdoms, known as the Twelve Doors of Mali. Collectively, their territory would be known as Manden, a reference to the Manding people responsible for its organization. As former subjects of the Ghana Empire, the Manding were familiar with imperial rule, and central authority. However, they would not immediately become the region's dominant force. The Manding would wait for additional pressures that would make conquest their only option. Immediately following the collapse of Ghana, another of its former vassals, an ethnic group called the Sosso would seize the opportunity to establish their own kingdom, and dominate their neighbors. Their kingdom would be called Kaniaga, and would be established in 1140 A.D. However, the Sosso would not attempt to build constructive or mutually beneficial relationships with the surrounding tribes. Instead they would rule through terror, and force. They would concentrate their efforts within the

Manden territories of the Twelve Doors of the Mali province. The Sosso would kidnap women, and raid towns for goods (especially Dodougou, and Kri which were within Mali). They would concentrate their ferocity on members of the Keita Clan, which was a sub-group (clan) within the Manding people. Little did they know; their persecution of the Keita Clan would bring about the abrupt end of Sosso dominance. Over time, the assaults on the Keita would grow, and the people of the clan would long for deliverance. In the Mali province of Niani, a child would be born, and a prophecy would declare that he was destined to conquer the enemies of the Manding people. The foretold child was the son of the Faama or Prince, Maghan Kon Fatta, and his second wife, Sogolon Kedjou. Unfortunately, the Faama's second wife, was a hunchback and she would pass on her propensity for infirmity to the child. As a child, Sundiata Keita would not walk until the age of seven, which would bring the prophecy into doubt. His capacity for conquest would not seem certain, yet despite his slow start, Sundiata would grow to be a strong and respected warrior. Over time, his fame would grow, and he would be held in high regard among the Manding elite. However, the sudden death of his father, would leave the young warrior exposed to the political aspirations of the Faama's first wife, and her son. Following the death of Sundiata's father, his half-brother, Dankaran Touman would take the throne. The prophesied leader would be banished along with his mother and two sisters. And the family would seek refuge in the court of the Emperor of Ghana, whose kingdom was now a vassal of the Sosso. However, fate would reward the treachery of Dankaran Touman and the first wife, as both would be driven from the throne of Niani by Soumaoro, the Sosso King. A desperate Niani delegation would seek out their prophesied leader, and implore him to confront the savagery of the Sosso. At the age of 18, Sundiata would lead a military alliance composed of the Ghana-Wagadou, the Mema people, and his own Manden. The coalition would converge on the Sosso, at the Battle of Kirina (1235 A.D). The young warrior would crush the opposition forces, and end the Sosso reign of terror. Following the battle, each King of the Twelve Doors, knelt before the throne of Sundiata, stabbing their spears into the ground. In this scene of solemn submission Sundiata, and his Keita Dynasty was given dominion over each of the twelve kingdoms. He was now, as foretold, the sovereign of the Twelve Kingdoms in an alliance called the Manden Kurufa. Sundiata Keita, the Lion Prince would be known to history as the founder of one of the world's most wealthy kingdoms; An empire that would cover 1,294,000 sq. km, or 500,000 sq miles (an area the size of Texas, California and Florida combined). Sundiata, would be called by several titles; the "Faama of Faamas' or Prince of Princes; and The Mansa or Emperor. The most lasting of Sundiata's monikers would be, The Lion Prince.

THE HISTORY OF THE MALI EMPIRE

When the Kings of the Twelve Doors gave Sundiata authority over their kingdoms, they ceased to be Kings, and instead became *Farbas*. Their new title, which meant Great Farin (Farin, means northern commander) allowed them to continue to rule their kingdoms in the name of the Mansa (which means Emperor). They would be a part of a complex administrative network, established by Emperor Sundiata. Following the Battle of Kirina, Sundiata would arrive in the town of KaBa, where he would present the "Kouroukan Fouga" -the Constitution of the nation of Mali. The term Kouroukan Fouga means the "Division of the World", and in many ways, the document essentially divides the world of the Mali kingdom. This new framework, would divide Mali into its ruling clans, but more importantly, it would establish The Gbara, or Great Assembly, as a deliberative body, with elected delegates that ensured representation for each of those clans. Each clan was encouraged to elect a delegate for the Gbara, however they could choose their representative in whatever manner they preferred. Initially 29 delegates (it would grow to 32) would be led in deliberations by the "belen-tigui" or the Master of Ceremony. Adding to the revolutionary character of the document, West Africa's first constitution would give no preference to men over women, or to free men over slaves. Centuries before western powers would even begin to approach the topic, the Kouroukan Fouga would declare that all would be equal in the eyes of the law. With an eye towards administration, the constitution would set forth a division of labor amongst the clans which ensured the functionality and long term prosperity of the kingdom. In all, 16 clans were responsible for leading and defending the empire. They were called the Djon-Tan-Nor-Woro; the Carriers of the Quiver. Four additional clans called the Mori-Kanda-Lolou, or the Guardians of the Faith, were responsible for leading in matters of Islamic Law. Four more, called Nyamakala, were given a monopoly on certain trades, such as smelting, woodworking, and tanners. Lastly, four more clans, called Djeli, or Masters of Speech, recorded their history in enigmatic songs. This Division of the World, not only ensured that tasks critical to the function of an empire were fulfilled, it ensured that every person and every clan had a place in the empire. The Kouroukan Fouga ensured that uniform laws governed the realm, with its 44 edicts and four sections. The first thirty sections, (1-30) concerned "social organization". Section two,

(31-36) defined property rights. The third section, (37-39) established policies related to "environmental protection". Lastly, section four, (edicts 40-44) specified "personal responsibilities". The Kouroukan Fouga was unique in the world, not simply because of its declarations on human rights, and equal rights, but also because it derived no inspiration from outside influences. Throughout the rest of the world, political ideologies would evolve as a rarely acknowledge amalgamation of cultural influences. As ideas would spread from one nation to another, the civilizations of Europe, the Great Islamic Empires, and even the Americas would borrow heavily from disparate cultures whose thoughts on human rights, and political organization would migrate across the globe. But in Mali, these progressive values would not only mature earlier than in many other nations, they would be singularly inspired innovations of the African political genius. The architects of Mali, would require no outside inspiration to develop sophisticated, and comparable concepts of political organization. In Africa, religion was of paramount importance. Faith was in many cases the glue of each civilization. Religion gave legitimacy to an administration. And gaining legitimacy meant that rulers needed to connect their own blood lines to pivotal figures in their respective faiths. Christian monarchs would claim heritage from their notable characters and Muslims would do the same. In the case of the Islamic state of Mali, the heritage of the Emperor was connected to Bilal, the favorite muezzin of the prophet Muhammad. In the Koran, Bilal was an Ethiopian slave, born in Mecca in 578 A.D. He was one of the first converts to Islam, and suffered intense persecution from his master, for his new-found faith. He would be freed from bondage by a fellow Muslim, Abu Bakr. In time, Bilal would become one of the Prophet's most trusted companions. Because of the beauty of his voice, he would also be named as the first muezzin, which is the person who sings from atop the minarets of modern mosques, and calls all Muslims to prayer. Bilal is also sighted as the basis or inspiration for racial equality, and the Prophet's anti-slavery stance. It is upon his name that the Emperors of Mali, would build their legitimacy, and trace their heritage. While clearly erroneous, the connection to Lawalo, one of Bilal'seven sons, is more convincing than other pseudo lineages of other African kingdoms.

THE LEGACY OF THE MANSAS

In the history of Mali, no leader in the pantheon of great Mali rulers would eclipse the fame of Sundiata Ketia. However, a few Mansas would have reigns that in the long-term were almost as consequential as Sundiata's impact. Mansa Mari Djata would annex a tremendous amount of territory. His "manifest destiny" and westward expansion would make Mali larger than Ghana. Gold fields, and commercial towns, would be added to the kingdom. His successors would expand the dominance of the Manding ethnic group, over the other ethnic peoples. The rule of Mansa Mari Djata would leave a legacy, as his direct descendants would rule for 25 years, and 21 Mansas in all would build onto his accomplishments. However impressive his achievements in life, it is the events that followed his death that are the most interesting. In life, the Mansa was recorded as merciful and kind. However well-intentioned his acts of generosity may have been, they would have terrible consequences for the future of his kingdom. During his life, he would adopt the sons of his generals as a reward for superior service. These children would live at court, and be raised as if they were his own. After his death, these adopted sons would come to feel entitled to the throne of their "father". They would seize power, and set Mali on a nearly fatal path. Their reigns are excellent demonstrations of the superb normalcy of events in African kingdoms, which were plagued with all the same pathologies, and dynastic struggles that would destabilize other nations in the world. Many of Africa's most infamous characters are strikingly familiar personality types, and can evoke comparisons to other actors on the world stage. In 1270, the first usurper, Mansa Quati- the first adopted son to assume power- would spend the treasury recklessly and treat his subjects with infamous cruelty. But in 1274, his death would usher in an even more wasteful administration. Mansa Khalifa, another adopted son, was tragically similar in behavior to the Roman Emperor Nero. Just as Nero slowly lost his grip on reality, and would most famously "fiddle while Rome burned", Khalifa would wade into a state of whimsical insanity. Just as Nero would be noted in history for acts of hysterical violence with which he would amuse himself, Khalifa would stand atop the roof of his palace, and fire arrows at pedestrians outside of his court. And just as Nero would nearly bankrupt Rome, the tyrannical Khalifa, would spend extravagantly (although, for less noble causes), and when he died, Mali was nearly bankrupt. Unlike Nero, Khalifa would not be left by his subjects to commit suicide. According to the historian Ibn Khaldun, the citizenry of Mali, having suffered long enough from his villainy would trample the Emperor to death. As the time of crisis ended, choices would have to be made to revive the terribly mismanaged kingdom. The deliberative Gbara would elect Manding Bory who, according to the constitution had been the rightful heir to the throne of Mari Djata all along. They would crown him as Mansa Abubari I, in 1275. Despite the election, the Court's officials would administer the government from 1275-1300, and it was under their leadership that Mali was restored to its former glory. In violating the laws of succession, written in their constitution Mali exposed itself to peril. And yet the consequences resulting from the actions of the two adopted usurpers, would not discourage all future coups. In 1285, Mansa Sakoura, a slave freed by Mari Djata would capture the throne. However, the outcome of this violation of the Mali constitution would pay off, as Mansa Sakoura would be a very successful ruler. He would add numerous territories, like Tekrour, and Djara. He would campaign into Senegal and Wolof. East Takedda, Macina and the always troublesome city of Gao would be forced to contend with his military. The usurper would establish diplomacy with Tripoli, and Morocco. His reign was distinguished and accomplished. As a Muslim, and as one who understood the value of forging connections with the larger Muslim world, the slave king would take the pilgrimage to Mecca. In a cruel irony, the Mansa, having fulfilled his spiritual obligation to Islam, would be murdered during the return from his Hajj. Near modern day Djibouti, common thieves would accost the Emperor, and deprive Mali of his able stewardship. Despite his status as a former slave, and illegitimate monarch, the success of his administration, would demand a royal burial. The legacy of Mari Djata would extend far into the future, with monarchs that were the direct result of his actions.

THE KOLOKAN MANSAS

In 1300 A.D., the Keita Dynasty of Mari Djata would end. It would be followed by another dynasty, whose leadership would result in unprecedented wealth and prosperity for the kingdom. The leaders of the new dynasty were chosen by the Gbara, from among the descendants of Mari Djata's sister Kolonkan. They would add new gold mines in Bambuk, Boure, and Galam, which would supply half of the entire worlds gold supply (supplying Asia, Europe, and Africa). They would bring salt and copper from towns like Taghaza and Takedda. And gold dust would effectively become the currency of the realm, as laws would decree that only the Mansa could possess gold nuggets. Whole gold, or nuggets would be confiscated from all merchants, consumers, and citizens. A fixed rate of exchange, called the mithqal (4.5 grams of gold dust) would be the primary measure for exchange.

THE ARMY OF THE KOLOKAN MANSA'S

The Kolokan Mansa's would build a professional army of 100,000 soldiers. The formidable military machine of Mali would be, for any foe, a terrible sight. A professional force of colorfully armored cavalry, horse mounted archers, and well-armed soldiers, were supported by a highly-trained infantry, and significantly less adorned bowman and slaves, recruited from the tribes. As we have previously discussed, in African Empires, rulers would balance the cultures of their urban lifestyle, with the village cultures of tribes and clans. The seemingly savage or less refined, would interact with the more civil or more refined. In the armies of Ghana, Mali, and many other empires, horses and warriors were fitted in heavy, brightly colored suits of quilted cotton cloth. The cloth was stuffed with woolen strands of kapok (which surround the seeds of the silk cotton tree). The soldiers and war-horses would also wear chain mails, and leather to protect the horse's flanks. The head would be covered with a chamfron or helmet of metal or cloth. The use of Quilted

Armor, and chain mail reflected the African emphasis on aerial warfare. While the use of swords, and other close combat weapons was common, the emphasis in African military strategy was on archery with poisoned and barbed arrows. Quilted Armor would evolve as a reaction to this strategic preference. Cavalry and elite warriors would wield swords, long metal lances, poisoned javelins, and shields. The remainder of the military would vary in equipment and clothing. The massive military would be maintained through the taxation of gold, salt, and traded goods, as they crisscrossed the expanse of the empire. Soldiers would come from clans, which were given quotas to fill. Volunteers would also come to the army from the "Horon" or the caste of freemen. The army would have two separate regional commanders. The Farim Soura and Sankar Zouma would lead northern and southern commands. A hodge podge of tribesmen, armed with reed and hide shields, and fierce spears or "tamba", would fearlessly wade right into the heart of battle. Bowmen outnumbered spear men by a factor of three. Barbed iron heads, and flaming arrows were used for sieges. Those soldiers of lower ranking, often coming from tribes were clearly less adorned. They would have whatever clothing was traditional for their tribes, and often less sophisticated weapons. This menacing mixture of warriors, created a frightening force that was organized, sophisticated, and effective.

THE END OF KOLOKAN DYNASTY

The Kolonkan line would continue for some time, but would end with the reign of Mansa Abubakari II, in 1310. It is believed that The Mansa set sail, with 4000 boats or pirogues into the Atlantic Ocean in 1311. The specifics of the event can be questioned, as it may possess some mythology, but the event is recorded in North African Records, and Mali's Oral Records as well (the djelis). Some scholars speculate that West African Muslims made the journey to the New World and they point to the Mansa's voyage as a source of inspiration. There is however, insufficient evidence for this conclusion. In the King's court, a man named Kankoro-Sigui, was serving at the pleasure of the emperor. When a full year had passed, and the Mansa Abubakari II failed to return from his Atlantic Ocean voyage, a new emperor would be chosen. The first ruler of this new dynasty would also be one of its most spectacular. Kankoro-Sigui would be known as Kankan Musa and he would be crowned under the title Mansa Musa. He was a devout Muslim, but would not attempt to force his faith on his subjects. He would establish the Islamic holiday of Eid as a national ceremony during Ramadan. As a Muslim, the Musa would take the Hajj pilgrimage to Mecca, from 1324-1326. His trip was a seminal moment for the Islamic world which was astonished by the spectacle of his wealth and power. On his journey the Emperor would be accompanied by 60,000 soldiers and a personal guard of 500 slaves, each carrying a wand made of 500 mithqals of pure gold. The Mansa brought 22,000 lbs of gold with him. As the Mansa travelled, he would give alms to the poor, as his faith required. He would patronize numerous vendors and would lavish his gold and wealth throughout the Islamic communities. The wealth of the Mansa seemed to the Muslim world to be almost inexhaustible. He lavished gold on the populace wherever he went, often throwing gold from atop his caravan. He distributed so much gold to the poor, and to vendors, that he crushed the price of gold. Twelve years would pass, before the price of gold would recover. According to Al-Maqurizi:

"the members of his entourage proceeded to buy Turkish and Ethiopian slave girls, singing girls and garments, so that the rate of gold dinar fell by six dirhams"

The Syrian scholar Al-Umari would arrive in Egypt two years after the arrival of Mansa Musa, and he would find the local populace still enthusiastically discussing the Mansa's Hajj trip. He wrote that Mansa Musa *"flooded Cairo with his benefactions. He left no court emir nor holder of a royal office without the gift of a load of gold. The people of Cairo made incalculable profits out of him and his suite in buying and selling and taking. They exchanged gold until they depressed it's value in Egypt and caused it's price to fall"*. Al-Umari also records a curious bit of conflict involving Mansa Musa, during the trip which gives us a very good indication of how the Mansa viewed himself, his empire, and the rest of the Muslim world. Al-Umari records that:

"From the beginning of my coming to stay in Egypt I heard talk of the arrival of this sultan Musa on his Pilgrimage and found the Cairenes eager to recount what they had seen of the Africans' prodigal spending. I asked the emir Abu, and he told me of the opulence, manly virtues, and piety of his sultan. "When I went out to meet him, he said that is, on behalf of the mighty sultan al-Malik al-Nasir, he did me extreme honor and treated me with the greatest courtesy. He addressed me, however, only through an interpreter despite his perfect ability to speak in the Arabic tongue. Then he forwarded to the royal treasury many loads of unworked native gold and other valuables. I tried to persuade him to go up to the Citadel to meet the sultan, but he refused persistently saying: "I came for the Pilgrimage and nothing else. I do not wish to mix anything else with my Pilgrimage." He had begun to use this argument but I

realized that the audience was repugnant to him because he would be obliged to kiss the ground and the sultan's hand. I continued to cajole him and he continued to make excuses but the sultan's protocol demanded that I should bring him into the royal presence, so I kept on at him till he agreed. When we came in the sultan's presence we said to him: 'Kiss the ground!' but he refused outright saying: 'How may this be?' Then an intelligent man who was with him whispered to him something we could not understand and he said: 'I make obeisance to God who created me!' then he prostrated himself and went forward to the sultan. The sultan half rose to greet him and sat him by his side. They conversed together for a long time, then sultan Musa went out. The sultan sent to him several complete suits of honor for himself, his courtiers, and all those who had come with him, and saddled and bridled horses for himself and his chief courtiers"

Al-Umari is describing the arrival of Mansa Musa and his encounter with the Sultan. As a visitor, Mansa Musa was required to bow and kiss the ground, when meeting the Sultan. The Mansa considered the typical protocols to be beneath him. His empire was larger, as scholarly and wealthier than the Egyptian Sultans. By every measurable standard, the Mansa considered himself and his empire to be equal to, if not superior to any in the Islamic world. He thus found any suggestion or demand for a posture of subservience to be insulting. He could only bring himself to bow in the presence of someone he considered to be his superior. He gave the gesture a religious meaning, hence his statement *"I make obeisance to God who created me!"*. Although the Mali empire and West Africa in general was well known throughout Europe and the Islamic world, his trip was so spectacular that Mali was immediately placed on

14th century maps. Mansa Musa, was depicted, holding a golden scepter and a nugget of gold, symbolizing his incredible wealth. The Hajj trip did not simply expose the outside world to Mali, the nation itself would import external influences. Mansa Musa would invite the famous Islamic poet, and architect, Al-Sahil to beautify Mali. The architect would innovate a new style for Mali's buildings, mosques, and palaces. The poet, scholar and architect would build a scholar's district called the Sankore Quarter and the Djingereber Mosque. Mansa Musa would also annex the scholarly city of Timbuktu in 1324. While the city was a major center of learning, Mansa Musa would direct a lady of his court, to transform the humble madrasa, or Islamic school into a famous Islamic University. Timbuktu would become a world-famous destination for Islamic scholars. The doctors, lawyers, mathematicians, and scientists there, would be some of the most educated men in the world. The libraries of Timbuktu would house 700,000 manuscripts, most of which remain today as untranslated texts, in the hands of individual families and collectors. Today these families see themselves as the keepers of Mali's glorious past. Many of Mali's books have been translated. The academic programs of Timbuktu have been found to have been on par with the most challenging programs in the Islamic world. The algebra program, for instance was the equivalent of a modern second year college program (algebra was still new to much of the world). The scholars of Timbuktu would prove themselves to be equal to any, anywhere in the world.

The Mali Empire mastered the art of administration. A robust central government, powered by a representative body, balanced the authority of its monarch with the need to ensure fair representation for all of its clans. On the local level administrators called the Kun-Tiguis, would elect village masters from the bloodline of its semi mythological founder. County level administrators were called the Kafo-Tigui, and they were appointed by the governors of each province. Provinces could choose their own governors, or Dyamani-Tigui (province master) by whatever method they chose. The province master, required the approval of the Mansa, who could assign a Farba in his place, if he was dissatisfied with the choice. For newly acquired territories a Farin could be assigned to an area until locals could be trusted to choose an acceptable Dyamani Tigui. The Governors were responsible for collecting taxes, building the local army, and ensuring that locals remained loyal to the Mansa's authority. If necessary, the Farba could strip the local council of its legitimacy, if their loyalty was in question. He could even put down rebellions when necessary. The successful reign of Mansa Musa was succeeded by his son Maghan, who spent wastefully and was the first poor ruler since Khalifa. The empire however, was so strong that not even his incompetence could destroy it. His brother Souleyman would become Mansa in 1341.

We can conclude our survey of Mali with details from the Islamic scholar Al-Umari. He would write a description based on the first-hand account of Abu Sa'id otman ed Dukkali, a 35-year resident of Mali. The country, he reported, was square, and required an astonishing eight months to cross from its coast at Tura (the mouth of the Senegal River) to Muli (Tuhfat). Al-Umari confirms for us the density of the population centers by reporting that the country was almost totally inhabited. He reports the expanse of the Empire and that its authority extended into the desert, over the Antasar, Yantar'ras, Medussa, and Lemtuna tribes of Berbers. He estimates 400 cities and towns, with villages of various religions and beliefs. Al-Umari would report that there were 14 provinces, but he would only name 13 provinces.

THE REIGN OF SOULEYMAN

The Palace intrigue and dynastic struggles of African Kingdoms, including Mali, were as interesting, contentious, and persistent as those of any of the world's kingdoms. During the reign of Souleyman, a series of events that would have been familiar to many of the governing dynasties of Rome, Europe, or China, would unfold. The Queen or Qasa would attempt to overthrow the king. As the Fula people began raids on the city of Takrur, the Queen along with several army commanders would attempt to seize the throne. We can only speculate as to the motivation of this coup. Perhaps she felt her husband was weak. Perhaps infidelities played a role. Perhaps the familiar Roman tale of love between a Queen and a General outlined the storyline of the events. Whatever her reasons, the Queen and her co-conspirators would fail. Souleyman's generals fought off the Fula, and the King ordered his Queen to be imprisoned. During Souleyman's reign Mali would lose control of the Dyolof province of Senegal, and the Wolof people would break away from the Mali empire, to form the Jolof Empire in the 1350's. The famous Islamic explorer Ibn Battuta would come to Mali in 1352, and despite the turmoil, he bears witness to the strength of the Mali empire. He states emphatically that Mali was on par with any place in the Muslim and Christian World. He would state that:

"The negroes possess some admirable qualities. They are seldom unjust and have a greater abhorrence of injustice than any other people. There is complete security in their country. Neither traveler nor inhabitant in it has anything to fear from robbers or men of violence".

Mansa Souleyman would go on Hajj, and maintain his correspondence with Morocco and Egypt, further strengthening ties with the larger Muslim world. The Mansa would build an earthen platform at Kangaba, which he called the Camanbolon. Here he would hold court with his provincial governors, and deposit holy books brought back from Hedjaz (Hajj). Mansa Souleyman died in 1360, but was succeeded by his son Camba. The Laye Dynasty would continue with a parade of Mansas. Each of leader met with varying success. Mansa Camba would be deposed after nine months. Mansa Mari Djata II, crowned in 1360 would be an oppressive tyrant, and waste the treasury. The financially ruined empire would then be run by court officials and Konkoro-Sigui, under Mansa Musa II. The most important event during this period of dysfunction and decline, would be the declaration of independence by a settlement called Gao, occupied by an ethnic group called the Songhai. Although the empire would recover financially by 1387, Gao would continue its independence. The Laye Dynasty would end in 1387 with Mansa Maghan II being deposed, in 1389.

THE END OF MALI & THE PORTUGUESE

By 1450 the Portuguese were sending raiding parties on the Gambian Coast. Portugal's Diogo Gomes testifies that Mali was still the dominant power along the coast. A succession of different dynasties now ruled Mali. No real pattern exists among the Mansas, and Mali would spiral downward, between 1389-1545. In time, the competitive churning of African societies would tear the Mali Empire apart, one piece at a time. The Songhai which led an important center of trade, would assert themselves, and conquer Mema, which was one of Mali's oldest territories. The Songhai, under Sunni Ali Ber, seized Timbuktu from the Tuareg, who had already taken the city in 1468. The Mossi would raid Macina, and conquer the province of Ghana. In the end, Mansa Mahmud II would be relegated to begging the Portuguese for assistance in facing the Peuhl, who were now seizing territory from Mali. The Portuguese would wisely stay out of the conflict (1495). The Last Mansa, Mahmud III, would come to power in 1496. Under his reign, Mali would lose most of its territory. Songhai's fabled king, Askia Muhammad would defeat the Mali General Fati Quali in 1502, landing another blow to the embattled kingdom. He seized the province of Diafunu. The persistent conflicts would continue to tear away at the nation in 1514, when the Denanke Dynasty was established in Tekrour, and the kingdom of Great Fulo went to war with Mali. Songhai continued its efforts to liquidate the former kingdom, when it seized the copper mines of Takedda. In 1534, Mahmud III would again beg a Portuguese envoy, Pero Fernandes, for Portuguese assistance. No help ever came from the Portuguese. In 1545, the Songhai under Askia Ishaq's brother Daoud launched an assault on Niani and even occupied the palace. Mansa Mahmud III fled to the mountains and hid. The displaced monarch gathered his resources and plotted his response. He eventually led a successful counter attack which forced the Songhai out of Manden permanently. The success of his campaign would not stop Songhai from becoming the undisputed power of the region but it did prevent them from returning to Manden. The fall of Mali, was merely another step in the harsh Darwinian evolution of African Empires. It would be followed by the larger, stronger, and wealthier Kingdom of Songhai.

SONGHAI: The Last Great Empire

The Rise of the Songhai Empire would follow the Empire of Mali. Just as Ghana was larger and more prosperous then the settlements that preceded it, and just as Mali would be larger, and wealthier then it's predecessor (Ghana), Songhai would follow the trend of increasingly sophisticated powers rising in West Africa. Songhai would be wealthier than all its predecessors. Two of the greatest indigenous sources of information on West African Kingdoms are the Tarikh al-fattash and the Tarikh al- sudan. Both are impressive historical chronicles written by native scholars, in the 17th century. They offer an indigenous perspective on the history of the region and are exceedingly valuable sources to consider, in addition to the extensive works of Arab historians. Through the combined historical efforts of West Africans, Arabs, and even European governments, we know that Songhai was in fact one of the world's wealthiest and most sophisticated kingdoms. Its administration would be more efficient than any of its predecessors, extending the authority of its ruler to even the far flung reaches of the preceding empires. Scholarship would reach even greater heights, and its armies would become even more formidable-scoring victories against the armies of major nations, like Morocco. Gold continued to be in obscene abundance in Songhai, and its rulers would continue to flaunt their wealth, for all to see. It would be Songhai's deep treasury that would ultimately attract the aggression of a nation that would conquer Songhai at a moment of political instability. The Songhai Empire is officially recognized as existing between 1350 -1600 A.D. However, the 250 year-period, is not truly representative of the nation's roots, which are considerably more ancient. The rise of Songhai, was the result of a growing political void, caused by the disintegration of the Mali state. The Empire of Mali would fall, in part, because of persistent rebellions in troublesome territories like the City of Gao. The settlement, which was established in approximately 800 A.D, would be the site of numerous uprisings, by an ethnic group called the Songhai. During the 9th century, Gao was transformed into a major center of trade and commerce. The city capitalized on its location along the Trans Saharan trade routes. The city, and its merchant residents became very wealthy, as Gao was filled with gold, cotton fabrics, and agricultural products like rice. In 1340, perhaps because of hubris, or perhaps as a result of age and maturity, the 500-year-old Songhai settlement would declare its independence from the Mali Empire. As the remainder of Mali's loosely tethered states would break away, the Songhai would establish themselves as the heirs to the regional throne and become the dominant power in the region. A ruling family called the Dia Dynasty, under the leadership of Dia Kossoi established the Songhai Capital, in the 11th century, but it was The Sunni Dynasty under the direction of Sulaiman-Mar that would end the long period of dominance by Mali in 1340. The 18 kings of the Sunni Dynasty would prove themselves to be experts in the art of state construction. They would secure their vast land holdings by assembling a military of unparalleled might and efficiency. Then a new Askia Dynasty distinguished itself by strengthening the empire structurally, with a proficient administration, capable of ensuring stability and long term economic prosperity. They assembled a strong administrative apparatus, a formidable military, and a vast network of trade and commerce. The population of Gao, would rise to over 100,000 people. The Songhai Empire would give birth to new settlements, while pre-existing cities would continue to grow. Timbuktu would continue to grow in economic and scholarly prominence. Its universities would continue to garner acclaim and build upon their reputation, while new institutes of Islamic learning began to rise throughout the empire. The City of Djenne became famous for its scholarship, and university. Djenne was the oldest city in west Africa and it became one of the most prosperous economic centers in the Songhai Empire. The city possessed one of the greatest markets in the Muslim world, and even after the downfall of the empire, Djenne prospered. As a major destination for scholars in West Africa, and a fantastic market town, the city was an important location for travelers and merchants. A network of streams and canals surrounded the city. Visitors to the city, would sail in boats or canoes down streams, entering the city through one of eight gates. Its houses were built with sun dried mud bricks. They were often 2 stories high, with central courtyards. The multi-story homes had flat roofs, with ceramic piping for drainage which prevented rainwater from damaging the homes. Decorative facades served a dual role as scaffolding for scaling the large buildings to ease maintenance. And grand, massive covered entrances accented the front of their homes. Many buildings were equipped with drainage systems, long before many places in Europe would sport similar facilities. The architecture of Djenne, could be extremely large. The Great Mosque of Djenne, is the largest adobe, or mud brick structure in the world. Ninty-nine wooden pillars support the interior which provides ample room for over 3000 supplicants. Massive walls are used to support the tremendous structure, which rests on a bed of plastered, and mortared mud brick. Beautiful mosques are spaced at near equal distances, throughout the region. The city of Agades was also a great market city. Its population was well over 70,000 people, and was filled with "splendid" homes. The short-lived Songhai empire would climax under the skilled leadership of the Askia Dynasty, whose able administration would not be sufficient to prolong the meteoric rise of the Songhai Empire. In size, and wealth, Songhai would eclipse all the West African Empires that came before it. Despite its brevity, the Songhai Empire would become one of the world's most prosperous powers. It would reach its apogee, and just as rapidly as it ascended, Songhai would fade into the backdrop of history.

THE FIRST GREAT EMPEROR: SONNI ALI BER

In 1464, the Great Sonni Ali Ber would take the throne (also spelled Sunni Ali). He was an animist, who worshiped the gods of his ancestors. His people called him a magician, and perhaps in military matters he was. Sonni Ali Ber, is remembered in all accounts, as a remarkably skilled military strategist. The additions he made to the empire, have earned him, in the eyes of historians, the distinction of being the first great emperor of the Songhai Kingdom. Through numerous military campaigns, he would not only build an Empire that was larger than that of Mali, but by capturing critical trade routes, he would build a kingdom even wealthier than its predecessor. While Sonni Ali, is revered in the eyes of most of his descendants, the high opinion of the ruler, is not shared by all. In 1468, the relentless conqueror would add the city of Timbuktu to his list of conquered territories previously held by Mali. The Islamic historian Al-Sa'df would describe Sonni's conquest of Timbuktu as thus:

"Sonni Ali entered Timbuktu, committed gross iniquity, burned and destroyed the town, and brutally tortured many people there. When Akilu heard of the coming of Sonni Ali, he brought a thousand camels to carry the Fuqaha (Islamic judges) of Sankore and went with them to Walata. The Godless tyrant was engaged in slaughtering those who

172

remained in Timbuktu and humiliated them".

In the eyes of some Muslim historians, the courageous warrior was little more than a ruthless tyrant. However, perspective must be applied to this passage. Sonni Ali, is not regarded as a devout Muslim, in any source. He certainly converted at some point, but in the accounts of many, he remained an animist. In either case, the African monarch may have to be added to the list of African Kings whose embrace or tolerance of Islam was largely motivated by commerce. Sonni Ali did not institute Islamic Law in his kingdom, nor did he force Islamic practices on the Songhai people. In West Africa, many citizens converted to Islam, but maintained their indigenous practices. Sonni Ali, allowed the indigenous beliefs of his people to be practiced freely. This progressive attitude toward religious freedom may not have sat well with the prevailing Islamic orthodoxy that was anxious to enforce a stricter interpretation of Islamic law. When Sonni Ali entered Timbuktu, he was invited into the city by the scholars of the city. During the decline of Mali, Timbuktu had fallen into the hands of the Tuareg. The Tuareg were nomadic traders, known more for their treachery and propensity for violence, than anything else. However barbaric the Tuareg were, they were also impressive warriors. Cloaked in their mysterious, and oddly regal robes, they were known as the blue men because of their common use of blue robes. In the hot desert sun, the dye eventually seeps into their skin, giving their faces a blue tint. The Tuareg are 80% Sub Saharan African, and mixed with Arabs and Berbers which comprise the rest of their heritage. The Tuareg are like desert dwelling Samurai, excellent swordsman that hold an almost spiritual connection to their blades. They were known best for their robbery of caravans in the Sahara. The Tuareg would often offer their services as guides through the desert, only to murder their unsuspecting customers. The fierce Tuareg would begin to expand and conquer territory, which included Timbuktu. The academics of the University of Sankore, appealed to the leader of the Songhai to rescue them from Tuareg domination. But instead of being a tireless crusader for Islam, Sonni Ali was an idle worshiping pagan with a tolerance for other faiths. The scholars were hoping for a champion that would spread and impose Islamic law on the pagan worshipers of the kingdom. However, as a practitioner of the local religions, Ali was not willing to give sanctuary to those he deemed to be religiously intolerant. Instead of an Islamic hero, the scholars were surprised to find that Sonni Ali, was a champion for traditional African customs. As one of the many Africans that practiced Islam, while maintaining a connection to the indigenous religious practices, Sonni Ali would choose to evict or kill anyone with an unyielding commitment to eliminating the local customs. It is this eviction that earned Sonni Ali the title of "Godless Tyrant" from Al-Sa'df. Whether this was truly the "gross iniquity" that Al-Sa'df claims, or a cleansing of intolerance is a matter of perspective. However, we can agree that, whatever his intentions, The Great Emperor probably did humiliate many of the Islamic purists in Timbuktu.

A MAN OF HONOR

Sunni Ali would continue his conquests with an assault on the City of Djenne, a major trading city and University town, in 1473. In Djenne, the venerable leader would face his most persistent opposition. The siege to take the city would last seven months, with the inhabitants forced into submission by starvation. Upon entering the city, Sonni Ali would not slaughter its inhabitants. He would not be filled with anger, vitriol, or contempt for the insolence of its population. He would instead be overwhelmed with respect for their strength. After seven months of waiting at the gates of Djenne, Sonni would spare its leadership, in admiration of their spirited defense of their home. His regard for honor; his prowess as a military commander, and his defense of religious freedom and traditional African culture have earned Sonni Ali Ber high regards in the oral tradition of the Songhai. After the Sunni Dynasty, a new family would take the reins of power. They were called the Askia Dynasty.

THE ASKIA DYNASTY

"One cannot count either the virtues or qualities of Askiya Muhammad'
-Chronicle of The Tarikh al- fattash

The astounding reign of Sunni Ali would be followed by the brief reign of his son, Sonni Baru. The entire Sunni Dynasty would come to a violent end, when an audacious general named Muhammad Ture, would effectively remove Sonni Baru from the throne. The general would rise to power on the wings of discontent caused by Sunni Ali's infidelity to Islam. The scholars and religious leaders that Sunni Ali disrespected would find their revenge by supporting his overthrow. The new dynasty would be born at the Battle of Anfao. In the battle, the general was outnumbered but he would win a decisive victory over forces loyal to the rightful heir to the Songhai throne, and seize control of the empire. If Muhammad Ture was ashamed of his coup, he gave no indication of it through his actions. Instead, he would flaunt his status as a usurper. The remaining daughters of the Sonni Dynasty would curse the general saying, "A Si Tiya" or "He Will Not Be". The general would mock the daughters of the former crown by using their words of protest as the basis for the name of his dynasty. He would found the Askiya Dynasty and be installed under the name Askia Muhammad (also spelled Askiya). Askia, which means usurper, became his official title. He would wear the moniker proudly, and lead the Empire of Songhai to new heights. The reign of Askia Muhammad was in many ways a direct rejection of everything Sunni Ali stood for. The most consequential difference was that Askia was a devout Muslim, in contrast to Sunni Ali whose embrace of the faith was half-hearted at best. Songhai would become a nation rooted in Koranic law. Unlike Sunni Ali, Askia was not a descendant of the Songhai. He was a descendent of the Soninke, whose ancestors built the Empire of Ghana. And whereas, Sunni Ali was a man of war, Askia Muhammad would be a head of state focused firmly on the kingdom's administration. Instead of concentrating his efforts on military affairs, Askia would focus his energy on the art of state craft. He would enact broad political reforms and establish organs for his administration in all the lands under Songhai control. He would enhance the bureaucracies, by establishing departments of agriculture, army, treasury, and assign supervising officials. Governors and mayors presided over local tributary states, around the Niger valley. Local chiefs were granted authority over their respective domains provided they did not undermine Songhai policy. Taxes were levied on outlying chiefdoms and provinces to ensure Songhai dominance. However, in their daily affairs, the provinces had almost total autonomy. The central government of Songhai would only intervene when circumstances became volatile. Government officials and bureaucrats represented each town. Askia would innovate creative schemes to centralize Songhai authority. He encouraged learning by rewarding professors with larger pensions and incentives. He gave generously to the poor. He would build mosques, which would not only nourish the spiritual needs of his people but would also serve as educational centers for scholars, and poets, from all over the world. He would fulfill his religious obligations by completing the Hajj. The Tarikh al-fattash, lauds the leader by stating that " *One cannot count either the virtues or qualities of Askiya Muhammad, such is his excellent politics, his kindness towards his subjects and his solicitude towards the poor. One cannot find his equal either among those who preceeded him, nor those who followed. He had a great affection for the scholars, saints and talebs (men of learning).*

Despite his focus on issues of administration, Askia Muhammad would not divorce himself entirely from military endeavors. As a devout Muslim, the Askia would declare numerous Jihads, and campaigns. Having outfitted his military and expert cavalry with protective armor, and iron tipped weapons, he would send his enhanced military against the Mossi. His war canoes and organized militia were positioned throughout the empire to ensure security and stability. The presence of the standing army throughout the empire made trade and travel safe. Throughout Songhai lands, numerous tribes would fulfill predetermined roles, each critical to the success of the Kingdom. The clan of a person determined occupation. Crafts guilds, which were precursors to the modern union represented the craftsman. These individual efforts would converge on the sophisticated cities of Songhai. There is a cooperative aspect to the governance of African Kingdoms that is rarely appreciated. Each tribe would submit to the authority of the central government, fulfill its assigned duty, pay proper tribute to the central authority, and finally benefit from the intricate networks that empires offered. For instance, salt would be mined by one tribe, gold by another, and agricultural products by yet another. The tribes mining gold would need salt, and those mining salt were desirous of fabrics, textiles, or produce. As most of the people lived in small, family owned farms of a few acres, agricultural products were abundant. By facilitating the exchange between tribes, and international customers, the Songhai king would maintain an infrastructure that could provide products for the entire known world. But this delicate system relied on a respect for village and tribal life. African Kingdoms were not necessarily culturally homogenous. Tribes could keep their own beliefs, and practices, and still interact with the sophisticated life of the empire. The life of an African Empire, was one of interdependence, and cooperation. Tribes, while less couth in dress, or education were still valuable, willing participants in African Society. In Africa, the misnomered savage would interact regularly with the civilized. The trans-Saharan trade consisted of gold, salt, and occasionally slaves. The Julla or merchants-would form partnerships and were protected by the state. The empire would become financially stable, militarily, and administratively secure, and would utilize a sophisticated bureaucracy. There was a hierarchy in the society. Lower castes were mainly non-farm working immigrants. At the top of the hierarchy were nobles, who were direct decedents of the Songhai. Adjacent to the nobles were freemen and traders. At the bottom were war captives and European slaves-used in farming. Craft guilds were akin to modern unions, and they consisted of various specialists and artisans. Under Askia, Songhai and Timbuktu became thriving commercial and cultural centers. Arabs, Italians, and Jews traded extensively in his realm. Islamic scholarship would reach new heights, in many of the empires cities. The justice system was based in Islam. In addition, local Qadis or Islamic judges, maintained order by enforcing Sharia law. Kings did not usually judge defendants, but in special cases, such as treason, they would get involved as a show of their authority. The town crier would announce the results of trials, and numerous prisons would house criminals. While Qadis worked on local levels in towns like Timbuktu, and Djenne, the Assara-munidios were enforcers working as police commissioners who executed sentencing. Jurists were chosen from academic communities. Professors took administrative positions from within the empire-and many aspired to become Qadis. By 1500, 1.4 million sq. km would be under Songhai dominion.

THE BLACK SULTAN & THE END OF SONGHAI

After the death of Askia Daoud (the ruler of Songhai from 1549-1582), a civil war weakened the empire. The Saadi Sultan of Morocco, Ahmad I al-Mansur, took the opportunity to send an invasion force to Songhai. The incredible irony of history, is that the final and most grand West African Empire, was destroyed by the orders of the black African Sultan of Morocco and not European powers as the poor instruction of African history might lead some to expect. Ahmad Al-Mansur, the Sultan of Morocco, was the son of an African Fulani woman. He was known as Ahmad "The Victorious", and al-Dhahabi "The Golden" and most importantly for our purpose, he was known as "The Black Sultan". Father Luis Nieto, a Spanish priest familiar with Al-Mansur, described him as "Black in Color". And yet the black sultan existed in an Islamic world that promoted the notion that an attractive appearance was a sign of God's favor and religious piety. Therefore, the definition of "attractive" in the Islamic world would literally color the images historical documents have left of al-Mansur. Despite constant references to al-Mansur as the "Black Sultan" and our knowledge of his mother's identity as Lalla Mas'uda, or Lady Mas'uda- a Sudenese Slave from the Fulani people, descriptions of Al-Mansur would be left for posterity that seem to alter his appearance. Mohammed al-Ifrani, a Moroccan historian would record that al-Mansur was "*tall in height, with broad shoulders, full cheeks yellowish in color, [with] brown hair and black eyes*". Despite these contradictions in his reported physical appearance, the truth of the matter is recorded in an anonymous description that states that Ahmad was, "Brown, his eyes deep-set in their sockets, and his beard thick; he had a scar on the left cheek: and he was corpulent". We can further solidify our physical description of Al-Mansur by recognizing how Al-Mansur was received in popular culture closer to his actual lifetime. Al-Mansur formed a tenuous allegiance with Queen Elizabeth of England and this affiliation made him a familiar character to English writers for generations. In the works of Shakespere, Al-Mansur was the inspiration for "The Prince of Morocco" in Shakespere's Merchant of Venice. The Prince of Morocco is always depicted as extremely dark-skinned and black. Yet the conventions of his time have resulted in contradictory descriptions and depictions of al-Mansur. In some ways, this distortion is the result of the ambitions for grandeur Al-Mansur placed on his own legacy. Al-Mansur made the audacious claim that he was the long-awaited for Mahdi, the Messiah of the Islamic World. The Mahdi, according to Islamic theology is the Messiah that the Prophet Muhammad predicts will return to lead all Muslims to salvation. The Mahdi is predicted to arrive at a time when Muslims globally have gone astray and witnessed the decline of Islam. When Al-Mansur came to power, the Islamic world was witnessing a decline, as the political powers of the Christian World were pushing back on the conquests of the Islamic World. Muslims witnessed the fall of their empire in Spain, the growth of Christian powers like Portugal, the temporary success of the Crusades and numerous declines in the general power of the global Muslim community. In the minds of Muslims in antiquity, the time was ripe for one who would restore Islam to its former glory. Ahmad-Al Mansur claimed to be the hero they longed for, as the Mahdi. As Mahdi, he needed to promote a public image that would be expected of the personified myth. The Mahdi would have immense power, wealth and would also be dashing. The need to present his myth as handsome which was synonymous with morality and sadly "whiteness" has altered the presentation of his race in some depictions. Despite, the revisions to his physical description, we know without doubt his true lineage. The monetary costs involved with presenting himself as the Mahdi were substantial. As

Mahdi, he needed to be charitable and he needed to have resources that would be sufficient to finance the re-conquest of lost territories by an Islamic army. His need to finance his empire, and its wars with Europe, would end the legacy of grand empires in West Africa. As Al-Mansur spent lavishly to maintain his façade as the Mahdi, the coffers of his kingdom would shrink and new sources of financing would need to be located. There was one place, popularly known throughout the Islamic world to be overflowing with endless supplies of gold. The wealth of West Africa and the Songhai Empire would attract the terminal aggression of The Black Sultan. At the time, Al-Mansur met resistance to his desire to sack West Africa. The notion of an unprovoked attack on a well known Muslim kingdom was an anathema to most Muslims. Songhai was a heralded Islamic nation that kept the tenets of the faith. It was not filled with heretics or abdicators which might have been a reasonable pretense for an attack. Songhai was famous for the piety of its citizens and the qualifications of its scholars. Timbuktu was called the "City of Knowledge" and the tranquil Niger River that led to Songhai's cities was called "The River of Heaven". The idea of killing fellow Muslims, and co-religionists without cause was a direct contradiction of any reasonable interpretation of the Koran and all Islamic law. Al-Mansur argued that by refusing to pay tributes to him and by refusing to honor his request to annex their territory, Songhai relinquished their right to be called Muslims. He was the Caliph of the World, the Imam of the Time, the Lord of All Muslims, who's coming was foretold by the Prophet Muhammad himself. The "Muslims" of Songhai effectively became infidels when they refused to acknowledge him as their Messiah. To gain popular support for attacking Songhai for the plainly stated reason of stealing its wealth, Al-Mansur promised to use the wealth of Songhai to fund a campaign to retake Spain for the Muslims who were expelled with the fall of Andalusia. Andalusia or Al-Andalus was the name given to the Iberian

Peninsula when the Muslims conquered Spain and Portugal. The Muslims maintained their incredible kingdom from 711-1492 and were effectively the light of European civilization during the Dark Ages. While most of Europe was literally "dark" in aesthetic and progress, The Moors would build an Islamic kingdom in Europe that advanced science, art, architecture, and commerce. Europeans that were still interested in education and knowledge during the Dark Ages, would find instruction in Andalusia. The opulent Andalusian kingdom of Spain was cosmopolitan, wealthy and a source of pride in the Islamic world. The fall of Andalusia and the expulsion of Muslims throughout Europe was traumatic for the global Muslim community. As the proposed Caliph of the World, Al-Mansur offered to re-take Spain for the Muslims if he could simply take Songhai's gold. Anyone who opposed him was effectively opposing the re-establishment of Islam on the Iberian Peninsula and disobeying the Messiah. Songhai's armies roundly defeated the Sultan's first invasion attempt. After their first attempt failed, Morocco would hold all efforts until political instability overtook Songhai. The next attempt would require more planning and a recognition that war is won on the battle field and in the minds of men. Al-Mansur began his assault by planting the idea that he was the Messiah in the minds of Songhai's elite. The Sultan sent letters to men like Umar b. Mahmud, the Qadi of Timbuktu (Chief Islamic Judge). In his letters, he declared himself to be the Imam of the World and he implored faithful Muslims to recognize the enormity of his challenge in leading all Muslims worldwide. *"God appointed us to be the Great Imamate and through it made unquestioning obedience to us binding upon people"*. He warned that he would send an army that would be so great and terrible that its arrival would seem like the end of the world had come. These warnings may have not been taken seriously but a seed of fear was planted in the hearts of Songhai Muslims. Those who would not bow were risking disobeying the Messiah of the world, foretold by the Prophet Muhammad himself. Al-Mansur saw his effort to tackle Songhai as an exercise in multi-dimensional strategy. He installed spies throughout Songhai and one of his greatest double agents was Bukar Lanbaru, the Imperial Secretary and personal Chaplin of the Emperor Askia Ishaq II. He was the Songhai Emperor's most trusted advisor and spiritual guide in matters of faith. He was also the personal mole and spy of the Moroccan Sultan, Al-Mansur. In the annals of effective espionage, Bukar Lanbaru deserves the highest recognition. His role would be pivotal to the invasion of Songhai. The army of the Moroccan Caliph was placed in the capable hands of the eunuch Judar Pasha, a Spaniard-captured as an infant and educated at the Moroccan Saadi court. He would lead the second invasion. His army crossed the vast expanse of the Sahara, and half of his men perished from the journey alone. The Songhai worried very little about invasion because the Sahara was previously, a nearly impregnable barrier of protection against outside conquerors. For Judar, the wildly fluctuating climate of the Sahara would batter his forces. Sunstroke during the day, followed by the freezing temperatures of the desert night would cause convulsions of confusion that dehydrated the bodies of Pasha's army. But in the service of their Caliph, the army persevered. They assaulted the salt mines of Taghaza and more importantly concealed their approach toward Songhai. In Songhai, each tribe and ethnic group had a function and in the desert, The Taureg were commissioned as scouts for the Songhai. They should have provided an early warning to the empire of invasion but, true to their reputation for treachery they aligned themselves with Morocco. In truth, the Taureg were still morose over the execution of their chief for his participation in a revolt. They should have attacked the Moroccan army but chose not to in their state of dissatisfaction. The lack of a warning coming from the great expanse of the desert meant that when Al-

Mansur's army appeared out of the desert at the great city of Gao, it seemed like a miracle to the citizens of Songhai. When the army of the Messiah seemed to appear out of thin air, the letters of warning to the elite men of religion seemed to be prophetic. There was no army present to fight Judar's forces because the Songhai army was dispersed throughout the ample country on other campaigns. When word of the invading army finally reached Askia Ishaq II, the spy Bukar Landaru sprung into action. As the Imperial Secretary, he received the letters of warning first and when the Emperor's councilors began to debate a proper course of action, Landaru used his trusted position as advisor to prevent the group from coming to a concensus. He skillfully massaged the mind of the Emperor, sowing doubt and dissension, making it impossible for the group to respond effectively. Once the Songhai army was recalled, they met Judar Pasha's forces on the battle field, outside of the town of Tondibi. Historical sources have mixed feelings on the precise number of soldiers in the Songhai army. Some sources claim there were over 100,000 soldiers, and others put the number at closer to 80,000 warriors. Whatever the precise number, Ahmad Al-Mansur wrote that *"their number was so great that one imagined the gathering of humanity on Judgement Day"*. When Askia Ishaq II (1588-1591) met Judar in 1591 at the Battle of Tondibi, his Songhai forces were a superb medieval army. They were a fearsome force for the time, which consisted of Cavalry with lancers, javelin throwers with poisoned tipped iron spears, archers with flaming arrows and a monsterous infantry. Their incredible numbers however, were no match for the much smaller force of Al-Mansur which was outfitted with modern artillery. The true downfall of the Songhai empire was due to their failure to modernize. According to sources, the battle raged from mid-morning to mid-afternoon and the guns of the Moroccan army cut down the larger Songhai force. As the Mahdi's army fired their guns, unseen in the history of West African warfare, the terrible sound they made convinced the superstitious men of religion that the end of the world was near, just as Al-Mansur's letters predicted. As Askia Ishaq II peered across the battle field, he could see that his significantly larger army was being torn apart by the Mahdi's mysterious weapons. In this frightening moment, Bukar Landaru resumed his assault on the Emperor's mind. The entire time, he attempted to dissuade the Emperor against resisting the might of the proposed Messiah. He placed the salvation or eternal damnation of the entire nation at the feet of Ishaq II. As the Emperor's Chaplin, Bukar would advise Ishaq to "*Fear God, do not go to death, do not kill your brothers and do not cause all of Songhai to die at the same time in this one spot. God will ask you for a reckoning for the lives of all those who were killed here today for it is you who have caused their deaths if you do not flee*". While the Emperor was trying to make pivotal adjustments on the battlefield, the Emperor's most trusted advisor would continue to whisper into his ear that retreating from the Messiah's army was the only way to prevent the eternal damnation of the nation. As his forces were overcome, Ishaq II would submit and Bukar Landaru would turn the Emperor's horse and lead him off the battlefield. The army of Songhai would be demoralized by the submission of their emperor. As the Moroccan forces would continue their merciless assault, the soldiers of Songhai would plead for mercy, saying "*We are Muslims; we are your brothers in religion*". Al-Mansur's army held nothing back, continuing the slaughter. When the battle was all but lost, the famous Sunna warriors of Songhai would refuse to retreat. The Sunna were the elite guard that led the infantry. Their corp dawned ornate golden armlets and they were known for their oath to fight to the death. The Sunna honored their sworn duty and covered the retreat of the army after the Emperor fled. They fought until all others were ushered off to safety and then dropped their shields to the ground. As a final testament to their discipline and fearlessness, they sat on their shields, awaiting execution. Their fellow brothers in religion cut the Sunna down and stole their coveted golden armlets. This act of sacrilege was just the beginning of the theft that would follow. Judar sacked Gao, Timbuktu, Djenne and systematically destroyed every town of note in Songhai. His army pillaged every home and storehouse of treasure and even home furnishings. They burned towns and looted everything of value that could be used to finance Al-Mansur's future military expeditions. The scholars of Songhai's universities were kidnapped during the invasion, and taken back to Morocco. They would be forced to commit their genius to the advancement of a foreign culture. One of the most famous scholars, was Ahmed Baba. He was the author of 60 books. In Songhai, he was called "the imam, the erudite, the high minded, and the eminent among scholars". His reputation transcended the boundaries of the Songhai empire. Upon his arrival in Morocco, Arab scholars petitioned to have him released from prison. According to the French author, Major Dubois, " *All the believers were greatly pleased with his release, and he was conducted in triumph from his prison to the principle Mosque in Marrakech. A great many of the learned men urged him to open a course of instruction. His first thought was to refuse, but overcome by their persistence he accepted a post in the Mosque of the Kerifs and taught rhetoric, law and theology. An extraordinary number of pupils attended his lectures and questions of the greatest importance were submitted to him by the magistracy, his decision always being treated as final*". Ahmed Baba, made a point of complaining about the destruction of his precious book collection which contained 1600 volumes. He noted that his, was one of the smaller collections in Timbuktu. The professor, was forced to remain in Morocco, for 12 years, until he received permission to return to Timbuktu. When he arrived, he found that Timbuktu, the once great fount of wisdom, was in ruins, and the old kingdom was in tatters. Songhai never recovered from Morocco's assault. The incredible book collections Ahmed Baba referenced became the closely guarded collections of families that hoped to prevent their destruction by the Portuguese who banned reading and writing. While many families have granted researchers access to the secret hiding places of their family collections, many are still too scared to unearth their family books. Researchers believe that these still private protectors are harboring over a million African texts. This is highly possible because in medieval West Africa, the transcription and copying of manuscripts was one of the largest industries. Despite the popular notion that Africa was lacking in written records and literacy, these private collections prove otherwise. The university collections of West Africa were incredibly complete and consisted of current treaties on astronomy, mathematics, medicine, Islamic law, biology, and histories. Unfortunately, after its conquest of Songhai, The Saadi dynasty could not govern the empire, and after looting the nation of its material and intellectual wealth, the Moroccans let it splinter into chaos.

THE GREAT TRIBES & KINGDOMS

The Kingdoms of West Africa grew up along the banks of the Niger River, which bends and turns throughout the region. When the river floods, the banks of the river become extremely fertile. These rich zones of fertility made large scale agriculture and large centralized populations possible. The tremendous cities of West Africa, arose because of the annual process of fertilization which is strikingly like the flooding of the Nile, which made Egyptian (and Kushite) civilization possible. The process is so similar that early Arab visitors to the region, believed that the Niger was an extension of the Nile. All the great empires of Ghana, Mali, and Songhai came into existence because of the bounty produced by this flooding. But the great empires of West Africa were not the only kingdoms that rose because of the Niger's bounty. We can generally think of Africa as a vast universe, teeming with life. However, we must also contextualize the existence of Africa's civilizations by recognizing that the African continent is three times larger than the size of the United States. In between the space occupied by Africa's great empires was a vast formless expanse, filled by an innumerable variety of societies. The dramatic diversity, and constantly changing form of these societies means that there is no definitively African form for black civilization. African civilization varies wildly, in its form and even in its sophistication. If we accept this reality, we can properly contextualize the tribes, kingdoms, and empires of Africa. If we properly appreciate the diverse forms of African civilization, we can begin to see the seemingly strange and primitive tribes that dominate the popular stereotypes of African civilization, are singular points on a continuum of Black cultures. The African continent was filled with an incalculable number of admirable kingdoms and societies, outside of its major empires. The Kingdom of Fouta Djallon, is an excellent demonstration of the quaint but high quality of life that many Africans would have enjoyed prior to the western slave trade. The Kingdom of Fouta Djallon, was in Guinea, West Africa, near the banks of the Niger River. Fouta Djallon was a beautiful but simple kingdom, organized into nine provinces. Set amidst the rolling grasslands of numerous hills and valleys carved by the Niger, Senegal and Gambia River, Fouta Djallon was a picturesque society based on agriculture, animal husbandry, trade, and scholarship. The lifestyle of Fouta Djallon, was simple but comfortable. Its simple villages were well constructed, and well organized communities. Homes in Foutan Djallon were humble round houses, with thatch roofs. But manicured hedges and fences, defined the yards of individual houses, providing each family with privacy and personal space. According to early European visitors, the women were well adorned and wealthy. They typically wore ample blue togas, made from richly dyed fabrics. They adorned themselves in armlets and jewelry made from silver and gold. The provincial kingdom of Fouta Djallon was a major destination along the trade routes that crisscrossed the region. The nation was at the center of multiple trade routes, which provided numerous opportunities for the skilled craftsmen, and traders of Fouta Djallon. The kingdom was also a destination for professional scholars and academics. There were excellent schools for the children of this humble kingdom. The children of wealthy traders, artisans and nobles could further their academic pursuits in the major cities, at the Universities of Djenne and Timbuctu. The well-educated scholars of Fouta Djallon were a consequence of the nation's acceptance of the Islamic faith, however the indigenous population, was not the passive beneficiary of Arabization. Fouta Djallon became an Islamic kingdom, after a series of Jihad's expelled its pagan population, and those that were unwilling to convert. Its citizens learned Arabic as the language of religion. However, like many African societies, they would not bow entirely to Arabization. They accepted Islam and Arabic, but they made the language their own, by borrowing the Arabic alphabet, and using it to express their own indigenous language, called Pullar. Arabic is often called the Latin of Africa, because it served much of the same function that Latin did in the west. Arabic or more accurately an altered form of its alphabet was used by numerous African societies to express their indigenous language. In the case of Fouta Djallon, Pullar is the native tongue, but it is expressed as an altered form of Arabic. Despite the popular perception of Africa, as a land of illiteracy, more recent research has determined that many societies used the Latin of Africa. In addition to the tremendously large collections of texts written in Arabic, the ever-expanding collections of rediscovered texts from Timbuktu and West Africa, are filled with books written in indigenous languages with altered forms of Arabic. When we think of tribes it is important that we avoid assuming they were primitive or illiterate. Many tribes, especially those that converted to Islam would have been literate, simply because of their need to study the Koran. In Fouta Djallon, scholars would begin to conduct matters of religion in Pullar. They would even take the audacious, and often discouraged step of translating the Koran out of its original Arabic, preferring to study it in Pullar. The Pullar speaking academics of Fouta Djallon, would create a rich literary tradition, which they called Ajamiyya. Notable authors like Tierno Saadu Dalen, Tierno Muhammadu Samba Mombeya, and Tierno Jaawo Pellel would garner acclaim as accomplished authors. Poets, and even playwrights would spread the fame of the provincial kingdom. Despite its humble lifestyle, Fouta Djallon would become a destination for accomplished scholars, as ideas, books, and information were all exchanged along its trade routes. The nation was one of numerous provincially organized kingdoms, that may not have qualified as empires, but were certainly laudable achievements of culture and living conditions. It is worth contemplating the dramatic decline in living conditions African slaves would have experienced when they were taken from their homes and sold into the western slave trade. Fouta Djallon has achieved popular recognition in part because of the prominence of one of its citizens. Prince Abdul Rachman was the future heir to the throne of Fouta Djallon. When returning from a military engagement for his father, a small cadre of soldiers accompanied the Prince. The small company was ambushed by local slave raiders and the Prince was captured and sold into slavery. He was forced to board a ship to America, where he was sold to a man named Thomas Foster. Foster was an amateur cotton farmer. He knew very little about agriculture, but he was one of many entrepreneurial settlers that were willing to take their chances in the new world. In the beginning, Abdul Rahman resisted his enslavement. He even tried communicating the truth of his royal heritage to his new master. Foster would find humor in Rahman's claims and named him Prince mockingly. Foster was very lucky and very surprised to find that his slave, Prince was particularly adept at cultivating cotton. He was equally surprised to find that Prince was fluent in Arabic. The slave would be Foster's key to success, as Prince would manage Foster's farm, and turn the small plantation into a thriving colonial operation. There is very little about Abdul Rahman's story that is entirely unprecedented. Among early slave populations, the name Prince was somewhat common. There would be many colonial farmers that would mock the claims of their slaves to royal heritage. There would also be many slaves that came to America with a variety of skills. Many slaves came from sophisticated, although humble agrarian based communities like Prince Rahman. They would similarly become invaluable contributors to the success of their masters. On many plantations, the choice of crops, would revolve around the indigenous expertise of purchased slaves. Some farmers would even import African crops, which would become staples in the colonial economies. An often-neglected topic in the study of history, is the contribution of slaves and the skills they possessed prior to enslavement, to the agriculture of America. There were many slaves that were secretly the keys to their master's success. Many early European "Masters" knew little to nothing about agriculture and relied on the skills of their slaves. Prince Abdul Rahman would manage Foster's farm, and Foster would cling tenaciously to his most valuable acquisition. Prince was so valuable that he was granted an abnormal amount of freedom and autonomy. The slave was even permitted to sell his own crops, from his vegetable garden in the local market, for extra money. While in the market, Prince was reunited with Dr. John Cox, an Irish surgeon he met while still in Fouta Djallon. The surgeon was once near death, while in Fouta Djallon. He was taken in, and nursed back to health by Prince Rahman and his family. Dr. Cox was anxious to repay his debt, and attempted to rescue Prince from bondage. He made several attempts to buy his freedom, but Foster would not entertain the idea of losing Rahman. Cox would publicize the slave's history and attempt to raise funds to free him, but he would eventually die, still trying to buy Prince's freedom. Rahman's story would eventually reach the newspapers, and in time the Sultan of Morocco. In the fantastic tales spun about Rahman's captivity, the Arabic speaking Prince, was often referred to as a Moor. The Sultan of Morocco would seek the freedom of his fellow Moor, and bring the matter to the attention of President Adams. Because of this fame, Rahman would tour the nation, giving speeches to raise enough funds to free his wife and children. Prince and his wife, were only able to generate half of the funds necessary to free their children. The couple would leave America for Liberia, unable to free all their children. Within four months, Prince Rahman would die, and never reach his beloved Fouta Djallon.

THE SKILLS OF EARLY SLAVES

Ultimately Fouta Djallon represents a type of African society that would have been rather common prior to colonization. It was a literate, scholarly society based around a written constitution. Its people were artists, authors, sophisticated farmers, and warriors. They lived in simple but well-constructed villages, and enjoyed a high quality of life. Prince Rahman once commented on the comparatively deplorable conditions of his life on the plantation, in longing for his homeland. Rahman was one of many literate and highly skilled Africans enslaved during the colonial period. The still prevalent mythology of the unskilled African slave was never based upon reality. Africans arrived in the new world with a wide variety of skills and talents, developed in the villages and kingdoms of their origin. Some were excellent farmers, whose prowess contributed to their master's success. Books like Black Rice by Judith Carney focus on the African role in the knowledge of and production of agricultural products in the Americas. Many of the Africans that were kidnapped into slavery were village craftsmen, or expert traders and merchants. Many of these early African slaves were Muslims, and among them were scholars, doctors, and otherwise literate and highly educated men and women. Their talents and knowledge would be put to great use as captives and the knowledge they possessed would benefit Americans. In one such instance, the transfer of African knowledge, was pivotal in the early formation of what would become, the United States. Prior to the Battle of Valley Forge, General Washington's troops would be stricken with small pox. Among his troops were black men, but their story is a topic for another work. General Washington was set to engage the British in what would become the decisive turning point in the war, which had seen little to no previous success. Standing in the way of destiny was however, the growing plague of small pox. The disease was now sweeping through the Americas and was threatening to cripple Washington's troops. The general, desperate for options, turned to a West African method of inoculating his remaining troops from the disease. Inoculation, was not yet in the western doctor's medical kit. It was a practice that was not well understood by Western doctors and Washington was taking a tremendous risk by utilizing a method of protection introduced in the Americas, by slaves from West Africa. The first recorded transmission of this knowledge came from a slave named Onesimus who shared his knowledge with Cotton Mather. In the procedure, the pustules, or puss from the sores of an infected victim are scraped off or gathered, as several cuts are made to the arm of the patient. The puss is then placed in contact with the open wounds, which introduces a small amount of the virus into the blood stream. Immunity builds over time until the patient, and in this case the soldiers, were safe from infection. Washington and his troops went on to win the Battle of Valley Forge, which was the first major victory against the British. While we know very little about West African medicine, we are learning a great deal about

African Muslims in early America. They were literate and could leave traces of their history, and lasting impressions of their contributions to early colonial America. These men and women, along with their non-Muslim but highly skilled African brethren, constituted a tragic drain of African intellect and skill from the African continent, for the benefit of the early American colonies. Approximately ten percent of early slaves were Muslims, and there is a basic level of literacy associated with the religion which, quite nearly, requires literacy for proper practice. In Islam, to properly recite the required daily prayers and read the Koran, a practicing Muslim must be able to read Arabic. To live a proper Islamic life, a Muslim should be conscious of Fique or the highly complex laws which are derived from the Koran. Volumes are written on Fique which is used to govern, even the most mundane aspects of life (such as the permissibility of drinking coffee). The legal nature of Islam can seem foreign for unfamiliar non-Muslims but Islamic law is a science of remarkable complexity. In West Africa, many children were required to memorize the entire Koran. When they were taken as slaves many of them attempted to preserve their religion, against the tremendous pressure applied by their new masters. Many were brutalized, and beaten for merely mentioning their faith. Nearly all slaves were forced to convert to Christianity, but some continued to practice Islam in secret. The young West African children that were forced to memorize the Koran, as adults would make hand written copies of their holy book, from memory while in captivity in the Americas. These hand-written Korans, were written in the original Arabic and are a part of an incredible intellectual history that is being rediscovered in America. Even more astounding is the revelation that some Africans derived their own Fique, adapted to their captivity. These hand-written Korans, were not merely powerful demonstrations of African literacy and education, but they were difficult, emotional attempts to preserve sincerely held beliefs. African Muslims often could not even share their faith with their children, whose personal diaries often recollect the strange practices of their parents, who were uncommonly timely in making multiple prayers in a single day. These children and grandchildren often note that their elders could often be seen praying toward the sun, and often spoke a strange language. The children of these slaves were unaware of the meaning behind their parents and grandparent's practices, but to historians their meaning is unmistakable. In imagining African societies, we are often drawn to the strange and most outlandish tribes on the continent. The cultures of Africa are often stereotyped as odd and primitive, and in truth some of them are. But many more were neither odd nor primitive. We can effectively consider Africa to have been a continent with a wide variety of societal types. There were many large empires, and many smaller but influential states. In each of these empires, and most certainly outside of these empires, were African villages, often occupied by tribes. Some of Africa's tribes were very small and (because of our lack of understanding) seemingly savage, and yet others were very large and culturally accomplished. Africa has always been a place of such innumerable variety that those who observed its societies have been able to choose from among its societies in defining what we have come to think of as quintessentially African. The reality is that there is no such thing as a typically African society, and if there were, African culture could never be described as primitive. Each African civilization created its own customs, language, art, and even architecture. The tribes of Africa are incomprehensibly complex and varied. Provincial kingdoms like Fouta Djallon and major tribes like the Mossi were large (whose numbers once exceeded 30,000). The Mossi for instance, were once wonderful horseman and warriors. They built a large, and prosperous kingdom that maintained peace over a large region. When they were at war, they were formidable for any empire. There were also tribes like the Zulu whose strong organization and military talents made them formidable against other powers. The most famous ruler of the Zulu, was Shaka Zulu. While he is generally thought of as a fierce but barbaric king, he was a skilled organizer. He unified his tribe to fight the growth of competative tribes. He saw how the introduction of the trade left surrounding tribes vulnerable to aggression and ultimately led to their downfall. He was intent on protecting his tribe from the same fate. The numerous stories of his violence and willingness to kill any European within his territory are overblown and out of context. He led his tribe from being disparate and primitive to being fierce and strong. In many ways, his kingdom is a perfect example of the evolution of African tribes. Many began as little more than hunter gatherers, and competitive pressures would encourage innovation and improvement. Naturalistic artistry would evolve into more polished achievements. Humble huts, might grow into thatched meeting halls, which might then lead to brick architecture. Charging hoards with hide shields would evolve into organized, uniform militaries. This was the natural life cycle of African culture, when not interrupted. Doubts about the level of achievable sophistication should be quelled by African tribes with great artists that independently invented advanced artistic concepts such as cubism, and abstraction. Modern art, and sculpture have taken a great deal from African societies. In many African societies, the community's artisan or sculptor created housing. The modern movements in experimental architecture have been inspired by the incredible variety in African housing. Societies like the Musgum have become respected for their unique form of architecture. Many African societies seem to have been masters of sustainability long before it became fashionable. The Musgum designed easily repairable, durable forms that remained comfortable in the harshest of climates. The Musgum homes, for instance, are naturally cooled because of the carefully prescribed heights. The seemingly decorative facades are in fact used to scale the edifice for repairs. They are built in clusters, unified by an adjoining wall around a central courtyard, which makes it very easy to add a unit if the community expands. African societies were and still are creative, prosperous, and comfortable. We must always remember that what we see in Africa today, is the remnant of what once was. It is not all that has ever been. The civilizations of African culture have an ancient, and grand past that deserves our respect and admiration.

BEAUTIFUL BENIN

"The King's palace or court is a square, and is as large as the town of Haarlem (a town in Europe) and entirely surrounded by a special wall, like that which encircles the town. It is divided in many magnificent palaces, houses, and apartments of the courtiers and comprises beautiful and long square galleries, about as large as the Exchange at Amsterdam, but one larger than another, resting on wooden pillars, from top to bottom covered with cast copper, on which are engraved the pictures of their war exploits and battles".

- Olfert Dapper
Portuguese Explorer

In the late 13th century, Europe experienced a revival of culture, that would be known to history as the Italian Renaissance. During the renaissance, science and education were revitalized, after nearly 700 years of the Dark Ages. During this renaissance, the art of Europe reached unprecedented levels of quality and sophistication. If there were ever a renaissance in Africa, or a place where art achieved new heights, it must have occurred in Benin. Benin is where African artistic expression arguably reaches its pinnacle. Organized in the form of large city states, the Benin empire, was structured in much the same way that the early Greek city states were. Benin was one of several empires known to posterity as the Forest Kingdoms. These

199

citadels of civilization, amidst thickets of robust forests, are absolute proof of the resilience, innovation, and originality of African civilization. The people of this nation built one of the finest cities in the world. Very regular homes lined its broad streets, and centralized water collection units ran to each home. Romanesque courtyards and impluvium joined its houses and well-structured galleries displayed the nation's artistic acumen in the court of its king. The Emperor of Benin was at the head of a remarkably well administered kingdom, that included advisory councils, governors, and a court aristocracy. An incredible army of highly trained warriors protected the Empire. The Emperor of Benin could assemble 20,000 soldiers in a single day, and an approximate total of 80,000- 180,000 soldiers. The warriors of Benin were a well-armed war machine, that literally shook the ground beneath the feet of neighboring powers. The famous Benin Bronze Plaques, are superb depictions of Benin life, its kings and warriors. These plaques have become famous in artistic circles for the beauty and skill of their craftsmanship. From the earliest point of European contact, Benin art has captivated the artistic mind of the west. In fact, after the destruction of Benin, the early British attempted to claim that the Portuguese designed the art of Benin. They found it distasteful to admit that Africans could be masters of a medium as temperamental as bronze and produce such exquisitely detailed work. The bronze masterpieces give us an excellent idea of life in Benin, the dress of its people, and even the weaponry of Benin's security forces. The warriors wore lavish wraps around their waists, made from a red or blue, silk-like material. The Emperor, or Oba, maintained a massive armory of weapons, closely under guard inside of the palace. In the arsenal of Benin warriors, was an impressive array of weapons. The warriors were armed with short, curved broadswords, made of iron with a single-edged (about the length of a Roman gladius sword). Their arsenal included the bow with poison tipped arrows. They were also armed with both a long spear and a short spear. These Assegais (spears) were favored by Benin warriors. They were iron tipped spears, with hardwood handles, used for close quarter stabbing, and throwing. Warriors were protected by large shields made from wood, basketwork, and hides to cover the shield. In terms of material and construction, they were much like the shields of many other cultures outside of Africa (a Roman shield for example was made of 3 sheets of wood glued together and covered with canvas or leather). They were also curved at the bottom and were large enough to protect the full body of soldiers that could crouch behind them. Cross bows were used to fire heavy iron arrows, at distant enemies. Protective helmets were also made from wood, or padded basket weaving, and covered in crocodile skin. Quilted coverings of leopard skin fabric protected their bodies. The armor could stop an arrow fired even at close range. Armlets and charms for protection completed their outfits. When heading into battle, each warrior wore loud quadrangular bells. Altogether, the sound of 180,000 feet marching in unison, combined with the clanging of 180,000 bells, and the loud trump of war horns, were all intended to intimidate their doomed foes. These warriors, and the kings they served were immortalized in the breathtaking art, of Benin's talented artisans. These craftsmen were organized into guilds of metal casters, blacksmiths, and ivory carvers. They lived in the fine houses of a dedicated art district, built, and sustained by the Emperors, where they worked exclusively for him, perfecting their crafts, and celebrating their culture. It is their art, that has proved to be enduring and reminds us, of this ancient and accomplished culture.

A CITY AS FINE AS AMSTERDAM

The City of Benin was a metropolis, and a masterpiece of African urban engineering. In the 15th century, the City of Benin was one of the finest cities in the world. The Numerous European travelers that visited the city, spoke highly of its well-constructed streets, its homes, and the sheer size of the city. A visitor entering the city would have passed over the massive moats that protected Benin, and entered the city through one of nine wide gates. The gates would then open onto the broad streets of Benin. The streets were to visitors, remarkable in themselves. Composed of red clay, the unpaved streets were visually striking, in part because some streets were as wide as 131 feet. The main street, from which all others spread out like capillaries, was said to have been eight times larger than the Warmoes Street in Amsterdam. The palace was comprised of numerous incredibly large houses, some of which were four stories high. The palace compound was comprised of a private living quarter for the king. In the palace complex, there were various reception courts, separate quarters for the three palace societies, and a separate quarter for the king's harem. The King's court, which was used as a gallery to display the tremendous artwork for which Benin was known, was reportedly the size of an entire European town. In the 17th century, the gallery displays were supported by large wooden pillars that displayed the Bronze plaques of Benin. The plaques are artistically sophisticated mnemonic devices for the court's "Rememberers" to recall the history of Benin. Later, in the 19th century, the wooden pillars which supported the plaques, were replaced by clay columns which were decorated with depressed reliefs. The doors and beams of buildings were often covered in hand embossed bronze sheets or decorated with inlaid mirrors. Although the palace, homes and administrative buildings of Benin were built from red clay, the artisans of Benin treated the clay, giving it a reflective lacquered appearance. The red clay for building was mixed with palm oil, as opposed to water (as it is in the traditional adobe of most cultures). It is said, that this prevented the cracking that occurs with natural aging or weathering. Many European visitors were astonished, at the sight of their own reflections, in the walls of Benin constructions. The palace complex, and the courtyard galleries were segmented by another system of gates that also impressed European visitors. Eye witness accounts have been left for posterity, by numerous European explorers. According to a Portuguese ship captain, Lourenco Pinto, (August 1619):

"Great Benin, where the king resides is larger than Lisbon, all the streets run straight and as far as the eyes can see. The houses are large, especially that of the king which is richly decorated and has fine columns. The city is wealthy and industrious. It is so well governed that theft is unknown and the people live in such security that they have no door to their houses".

The Dutch arrived off the Nigerian Coast in the 17th century, and in 1602 they purchased a document called "A Description of Guinea" compiled by Pieter de Marees. Within his compilation was a description given by Dierick Ruyters. His description of Benin records the remarkable city of Benin. More telling though are his comparisons of the city to its contemporaries. He compares the city to Amsterdam, which at the time, was one of the world's most beautiful cities. Amsterdam was the standard of excellence in Europe. The willingness to make the comparison, and the fact that Benin was comparable in the eyes of those Europeans that visited the city, is compelling. It is a testimony to the achievement of the Forest Kingdoms and establishes the equality of African civilization on the world stage. Dierick Ruyters journeyed to Benin under the authority of Ehengbuda, King of Benin. Ruyters description was telling, but it is the drawings of the Portuguese Dapper Olfert that complete the imagery. Ruyters wrote that the city *"is very great when you go into it for you enter a great broad street, not paved which seems to be seven or even eight times broader than the Warmoes street in Amsterdam; it goes straight in and never bends"*. Ruyters lodgings were *"atleast a quarter of an hours going from the gate and yet I could still not see to the end of the street"*. Ruyters marveled at the number and length of streets adjacent to the main street: *"You cannot see to the end of them because of their great length"*. Of Benin's homes Ruyters said they *"stand in good order, one close and even beside the other as the houses in Holland stand. Those belonging to men of quality and others have two or three steps to go up, along the front of them there is a kind of gallery where you may sit in the dry."* The king's palace was a collection of the largest homes in the city, according to Ruyters, *"The kings court is very big, having within it many wide squares with galleries round them where watch is always kept. I went so far within these buildings that I passed through four such squares, and wherever I looked I still saw gate after gate which opened into other places"*. Olfert Dapper's unwitting contribution to the history of African civilization is controversial. While the verbal descriptions of European explorers are instructive and numerous, emanating from a variety of witness, they can leave the reader confused. The value of Olfert Dapper's drawings is that they provide context for the confusing details of verbal descriptions and bears witness to their claims. Sadly, the witness they bare is false. The engraver Olfert was not a firsthand witness. He never actually left his home in Holland, however he compiled the descriptions of many of Europe's explorers. His book "Description of Africa" became very famous. We can assume that his drawings possess some degree of truth, as they were never rebuked as inaccurate. The drawings which were commissioned as a part of his publications on Benin, were never disputed or declared inaccurate by any of the persons whose descriptions they purported to represent. But we should look on them, understanding that they are not precise. The drawings do, however allow our minds to formulate a renewed understanding of life in ancient Africa. Visitors to Benin were consistent in their praise of very lifelike bronze statuettes that sat atop many of Benin's administrative buildings. The towers that are visible in Olfert's drawings give us a hint of the architectural details that were typical in Benin constructions. The verbal descriptions of Benin describe an immense capital city. The Dutch compared it to Amsterdam; the Spanish compared it to Madrid; and the Portuguese compared it to Lisbon. The streets were said to be seemingly endless, and gate after gate lined the unpaved roads. In human terms, the most instructive detail of Dapper's work is his depiction of life in Benin. The normalcy of life in his rendering is unique, as it allows our imaginations to reconstitute themselves away from the impression of African kingdoms as tribal and primitive. There are many derisive drawings of Africa, most often depicting wild dances (which not put in their proper context seem strange), naked bodies, and an emphasis on tribalism. In Olfert's work, we see very regular people, walking the streets of their city, celebrating during the royal festivals, and armed cavalry accompanying the Oba. In short, what Olfert shows is the very normal existence of blacks in African kingdoms. What he emphasizes in his drawings is a basic humanity that is often neglected, if not omitted, in the most commonly available depictions of Africa.

THE BENIN MOAT

While many Europeans admired Benin's beautiful bronze plaques, and its tremendous court, the city's defensive fortifications equally impressed visitors. The City of Benin has become famous for its interconnected system of moats and walls. While it may seem strange that a simple moat would capture the attention and imagination of Europe's trading class, the sheer magnitude of Benin's moats was unlike anything else in the world. The length of the walls in Benin was so great that they are one of the largest structures ever constructed by men. The walls contained 6213.7 miles of Benin territory. The walls spanned 9,900 miles, and covered 2,500 square miles. The Great Wall of China is the only structure on earth that surpassed them. Enhancing the tremendous system of walls were earthen ramparts, which made up the moats. They were in some places 66 feet high, and according to the Guiness Book of World Records, remain the most extensive earthwork in the world. They are without equal, anywhere in the world. The ramparts and the moats, are called Iya in the language of the Edo, and cover 2485.5 miles of land. While archeology has established that construction on the immense system of defense began in between the years 800-1000, Oba Ewuare the Great is recognized as ordering the construction of the moat, in the heart of the city, in the middle of the 15th century. When they were constructed, the architects of the moats carefully created the moats in such a way that the banks of the moats became protective walls as well. The moats were a part of an ingenious scheme to control traffic into the city. The moats ensured controlled flow through nine gates, for those wishing to enter the city. The moat, completed in the year 1460, was the world's largest earthwork. In the ancient world, Benin's protective fortifications were not only formidable, they were nearly without equal.

TRADE IN THE KINGDOM

Attempting to reconstruct life in pre-colonial Africa is wrought with danger. There are numerous sources to choose from but they vary in reliability. Bias can be rife in both ancient and modern sources. Some cultures were prone to minimizing the achievments of black cultures while some modern afro-centric sources can be prone to embellishing some achievements. However, by utilizing conventional, and reliable sources, that tendency for embellishment is revealed to be as unnecessary as it is dishonest. Many cultures found themselves visiting Africa, and it is from their records that we can begin to understand the high level of achievement in African Civilization. One of the major misconceptions about Africa is the commonly held belief that it was a Dark Continent; An undeveloped continent covered in wild forest. This idea is the result of misunderstanding more than it is a consciously deceptive stereotype. In the case of Benin, tremendously dense Nigerian forests surrounded the city. However, the growth of these forests was not haphazard. In many cases (as in Benin) the growth of forest was encouraged. The forests, were a natural defense, and particular plants were chosen and cultivated in order to create an inescapable maze, protecting the cities. Visitors that were unfamiliar with the locations of the numerous cities within the forests would find it impossible to navigate through the region. These cultivated landscapes served their purpose for centuries, protecting the Forest Kingdoms and their cultures from outside interference. After first learning of Benin, the Portuguese would be forced to wait 16 years before being shown into the great city. Overtime, the merchants of Benin would establish trading arrangements with the Portuguese, the Dutch, and the British. All the European powers were in fierce competition for the attention of Benin. The city produced an astonishing variety of products. It is through the records of traders, visitors, and missionaries that we can develop an accurate understanding of life in The Great City of Benin. Africa has always been an international port of sorts. Trade has always been a mainstay of the continent's empires, and at times that international role has been used to discredit African civilizations. African's were, and continue to be very open minded. Lacking the xenophobia of other cultures, many African groups readily adopted the faith, habits, and cultural trappings of others. It has been consistently argued that various African cultures came into existence and reached grand heights of culture, only because of interacting with another (generally European or Arab) culture. In Benin, these arguments become as irrelevant as they are erroneous. Sheltered from the rest of Africa, by a maze of forests, Benin developed unmolested, and un-influenced by cultures of the greater ancient world. The result was a complex, highly artistic, and highly refined culture. Trade in Benin, between the European powers was extensive, sophisticated, and personal. The Portuguese were Benin's primary trading partners. They became aware of the empire in 1470, but never saw the city until 1486. The relationship began when Joao Affonso, the Portuguese envoy, successfully located the city. In the 16th century, the Oba sent an ambassador to Lisbon, and the Portuguese sent Christian Missionaries to Benin. From that point on, a high-ranking member of the King's administration would greet European traders at port, adorned in signature Benin coral or jasper necklaces. Trade was in products such as pepper, cotton garments of red and blue, jasper, leopard skins, ivory, and numerous other products. We can develop an understanding of the scale of trade by considering the cargo of various ships involved in trade. A Dutch Ship called the Olyphant transported 88,235 pounds of ivory, and 1337 pounds of pepper. The quality of Benin products was so great, that its wares became renowned, and the city itself was so impressive that it became the source of European lore. Trade was the corridor through which natural resources, finished goods, and most importantly ideas passed. It is quite easy, and quite common to attribute our modern world, and its culture to the contributions of singular groups or ethnicities. And while, we do live in a predominantly western culture, it is not exclusively western. It is more accurate to think of our modern culture as a composite of cultural contributions that were compiled in varying ratios. In truth, modern culture is a shared culture. It is an amalgam, of ideas, aesthetics, and technologies from all over the world. Trade improved the lot of the entire world, by refining and introducing innovations from one culture to another. For Africa, trade was a mixed blessing that came with many benefits and an equal measure of negative consequences. Many of Africa's civilizations were fully integrated in the ancient world. African Nobles, merchants, and royals, were by most accounts insatiable collectors of luxury goods from all over the world. Trade allowed Africa to interact with the entire world by sharing its innovations and resources, while experiencing the genius of other cultures. However, trade brought with it many destructive forces to Africa, and eventually lead to the downfall of many societies. When Europeans first arrived in Africa, they found fantastic markets, and numerous civilizations of wildly varying degrees of sophistication. Networks and trade routes were already well established. Trade was a cooperative endeavor that paired tribes, with empires, to create international supply chains. Tribes were often responsible for mining, and cultivating natural resources, while empires maintained the markets and protected the transport routs, for those products. These numerous markets sustained sophisticated kingdoms, that brandished all the pomp and circumstance, expected of civilization. These lucrative trading markets were powerful demonstrations of Africa's wealth and potential to the first European explorers. However, when the first

Portuguese (and other European) traders arrived in Africa's trading centers, they found very little demand for their wares. European products were known throughout Africa, but they were often already transported by third parties. In this established framework of trade, Europe struggled to find its place. The first European traders returned to Europe with fantastic tales of tremendous markets, but very little else. In time, high quality finished and manufactured goods earned the European powers a place at the table, but the slave trade paved the way for its dominance in African commerce. The slave trade was extremely lucrative for Europe. At first, slaves were taken as domestic servants. They were transported to Europe to serve in homes, but the presence of the New World changed everything. Many of the first African slaves were taken, not only for labor, but as translators. The Portuguese recognized the value of Africans in building relationships amongst Native Americans. Cultural similarities, and the linguistic flexibility of Africans made them preferred intermediaries between Native Americans and Europeans hoping to establish trading relationships. Slavery had a well-established history in Africa, but the European version was very different from the institution Africans had come to know. In Africa slavery was common, especially amongst tribes. Slaves were taken as captives in war, and utilized throughout the African and Islamic world in domestic capacities. However, within these iterations of slavery, one could find dignity. The role of a slave was not necessarily an undignified station. Slaves could command armies, administer kingdoms, manage businesses, and escape bondage by earning freedom or marrying into the family of one's master. Marriage between slave and master (or the master's family) was common in the African and Islamic world. Considering its history, and relatively softer nature, Africans saw little reason for concern, when Europe began to solicit slaves. The civilizations of Africa, were generally unaware of the vicious nature of the institution into which they were delivering other Africans. The slave trade would become a mainstay for some societies. Some societies were built on the bondage they delivered others into. There was no shortage of willing participants. Many of Africa's empires, were willing to prey on weaker tribes to fulfill Europe's desire for slaves. Tribes were willing to go to war with one another to obtain the benefits of wealth and European products. Europe could provide superior weapons that made conquest and territorial expansion possible for even the weakest tribe. With European weapons, and periodic infusions of wealth, humble tribes could envision a future for themselves as empires. The prevalence of strong tribes, weak tribes, and large opportunistic empires, was paradoxically Africa's Achilles heel. While slavery depleted whole regions of Africa, and weakened entire nations, few could afford not to participate. The refusal to engage in slave raids, could leave a kingdom, or tribe susceptible to less sympathetic neighbors. Kingdoms were forced into the unenviable position of choosing to enslave others, or be enslaved by neighboring regimes. As Europe's position in the African trade improved, the powers would eventually begin to leverage their position in the slave trade. Europeans began to demand that the African powers sign exclusive trading contracts, many of which required that tribes and empires alike surrender their sovereignty. If an African power refused, there was usually an ambitious neighbor that was anxious to cooperate. Benin refused to participate in the slave trade, hindering the economic prospects of European merchants.

THE BRITISH, BENIN, AND WAR

The Portuguese contacted Benin City in 1486, and set up trade by 1553. After a 339-year trading relationship, in March of 1892 the British Vice Consul of The Oil Rivers Protectorate visited Benin hoping to annex the city, because of frustrations from merchants whose profits were hindered by the policies of the Benin Oba. The Vice Consul came with an agreement, that the King of Benin believed was a friendship and trade agreement. Upon reviewing the British offer, the King of Benin discovered that the agreement was a deception that would make Benin a colony of Britain. He subsequently barred the British from all Benin territories. Major Claude Maxwell Macdonald, the Consul General of the Oil Rivers Protectorate considered the Kings willingness to endorse a relationship of friendship and trade, as acceptance of the treaty, and declared his subsequent actions baring Britain's from Benin to be illegal. From this point on there was a steady escalation of tensions. The British Royal Navy and the Oil Rivers Protectorate (also called the Niger Coast Protectorate) destroyed Brohimie which was a successful trading town, near the rivers of Benin, built by the Itsekiri ethnic group. The Chief of the conquered territory was Nana Olomu. After this the Oba of Benin enhanced his military posture along the southern borders. This posturing was sufficient to cause the Colonial Office to scrap any invasion plans. Later, three attempts to enforce the treaty were made. In March 1896 Benin began to enforce a trade embargo, as a response to price fixing and itserki stubbornness to the payment of tributes. The trade embargo sealed the fate of the conflict. All trade nearly ceased, and the British traders that were anxious to invade Benin, now found a Protectorate's Counsel General that was receptive to their point of view. In 1896 James Robert Philips, the acting Counsel General agreed to military action in Benin. In December of 1896, without waiting for permission from London, Philips went forward with an assault plan. It is instructive to note that the European powers would rarely act alone militarily. In this case, the British enlisted the assistance of 250 African soldiers. There were only five British officers. The mission was to kidnap the King and have him replaced by a subservient ally on the Native Council. The itserki secretly sent a warning to the Oba that "*the white man is bringing war*". Upon summoning his nobles, the Oba discussed the situation with his advisors. While his advisors insisted on confronting the force, the Oba was more cautious. He wanted to allow the British to enter the city, so that he could examine the men and divine their intent for himself. His advisors disagreed, and without the King's knowledge, they sent a quick moving action force to intercept the invaders. The action force was composed of the chief's servants, and border guards. By all accounts, they slaughtered the British, and their African compatriots. Only two British survived the assault. On January 12, 1897, 1200 British Marines, sailors, and Niger Coast Protectorate Forces joined three columns of Sapoba, Gwato, and Main (African tribes) in a march for Benin. The Gwato column was decimated before reaching the city, and the others endured 10 days of brutal combat. When the British successfully penetrated Benin, they looted the entire city. They stole its famous artwork, emptied its warehouses, and intentionally set the King's palace on fire. The British then turned their sights to the tremendous walls of Benin. They smashed through the portions they could destroy, and set fire to the rest. Imagine the loss to human culture, if the Great Wall of China were to have been destroyed in this manner. The bronze plaques, which recorded the entire history of the empire were now in the possession of the British. In a letter to Lord Salisbury, Philips proposed using the Oba's own ivory to pay for the invasion. The art was auctioned to pay for the expedition. The Germans bought much of it, and the rest went to the British Museum. The British would actively promote the idea that the art of Benin was the work of Portuguese sailors and tradesmen. Some in Britain even argued that the Benin Bronzes were from the lost City of Atlantis. The theft of Benin's brilliant Bronzes gave Europe it's first exposure to African art and it kicked off an era defined by the looting of Africa's innovative creations. Despite denying the genius of Africa's artists, the stolen art of Africa gave birth to new movements in European art. Influenced by African creations, the foundations for "Modernism" were laid in western art by celebrated artists like Henri Matisse. Picasso would incorporate African concepts in his new work during a period known in art history as Picasso's "Negro Period". The foundations of Modernism and Cubism were established on a clearly African foundation as Europe's most exceptional minds incorporated the stolen art of African societies in their work. In an act that exemplified the hypocrisy and self-delusion that characterized Europe's actions during this time, Picasso would deny being influenced by African art.

THE ORIGIN OF BENIN

The Kingdom of Benin, was the result of a long pattern of regional development. While the art of Benin, is astounding, it was not without precedence. It's art, and civilization were the culmination of artistic evolution throughout Nigeria. The entire region, functioned as an incubator for highly developed African art, as one civilization followed another, and the sculpture and skill of one, lay the foundation for the next. The first of these artistically obsessed cultures entered the region, in 1000 B.C. The Nok culture was the first in a region that would make artistry it's cultural focal point. The Nok, produced life sized Terra-cotta sculptures of people and animals. The pieces are highly refined sculptures that blend realism and abstraction. They are striking for their emotive power and the inescapable humanity of the pieces. Unlike artistic traditions that emphasize idealized representations, Nok art never hesitates to capture sickness, sadness, or deformities. The pieces are hollow, and adorned with the jewelry common in Nok culture. While the Nok terra-cotta sculptures were once full body statues, like the Chinese Terra-cotta army, the heads of the figures are generally all that remain. Nok art is unique, for its artistic sophistication, as well as its subject matter. Many of the Nok pieces are specifically designed celebrations of Nok hairstyles. The sculptures capture the complex hair braiding and hair styles of men and women in Nok culture. The Nok, lived in large agricultural villages, that mastered iron smelting and tools as early as 500 B.C. Their culture disappeared around 200 A.D. The Nok would be followed by another culture that would take its artistry to a level that was nearly unmatched anywhere in the world. The Nri Kingdom would be established by a group called the Igbo. Whereas, the Nok were primarily known for their terra-cotta, the Igbo would immortalize their culture with sculptures in metal. Their metal work began in the 9th century. They were the first West Africans to use a technique called The Lost Wax Casting method. Several Igbo sites (approximately 3) have revealed hundreds of aristocratic castings, ritual vessels, and sculptures that are among the most technically sophisticated bronzes in the world. Their castings were made in stages. At a site called Igbo Ukwu, a bowl, found on a flat stand, was discovered. Intricate details, such as spirals, and insects accent the piece. The small decorative adornments, were cast first, and then placed in the wax mold, before the main part of the bowl. The vessel, was then cast in two parts, and joined together by the casting of a middle band. The level of detail, in the Igbo castings, is a testament to the skill of their artisans, who were, at the time, among the world's greatest metal artisans. The manipulation of metal, on this scale, and with this degree of mastery, is a science. It requires a sophisticated knowledge and awareness of the behavior of these metals. They created breastplates, swords, staff ornaments, crowns, and pendents. The Nri Kingdom of the Igbo, was, artistically, socially, and architecturally sophisticated. They lived in well-organized settlements, that engaged in extensive trade, with nations as far away as India. An archeological site called Igbo Ukwu, was a burial site. In one of the graves, a richly adorned person, was displayed for burial on a stool, in a chamber with fine clothing and luxury goods. 150,000 rich glass beads from India were found in the grave, along with bronze vessels, ornamented bowls, and numerous effects. One of the most interesting aspects of the Igbo culture and the Nri kingdom, was its government. While a king ruled most nations, often endowed with divine authority (as in Europe or any of the Islamic caliphates), the Nri were ruled by a king they considered to be truly divine, and sent to them from their God. They believed that the Eri, or the Sky Being established civilization. The Eze Nri, or priest kings created sophisticated administrations like many of the world's monarchs, however, it was their method of expansion and conquest that made them unique. The Eze Nri, had no military, and they did not believe in war. He exercised no military power over his subjects and maintained political control through entirely peaceful means. The Nri diplomats, would travel throughout the region, with palm leaves as signs of their peace, delivering the message of their divine ruler. Conquest was made by peaceful conversion to the Igbo religion, which in time established a wide area of influence. Unlike Christianity and Islam, the Igbo religion was not spread by faith-filled armies compelling conversion and submission by force. War and violence were a pollutant, and abominable blights upon the earth. Violence was forbidden and punishable by a form of spiritual excommunication. Province after province would fall to the peaceful dominion, of the Eze Nri. The Nri kingdom became a magnet for runaway slaves, as slavery was also forbidden in the kingdom. Outcasts, and those suffering persecutions were welcomed into the large kingdom. And the Nri, prospered through an impressive system of trade and commerce organized by the Eze Nri. The Igbo, and the Nri Kingdom, were fantastic stepping stones, which would lead to the foundation of another artistic enclave.

The Nri Kingdom of the Igbo would continue through modern times, but their influence, particularly in art would be followed by the Yoruba, and their capital of Ile Ife. The Yoruba began their cultural ascension by 1000 A.D. By their golden age, during the 12th-15th century, the Yoruba were producing fine works with copper, bronze, iron, and beautiful terra-cotta. Their art would continue the artistic progress and tradition of the region. The Yoruba, like their predecessors, would also produce breathtaking works, that celebrated their culture and the nobility that governed their daily lives. A fantastic tale from their history, recounts the reign of their only female King. It is said that during her reign, while traveling throughout her capital, her gown began to accumulate dirt from the ground. After noticing the soiling, she ordered the entire city paved. The innovative community created a lovely decorative pavement using pottery shards. Open air courtyards were constructed, for public gatherings. The Yoruba built numerous urban cities. Their cities were Popo, Owu, Ijebu, Ijesa, Oyo, Egba, Ketu, Sabe, Dassa, Egbado, Igbomina, six Ekiti principalities, Owo and Ondo. The buildings of the Yoruba, were made of sun-dried adobe bricks. In the capital of Ile Ife, earthen walls surrounded the entire city, and a progressively growing wall would encircle the royal center. The royal center, was 3.8

km (2.3 miles), and its first protective wall enclosed an area of 7.8 km. We can begin to comprehend the scope of their buildings by recognizing that the first layer of the defensive wall protecting the royal center was followed by a second wall with a circumference of 14km (8.7 miles). Both walls were 4.5 meters tall (14 feet tall) and 2 meters thick. This produced a sprawling royal center complex of 3 miles, covering an effective area of approximately 7 miles in circumference. The Yoruba went on to found the Oyo Empire, and its associated metropolitan cities and markets. The Yoruba were a large and influential kingdom, whose art, would lead directly to the grand artistic wonders of Benin.

THE ART OF THE FOREST KINGDOMS

The Kingdom of Benin was created in the year 1180 A.D, just before the Italian Renaissance. It was founded by a dynasty of rulers called The Ogisos, or the Sky Kings. Modern day Nigeria was once home to a cluster of domains called the Forest Kingdoms. Each kingdom represented the grouping and organization of a different ethnic group. The most prominent of the forest kingdoms were, The Kingdom of Benin, The Akwamu Kingdom, The Yoruba Kingdom of Oyo, The Kingdom of Dahomey and The Ashanti Kingdom. Each of these empires consisted of multiple city-states that were linked culturally and commercially. While Benin is, to posterity, the most famous of the forest kingdoms, it owes its existence, in part to The Yoruba kingdom of Oyo. The name Benin, is a Portuguese corruption of the empire's proper name Ubini. In its early years, the kingdom that would become Benin, was ruled by a dynasty of 36 Ogisos. The dynasty would come to a halt when the kingdom was engulfed in a scandal that resulted in the expulsion of the King's heir. The controversy arose, when it was discovered that the Ogiso's wife had altered a prophecy regarding the nature of her son's birth. The queen violated the sanctity of the prophecy by changing and hiding the truth of the oracle's revelation. The breech of protocol was onerous and unacceptable to the community. The local chiefs insisted that punishment for the indiscretion should be swift and severe. They demanded that the Queen's son be banished from the community forever. The ousted Prince Ekladerhan searched for a new home. He journeyed to the land of the Yoruba, where he found refuge in the city of Ife. An old Yoruba prophecy held that a great leader would come to them, from the forest. The arrival of Prince Ekladerhan seemed to fulfill the prophecy, and Ekladerhan was eager to position himself as the fulfillment of their mythology. He was given several titles; among them was the title Oba, which meant "ruler" in the Yoruba tongue. After many years, the Oba of Yoruba received word from his previous home (Ubini/Benin) that his father had died. Unknown to his Yoruba subjects, the Oba received a delegation of chiefs from his homeland, some of which were responsible for his exile. In a shocking Irony, the chiefs now begged him to return and rule over his father's kingdom. The formerly despised king refused their offer, adding that a ruler could not leave his domain. Instead, the Oba sent his son Oranyan to rule in his stead. Oranyan's arrival signaled the end of the kingship of the Ogisos and the beginning of governance by the Oba's. However, Oranyan's administration would be short lived. Upon arriving, Oranyan soon became disenchanted with his new kingdom, and decided that he would return to his life in Ife (Yoruba city). As the young King was leaving, he cursed the city calling it Ile Ibinu, which meant the land of annoyance and vexation, and this became the name of the kingdom that would become Benin. As the abdicating king was heading back to the Yoruba territory of Ife, he rested in the city of Ego. In Ego (still Bini territory) he impregnated Princess Erimwinde. The product of this union was Eweka, the future Oba of Ile Ibinu (Ubini/Benin). Eweka's ancestor Oba Ewedo changed the derisive name of his kingdom, Ile Ibinu to the simplified Ubini. The name Benin was given to the kingdom by the Portuguese, whose corruption of the local language continues to persist until today.

KANEM-BORNU

The Knights of Africa

The image of Knights in expertly crafted armor, and well-disciplined regiments of cavalry, typically conjure images of Europe's late middle ages. But these feudal lords could also have been found in the great African Kingdom of Kanem-Bornu. The name, Kanem Bornu, is more accurately a reference to two separate phases in the development of a single civilization. It is more accurate to refer to the Kingdom of Kanem, which preceded the separate Kingdom of Bornu. The dramatic rise of both, can be attributed to the ambition and drive of a tribe of Africans called the Kanembu. In time, after a long period of prosperity, the kingdom of Kanem would fall, and the Kanembu tribe would shift the center of gravity of their kingdom to Bornu. The name Kanem-Bornu, refers to a period after the founding of Bornu, when Kanem was resurrected, and in which both centers were unified. The sophisticated knights of Kanem Bornu would protect their realm, and ensure the safety of their subjects, utilizing a feudal structure just as their European counterparts would. The knights were the lords of the land, and were given authority over those living on their lands. These African knights wore all black armor and neck to knee chain metal armor. The cavalry would be supported by excellently skilled archers. The warriors would also be outfitted with muskets, from their Turkish affiliates. They carried the flags of their Sheikh, and utilized sophisticated military formations when charging into battle. Large boats would facilitate the transport of their military machine. This organized military force would wage war on opposing kingdoms, renegade tribes, and enemies of their allies to enforce the will of their Sheikh or Shehu (King). Kanem Bornu would grow into an economic power, because of its strategic location at a nexus of trade networks. Nations from all over the world would send representatives to the kingdom which would be visited by delegations eager to establish trade. The citizens of Kanem Bornu produced an impressive array of products that were coveted by many of the world's economies. The artisans of the kingdom were expert metal workers and blacksmiths, that displayed a mastery with iron, bronze and copper. Their array of magnificent products included beautiful jewelry. Bornu sent diplomats to North Africa, and Spain. The Kingdom maintained an embassy in the Ottoman Empire, with whom they had a treaty of "friendship and commerce". The people of Bornu grew wealthy off the demand for their industrial products. In time the kingdom became a destination for some of the Islamic world's most highly educated scholars. Kanem Bornu was an absolute monarchy, but the king was advised by several councils. The kingdom would also develop an Islamic orientation, in which men of learning and influential imams settled controversial matters of law and religion. The highest council was called The Majlis. The King still retained the ability to overrule the councils, but the councils, along with numerous regional governors established a sophisticated framework of law and administration in the kingdom. In the government of Kanem Bornu, women were equal to men. Women even held high offices in the government and had property rights.

THE ORIGIN OF KANEM-BORNU

The long road to building an empire began in approximately 700 A.D when the death of one African culture would lead to the birth of another. The Sao Culture, was an ethnic group located in modern day Cameroon. They lived south of Lake Chad, near the Chari river. The Sao, it seems were highly skilled artisans of bronze, iron, and copper. They lived in walled cities, and made terra cotta-clay statues and jewelry. All that remains of these Africans are their coins, pottery, and statues. This advanced civilization would be displaced by another group of immigrants called the Zaghawa. The Zaghawa were an ethnic group fleeing political persecution. Their homeland was also being transformed into a desert, prompting them to evacuate. The Zaghawa would enter the region as nomads, seeking land for their livestock but overtime, they would learn from the Sao and adopt elements of their settled-city dwelling culture. Through a combination of conquest, absorption, and assimilation the Dugawa Dynasty of the Zaghawa, would displace the Sao Culture. They would build the city of Kanem, a capital city called Manan, and Anjimi, all centered around the lush green oases of the region. Their major cities were primarily used by Zaghawa nobility, while the majority maintained a roaming, semi nomadic lifestyle, in which they would wield their military might over more settled populations and kingdoms. While the concept of a mobile empire seems foreign in our modern understanding of governments, it is not dissimilar to the fashion in which the Asian Mongols ruled their kingdom. According to the Arab traveller, Al-Ya'qubi their territory would stretch from Lake Chad to the Nile Valley, near the kingdoms of Christian

Nubia. One arab scholar, would even refer to the Zaghawa as a kingdom without cities. However strange the formulation of the kingdom might sound, it was nonetheless an effective, building block in the development of a greater society. Out of this protoplasm of civilization, a great power would be birthed.

ISLAM & THE KANEMBU TRIBE

The Dynasty of the Zaghawa would end, and a new ethnic group would take their place guided by the religion of Islam. In 1085 A.D. a Muslim noble, called Hummay would introduce Islam to the region and help propel a tribe called the Kanembu to power. Their dynasty would be called the Sayfuwa Dynasty, and it would be lead to Islam by King Umme Ibn Abdul Jalil, from a new capital called Njimi. He would rule from 1086-1098, and would introduce Islamic policies and mores to the Court at Kanem. An interesting byproduct of the acceptance of Islam was the tendency of African Civilizations to rewrite the history of their origins. In many African civilizations, especially Islamic nations, blacks would attempt to claim connections to, or heritage from notable Arab figures. For example, in the case of Kanem, they would identify their own Sultan Hummay as being of Berber origin. Later, in the 13th century they would rewrite his heritage, and claim that he was descended from members of the Prophet Muhammad's tribe (the Querish). They would continue the revisions with Mai or king- Sef, who founded the Sayfawa dynasty (which brought the Kanembu into power and displaced the Dugawa). They would link him with a legendary Yemenite hero named Sayf Ibn Dhi Yazan. This explains the spelling of the dynasty itself, which should be Sefuwa, but is instead renamed Sayfawa. According to Unesco's general History of Africa volume 4, this was done to demonstrate their "long fidelity to Islam". To understand why Africans would do this we must recognize that the goal of religion is not only to proselytize. Religion is often a vehicle for the propagation of culture. The notion that Islam and Arabism are implicitly joined essentially enshrined not only Arab culture, but Arabs by association. Leaders that attempted to gain their legitimacy through a belief in Islam, felt pressured to connect their own existence or heritage to a noble lineage of Islamic figures. This unfortunately gives future generations cause to question whether these kingdoms were the creations of black Africans, or the result of Arab intervention, trade, or Islam. These historical revisions are all too common in the civilizations of Africa, and we should understand that there are no substantive questions concerning the authorship of these African kingdoms. Viewing the kingdom of Kanem-Bornu as an example, and understanding the regional process of development, by which the Kanembu built upon the Zaghawa; and the Zaghawa built upon the Sao; We can understand the consecutive way in which each culture built upon the achievements of its predecessor. And we should understand that similar processes took place throughout Africa. This allows us to see the growth of civilization as the indigenous creation that it is. It also allows us to understand the way in which Africans benefited from the influence of outsiders, without ever relying on them for the creation of their kingdoms.

A KING WITH A VISION

The work of Hummay, and King Umme Ibn Abdul Jalil in introducing Islam would be furthered by North African traders, Berbers and Arabs who would also work to spread the faith. The Great Mai Dunama Dibbalemi would continue to spread Islam by declaring Jihad against the minor states surrounding Kanem. Mai Dibbalemi, was a militant monarch. He is one of the greatest leaders in the pantheon of African Civilizations. He was a military genius that brought the territories around Lake Chad into submission, which is modern Libya, his influence then stretched into Kano (modern day Nigeria). He would extend Kanem's authority into the Quaddi, and south into the Adamawa grasslands (modern day Cameroon). The administratively minded Mai would establish diplomatic relations with North Africa, build hostels in Cairo for pilgrims to Mecca, and devise an efficient, well organized system of governance. The Mai would give his warriors dominion over the people they conquered, and would encourage his warriors to marry into prominent families responsible for the region's agricultural production. By marrying into farming families, the Mai's warriors could gain control of the regions agricultural production. By trading these products, the King could generate the resources necessary to maintain his large, and well equipped army. The marriages and the authority granted to the warriors by the Mai, effectively established a hereditary system of lordship. The result was an authentically African structure that resembled Europe's feudal system, in which the warriors were, by definition African Knights. The Kingdom of Kanem, would reach its height, during the 12th to 13th century. After the death of Mai Dabbalemi, his sons would compete for power. The disunity would be costly for Kanem, and after the death of a successor named Mai Dunama II, Kanem would fall apart (in the 14th century). From the writings of Ibn Sa'id in 1270 we learn that Kanem had already become an independent kingdom. The death of four Mai's, at the hand of the remnants of the Sao Culture would pile on to the destruction of Kanem. In 1388, an ethnic group called the Bulala would conquer much of Kanem's territory. Because of the conquest, the Kanembu would return to the nomadic lifestyle they abandoned 600 years earlier. They would become the target of attacks from Arabs, Berbers, and the Hausa.

THE KINGDOM OF BORNU

Where "a lone woman clad in gold might walk with none to fear but God"
(King) Mai Idris Aluma

After 10-20 years of wandering and persecution the Kanembu would establish a new city, in approximately 1396 called Bornu. Bornu would last from 1396-1893 (approximately 500 years). The collapse of the Songhai kingdom would leave open a vacuum that the new city of Bornu would quickly fill. Apparently though, exile taught the Kanembu very little. Even after founding Bornu, the Mais' would continue to war against each other. From 1400-1472 fifteen Mais' would cycle on and off the throne. In 1472, under Mai Ali Dunamami a unification was finally affected which brought consistency to the throne of Bornu. He built a fortified capital at Ngazargamu in present day Niger. Because of the abundance of agriculture, Ngazargamu was favored as a residence for the monarchs. It is after this point that the Kingdom of Kanem and the Kingdom of Bornu would finally be unified by Idris Alawma in 1575-1610. The peak of Kanem Bornu would come under the reign of Mai Idris Aluma. Kanem-Bornu would become a world power, economically and would brandish its military prowess throughout the region. It's black knights, would dawn fully black armor, with chain metal dresses that covered the warriors from the neck and terminated at the knees. These highly disciplined warriors would ride similarly armored horses in sophisticated military formations. The entire force of Bornu was comprised of a large cavalry army, and a substantial infantry. Some sources claim that Mai Idris

Aluma leveraged his military to expand his territory through an astonishing 330 wars with over 1000 battles. The Mai cleared roads, created standards to facilitate the trade in grain and invested significantly in agricultural development. Security became a top concern for the trading kingdom. The Mai famously set a goal that "*a lone woman clad in gold might walk with none to fear but God*". The Mai also broadened the international reach of the kingdom by recognizing the importance of diplomacy for his trading nation. He forged relationships with the Ottoman Empire, the Egyptians and even Tripoli. The Ottomans are believed to have sent a 200-member delegation of ambassadors to the Ngazargamu court. Aluma would erect an Islamic state that would last for another 200 years. As we describe the once grand kingdoms of Africa, it is important to note that early Europeans and traders of every ethnic stripe visited these lands. We can always return to their personal notes, diaries, and published works for first hand accounts. These texts are instructive because they give us an unvarnished take on how Europeans perceived these African kingdoms at the time. Hugh Clapperton was a Scottish explorer who travelled with his colleagues Walter Oudney, and Dixon Denham to the noted trading kingdom of Bornu. The trio would leave Tripoli in 1822, and head south until they reached the Bornu city of Kuka on February 17, 1823. They were sent in service to the British government and their travels are recorded in the "Narrative of Travels and Discoveries in Northern and Central Africa in the years 1822-1823 and 1824 (1826)". Clapperton was also the first European to record observations of Hausa States. His descriptions appeared in the "Journal of a Second Expedition into the Interior of Africa: From the Bight of Benin to Soccatoo". These relatively inexpensive books are just a few of the firsthand accounts available to readers.

THE HAUSA
THE CHIEFS OF INDIGO

When imagining African Kingdoms, it is easy to envision these kingdoms as humble, or modest, or to allow the caricature of African civilization to influence the sophistication we imagine in these cities. But the architecture of the Hausa was known to be among the most beautiful styles of architecture developed in the medieval age. Mosques and palaces were bright, full of color, and intricately engraved with complex symbols which were etched into the facades. The Hausa lands, were established in iron rich territories, and they were as vast, and sophisticated as any in the world. One of the Hausa's most famous cities, was the industrial city of Kano. Kano was renowned for its production of superbly dyed cloths, in its Indigo dye pits. The sheer brightness of the indigo colored fabrics they produced made them a coveted commodity. An important fact about African productivity and Hausa productivity is that Africans met incredibly high industrial demands without destroying the communal fabric of their culture. This fact was noted by many Europeans that visited the region. The dye pits of Kano are like open air industrial facilities, that produced phenomenally vibrant, blue fabrics of nearly unmatched quality. In the 15th century Sarkin (King) Rumfa introduced his "twelve innovations", which included the palace and the Kurmi market place. His 33-

acre palace, continues today to house up to 1000 people. The palace possessed private houses for the King's guests, reception rooms for the public, and apartments for the Sarkin and his visitors. The entire complex was surrounded by a wall that was 20-30 feet high from the outside and 15 feet from the inside. The walls were renowned for their thickness and durability, which was as much as 15 feet wide in some places. The whole city of Kano was surrounded by a massive system of walls, that were sculpted with supreme artistry. The walls of Kano, were renowned for their beauty. They were tapered inward, and were rounded on top with openings for archers defending the city. The eleven mile walls of Kano were surrounded by moats with low earthen bridges which provided passage to the southern gates. The main gate of the complex was called Kofar Kodu, and was decorated with bronze paneling, adding to the artistic details. Beyond the outer wall, was an additional fortification; an impressive, two story doorway-gate buttressed by two adjoining gatehouses. It is called Soron Gabjeje. All along the rooflines are openings for archers. The Soron Giwa, or the Hall of Elephants leads to the grazing lands for the royal elephants. Audience rooms have walls and ceilings that are decorated with grooved patterns and paint. The Hausa use a substance derived from a locust bean shell, to stain timbers that give structure and scaffolding a deep black color. The walls are often plastered with mica, to give them a silver sheen. We should take the time to note how innovative these substances are. The timbers are resistant to rotting. The mica is non-static and prevents dust from accumulating, repelling spiders and hornets from the building. The use of substances like these, and the locust bean stain for wood timbers, display the innovative capacity of this early African civilization. The expertly sculpted walls of Kano were admired, and its vast, well organized markets were a credit to the administration of the Kingdom. The unique architecture, and beautifully sculpted walls which seem more like art than fortifications, still draw visitors to Kano's markets. The Hausa Kingdoms represented the propagation, and prominence of a single ethnic group in addition to those who accepted or adopted their culture. The Hausa represent the typical way in which African Kingdoms would grow and evolve in the ancient world. The Hausa Kingdoms, were composed of a total of seven states, but an additional seven states adopted Hausa culture, to participate as fully as possible in the prosperity of the culture. The seven official states, which were Hausa ethnically and culturally, were: Biram, Daura, Gobir, Kano, Katsina, Rano, Zaria or Zazzau. Each of these cities was founded at a different point in time. They are referred to as the Hausa Seven, or Hausa Bakwai. As previously stated, labor in African kingdoms was often divided to ensure the full functionality of African kingdoms. The cities of Kano, and Rano (especially Kano) were famous for producing beautiful indigo fabrics. Cotton, which was cultivated grew rapidly in the plains near the cities, and its farmers could supply the cloth in ample quantities to those responsible for weaving and dying it before shipping it off, via caravan. Kano and Rano became known as the Chiefs of Indigo, a reference to the beautiful blue hew of the fabrics they produced. Anecdotally some scholars highlight the communal nature of Hausa fabric production, often suggesting that it lacked some of the brutal production conditions of similar industrial scale systems in Europe. Our focus however, is simply on the scale and scope of yet another African culture that managed to satiate the ravenous appetite of global markets for African goods. The remarkable Hausa communities were another example of the capacity of African civilization to organize formidable and laudable kingdoms that upend stereotypes of black civilizations. The entire history of the Kano people is recorded in a document called the Kano Chronicle. It is written in Arabic. Translations of the Chronicle are available to interested readers.

THE ORIGIN OF THE HAUSA

Between 800 B.C. and 200 A.D. the Nok and Sokoto ethnic groups that had ruled northern Nigeria were in decline. The Hausa, an ethnic group which moved in slowly from Nubia (the home of Kush, near the east coast of Africa, centered around the Nile River near Egypt) began mixing with the local Northern and Central Nigerian inhabitants (between 500-700 A.D.). They established several strong states. When the first Kings of the Hausa determined that they would build large-walled and fortified cities in the regions between the Niger River and Lake Chad (present day Nigeria) they would find themselves locked in a century long conflict with the religious establishment of their day. The pagan cults of the most popular faiths derived their authority from shrines, and groves prominently located in the proposed paths for the King's cities. To modernize, the rulers would have to destroy their past, and they would face resistance just as visionaries throughout human history would. The point of import here is that the Hausa came into the region as immigrants, after the decline of Kush and in-between the transition period of the rise of new kingdoms in the Nile region. In the cumulative creation of civilizations, we can again see a connection between the fall of one empire and the creation of another. The civilizations of Africa were always linked in some fashion, through trade, through achievements, and through migrations. The Hausa were a part of this collective effort that gave birth to cultures and empires throughout the continent.

THE END OF THE HAUSA

Today, the Fulani are a semi-nomadic, and impoverished people. However, in the 1800's Muslim jihadists of the Fulani persuasion, would bring the Hausa Kingdoms to an end. They were led by a religious teacher named Usman dan Fodio. He is known in history as one of Africa's greatest political philosophers. He led the Fulani minorities in their famous crusade against Hausa oppression. The uprising he provoked would lead to the establishment of the Sokoto Caliphate. The Sokoto Caliphate was a loose confederacy, but it was also the largest African Empire constructed after the fall of the Songhai Empire. Usman was a well-educated, religious scholar, living in the Hausa state of Gobir. In the city of Dengel, in the state of Gobir, he was attempting to establish an ideal society based on strict Islamic practices. In our modern, terror-conscious, society, strict Islamism carries a connotation. We often think of sexism, and militancy. But Usman as a philosopher and teacher doesn't fit neatly into our modern understanding of Islamism. Usman for instance railed against the "Islamists" of his day that oppressed women, and confined them to their homes. He viewed the abuse of women as a violation of the rights guaranteed to them by Islam. Far from our modern understanding of an Islamist, Usman demanded freedom, literacy, and opportunities for scholastic achievement for women in society. In the beginning of his career as a reformer Usman was employed by the nobles of Hausa society to educate the ruling elites. However, while living among the privileged, he became overwhelmingly concerned with the plight of the poor. He began to write discourses on the excessive taxes imposed on commoners throughout Africa. He began to vocalize ideas about the role of government, the morality of governments (or the lack thereof), and the obligations of leaders in society. The political philosopher would write over a hundred books on government, religion, and culture. He began crusading against the corruption, injustice, and inequity endemic throughout the land. He linked the oppressive taxation, corruption and cruelty faced by citizens with the un-Islamic and pagan habits of rulers throughout the Hausa lands. His ideas would eventually raise concerns among the nobles, and one of his former students would attempt to kill him. Dan Fodio would be exiled, and live in the grasslands, occupied by the nomadic cavaliers of the Fulani ethnic group. He would teach them his beliefs and his ideas would spread like wildfire among the Fulani, until they exploded in numerous jihads by his supporters. He would be declared ruler, and he would raise an army with the intent to establish his longed for ideal society. The Fulani, following the teachings of Dan Fodio, would punctuate true Islamic practices, and bring books, set up Islamic schools and learning centers. It is worth noting that, in setting up an Islamic civilization, and in crushing the cult worship indigenous to Hausa civilization, the original Hausa kings were inadvertently crusading against the role of women. Women made up a great deal of the diviners, cult leaders, dancers, and mystics whose power was derived from traditional Hausa shrines and religion. Religion was, in a sense the way in which women attained power over their husbands, and in society. To conquer, Islam would have to find an acceptable, but no less dignified role for women. To this end, Islamic philosophers like Usman dan Fodio suggested new roles for women as Islamic scholars. Usman, the jihadist, created avenues in Islamic scholarship that allowed women to become poets, historians, and erudite scholars. In fact, three of Dan Fodio's daughters were renowned poets. Women were given titles which mimicked the pre-Islamic titles granted to women, in government and society. Prior to his reign women could be tax collectors, and government agents. In the new Sokoto Caliphate women would have to be equally prominent, although separate participants. Ultimately Dan Fodio's writings would inspire Jihad's throughout Africa and lead to the establishment of several states. Some scholars even believe that his calls for justice inspired uprisings among African slaves in the Americas.

AFRICANS IN ISLAMIC SOCIETIES

The Ethiopian state of Aksum was deeply involved in shaping the events, politics, and development of Arabia. Aksum possessed tributary states in Arabia as early as the 3rd century (200 A.D). Although it was an Aksumite custom to maintain indigenous rulers over a conquered population, these states were loyal to the Ethiopian crown. Axum, which was naturally wealthy because of gold and iron deposits, was also heavily engaged in the trade of valuable commodities like salt (and agricultural produce). The power of its navy, gave it commercial dominance over the Red Sea trade, as the crucial link in the trade between Rome and India. As one of the world's most powerful empires, Aksum intervened significantly in the politics of the Arabian Peninsula, and eventually displaced the Himyarite Kingdom, which was the dominant state in Arabia. In the early 6th century, Aksum invaded Arabia, as a response to the persecution of Christians by the Himyarite King. From the year 525 A.D., Abraha the Aksumite, was a dominant force on the peninsula. According to the historical record, Abraha's army consisted of approximately 100,000 soldiers, and hundreds of war elephants. By most accounts, Abraha was a competent ruler, that took steps to legitimize his reign by connecting his legacy with Arabia's historical kings (of Saba). He is credited with making crucial repairs to the famous Marib Dam, which was constructed prior to his reign. The dam which had long needed repair, was responsible for irrigating 25,000 acres. We can develop an understanding of how important this dam was, by recognizing that after his reign, the dam was destroyed and 50,000 people were forced to migrate away from the region. Abraha is also believed to have constructed a grand cathedral, rivaling any in the Christian world. He campaigned to spread Christianity among early Arabs, in the face of persistent paganism and Judaism. As a major political force in the region, Abraha is only a single example of the effect that African polities had on the world and in Arabia in-particular. The role of Africa and its kingdoms, on the world stage is one of the most misunderstood, or under-appreciated issues in history. Africa was once extremely influential on the world stage. It shaped events, contributed to the development of cultures, and was respected throughout the ancient world. In Arabia, it was the Aksumite kingdom that held sway, and it was through this portal that a healthy population of Africans made their way onto the Arabian Peninsula. These Africans would contribute to the culture of Arabia, and would also be heavily involved in the birth and propagation of the region's most important export; the religion of Islam. The first Muslims would conquer all of Arabia, displacing the influence of ancient powerhouses like Persia, and the Byzantines. They would conquer north Africa, Egypt, and eventually much of Europe to form one of the largest empires in human history. But Africans would be critical contributors to the growth and success of the Islamic Empire. During Europe's Dark Ages, the center of the world's gravity, was in the east. The light of civilization would burn brightly in the Islamic nations, and Africans would play a critical role in establishing this near global juggernaut. To understand the role of Africans in the growth of eastern civilization, we should examine Arabia prior to the foundation of Islam.

ANTAR: The First of All Knights

Antarah Ibn Shaddad al-Absi was born in pre-Islamic Arabia (before the life of Muhammad-and approximately 500 years after the birth of Christ), between Saudi Arabia and Yemen. Antarah was born into the pre-Islamic world, as a subordinate to his peers. His father, Shaddad, was a well-respected member of the Banu Abs tribe, but his mother Zabaibah was an Ethiopian, captured and taken as a slave, in a war against a rival tribe. As the son of a slave, Antarah would be raised as a slave himself. His skin was very dark, which betrayed the secret of his African heritage. Despite looking, very much like his father, his physical appearance made it impossible for him to be accepted as an Arab. He would be ostracized by his father, whose status in Arabian society discouraged him from acknowledging his black-son. Yet, despite the inattention of his father, Antarah would learn to excel in the military arts. He was the strongest, and most skilled warrior in his tribe, and yet he would be unable to distinguish himself in battle, for much of his life. As a slave, he was not permitted to participate in the battles that were common in early Arabia. The pre-Islamic period of Arabia is often referred to as Jahiliyya, or "The Time of Ignorance" by Muslims. The moniker is apt because pre-Islamic Arabian society was composed of an innumerable number of tribes, locked in an endless cycle of senseless bloodshed and violence. Wars and blood feuds would often erupt in the desert between tribes over issues that seem strange and often trivial, but to the Arabs of this time, they were serious issues of life and death. One of these wars would create an opportunity for Antar, to distinguish himself in battle. The Great War of Dahis and Ghabra would erupt over the ownership of horses, but when the war erupted Antar (same as Antarah) was not permitted, by the members of his tribe, to join in the fight. However, circumstance and desperation, soon changed the minds of the tribesmen. As Antar's tribe stood on the precipice of defeat, they accepted his offer to fight for the tribe. The swift, and strong Antarah charged fearlessly into battle, striking down the enemies of his tribe. His valiant efforts would secure victory for his tribe, and the skill he displayed would inspire his father to finally recognize the young warrior slave as his son. Antar would be recognized by his father, under the condition that he continue to fight for his tribe. It seems that only the premium placed on warrior skill, was sufficient to overcome the prejudice against Antar's African birth. The courage Antar displayed in battle would only be matched by the beauty of the poetry that he composed throughout his life. In pre-and post-Islamic Arabia, culture and entertainment often centered around the art of poetry. Poetry is arguably the definitive form of art in Arab culture. Islamic art is not centered around portraits and sculptures as the art of many cultures tends to be. The spoken word, provided Arab culture with imagery of a different fashion. The norms of the Arabic language itself, developed primarily to spread the poems of Bedouin traders in the desert. In pre-Islamic times the lives of these nomadic herders was rigorous, and the harshness of the desert produced an equally rugged disposition among early Arabs. There were very few reprieves from this harsh existence, but as nomads traveled from one settlement to another, they would find brief relief and entertainment in poems which celebrated the glorious battles and histories of their tribes. Over time, the need to communicate these poems necessitated the development of norms in the Arabic language (which, in earlier days varied dramatically). Arabic then, more than any of the world's other languages was designed to convey poetry. Poetry became central among pre-and post-Islamic Arabs, and one of the most celebrated poets in the entire pantheon of Islamic poetry is Antarah. Antarah is one of many Africans that contributed to the formation of this high art. His poems examine the values of chivalry, courage and heroism. He paints vivid images of the battles his tribe fought, the armor they wore, and the weapons that they used to ensure the continuation of daily life in Arabia. His life and poems have inspired enduring epics, and even films which have been routinely remade (usually with light-skinned Arabs in blackface), but the prestige of his legacy lies in his position among the Mu'allaqat- or The Suspended Poems. The Suspended Poems (also called The Hanged Poems) are the seven poems which are hung in the Kaaba, Islam's holiest site, in Mecca. The placement of Antarah's poem among the Suspended Poems, is a testament to his place, as one of the most celebrated poets in Arabic history. As an enigmatic Warrior Poet, Antar became the archetype for the Islamic Knight, which earned him the title of The First of All Knights. He was also called The Lion and The Father of Heroes. He was a lover, a warrior, and an artist. The black warrior of African descent would epitomize the "Arab" ideals of virtue and masculinity. Yet despite his valiance in battle, and his artistry as a poet, Antar could still not shake the discrimination in early Arab society. In the epic of Antar, a central theme, is his love for his cousin, Abla. Antar was deeply in love with her but Abla was a member of the tribe of Ansar. Her father was known as one of the most bigoted men in Arabia. When Antar told his father about his love, his father assured him that his blackness made the marriage impossible. Antar persisted, and proposed marriage to his cousin's father. The father refused, but offered Antar a single course of action. If Antar could secure 100 pure yellow camels, of the highest breed, from northern Arabia, the marriage could proceed. It is worth pausing to consider what a tremendous price Abla's father gave Antar for her marriage. In an Arabia where wars were fought over singular horses, the value of 100 healthy camels is nearly incalculable. Antar however, achieved this feat, and was finally permitted to marry Abla. His poems about Abla, are among his most celebrated works. In both pre-and post-Islamic Arab society, numerous Africans would contribute heavily to the poetic and literary life of Arab civilization. Some of the most significant contributions of black poets in pre-and post-Islamic society are grouped together and are often referred to as The Crows, or The Ravens of the Arabs. Though many African or dark skinned Arabian poets, are referred to as Crows, the actual group of Crows, consists of three black poets, from the pre-Islamic era. The official trio consists of Antar, Khufaf (or Ibn Nadba) and Sulayk ibn al-Sulaka. The Crows represent some of the best contributions to the tradition of Arabic poetry, but they are merely a sample of a vast reservoir of African work. While there are numerous other black poets, from both pre-and post-Islamic eras, it is the crows or The Ravens that are remembered together. Later poets, whose works are often attributed to the trio of Crows, would dwell extensively upon slavery, discrimination, and the plight of Africans in Islamic society. We can distinguish the works of later poets from the actual Crows, because we know that the weight of discrimination that these poets write about, did not exist in the early pre-Islamic society of The Crows. As we shall see, racism would grow over time in the Islamic World. In the pre-Islamic world, Africans could, and would express a variety of experiences. Antar, was The First of All Knights-and the model of pre-Islamic manhood and warrior virtue. Khufaf was black, and similarly rose to become the Chief of his tribe, "despite his dark pedigree". Sulayak, was a rogue and thief, that immortalized his exploits in poetry. The three represent different aspects of African potential in early pre-Islamic Arabia. Despite popular belief, while prejudice and discrimination existed in early pre-Islamic society, Arabia did not display systematic or inescapably crushing forms of overt racism against blacks. The discrimination Antar faced, was based in large part (though not entirely) to his status as the son of a slave, as opposed to a statement against his race, exclusively. In many ways, later Islamic culture would become an unfortunate foreshadowing of future European bigotries. The pre-Islamic world would begin with Arab cultural pride that often expressed itself as a prejudice against foreign cultures (but not blackness particularly). However cultural pride would evolve into a society that capitalized on African talent, intellect and labor while espousing overtly racist dogmas. The ancient Islamic world would be an unfortunate (although less extreme) premonition of the future for Africans. The Islamic habit of taking Africans (and many other groups) as slaves predates by several centuries the Western/Christian slave trade. A crucial portion of the African story is the forgotten system of Arab Supremacy, Islamic slavery and discrimination which would be replaced and surpassed by White Supremacy, European/Christian slavery, and outright hatred of blackness in later times. Islam would in time be used to justify bigotry in much the same way that Europeans would use later Christian doctrines. After several centuries of cooperation, interaction and dependency on Africans, Islamic society would author many of the same stereotypes, and theories of racial superiority that later Europeans would hold. Some Arabs, like later Europeans would come to claim that Africans were inherently inferior. Early Arabs lived contemporaneously with many of the African Empires previously discussed and they would in time assign Islam (and therefore Arabs) credit for the existence of these literate, academic, and economically prosperous African civilizations. Their claims would pre-date the claims of later

Europeans that would similarly claim that Europe, through the influence of Christianity had brought civilization to African savages. Some in Islamic society would claim that the "light of prophecy" through Islam (and implicitly the presence of Arabs) civilized otherwise barbaric Africans. In time, some elements of Islamic civilization would come to depict Africans as evil, untrustworthy and demonic. In this early system of prejudice and racism, after the flowering of Islamic societies into posh polities, it is notable that whites were also considered to be, intellectually inferior, morally deficient, and generally, uncouth barbarians. Whites, were also depicted as savage cannibals, possessed by evil, and the authors of an inferior civilization, absent of manners or refinement. In time, Islamic society would become an unfortunate and near perfect mirror image of what was to come for black Africans. The similarities in claims about Africans and African civilization are not indicative of any truth in their claims, rather the similarities reflect the common motivation to conjure myths that justify atrocities and injustices that existed both in Islamic civilization and Western Christian civilization. Both would have in common their respective slave trades, and (I would argue) those respective evil institutions drove both to distort, dismiss and conjure falsehoods about African culture. The enslavement of human beings is a naturally corrosive institution that relies on the slave being dehumanized but slavery is most importantly an economic institution. And in the case of both the Christian world and the Islamic world, it resulted from a growing sense of supremacy among singular groups and an economic (and perhaps intellectual or emotional) need to justify the act of enslaving. There would however be some substantial differences between the systems of discrimination in Islamic society, and those of European society. Islamic enslavement of Africans was substantially different from the later, western slave trade. Whereas the western trade was economically driven, and the construction of western industry was reliant entirely on slave labor, the Islamic slave trade was not based on a total economic reliance on African labor. Africans were not primarily used for hard, plantation style labor. Slaves were a sign of status, and were used primarily for domestic duties. Most Africans taken as slaves were women. While the process of capturing and transporting slaves was often brutal and cruel, once in captivity and sold, the treatment of slaves differed significantly from the treatment of western slaves. The doctrines of Islam discouraged poor treatment, forbade even striking servants, and made a virtue of freeing slaves. Of course, these dogmas were not often followed to the letter, but the brutal beatings, lynching's, mutilations, and deplorable living conditions that were common in the west were much less common in the Islamic slave system. The discrimination faced by blacks in Islamic civilization, was also significantly less oppressive than the suffocating, and ubiquitous bigotry of western society; although this is a terrible curve or scale to use as a measure. According to Islamic law, slaves (most often) were to eat the same foods that their masters ate, and were to wear clothing like that of their masters (a demand which fit in with their domestic and business duties). African slaves could, and often did progress significantly in Islamic society. As a rule, (especially in early Islam) only non-muslim blacks were eligible to become slaves. And as slaves, they were given considerably more liberties. Slaves could work outside of their master's employment (with permission), and save money to buy their freedom. Islam made a virtue of freeing slaves, for the atonement of sin, and as a sign of piety. Slaves were also used in a very different capacity in the Islamic world. Many businesses were conducted under the direction of slaves. Slaves could find themselves as their masters most trusted advisors, and in some cases, as their business partners. Slaves could achieve great status, as high level employees, or officials in government. In more modern terminologies;

while the C.E. O's of most businesses were free-men, the President or Vice President of many early commercial enterprises could be slaves. Islamic slavery, was much more comparable to the western system of indentured servitude, as opposed to slavery. Many slaves also married into the families of their masters. Freed blacks or Blacks born into Islam, had little to fear from the systematic oppression of other blacks. There is no evidence of free blacks disappearing into bondage. Free black Muslims may have suffered from some social discrimination, and would certainly have been insulted by the cultural theories about the nature of blackness, but we have very little indication that they were inhibited in their private ambitions, public business dealings, or in the status they could acquire as individuals. It is through the combined contributions of prominent black slaves, accomplished Afro Arabs of mixed heritage, and free born black Muslims (that became scholars, architects, poets, businessman and government officials) that the influence of Africans was felt on Islamic civilization. It is important to acknowledge these differences in extremes, between the western slave trade and the Islamic slave trade, without minimizing, or excusing racism and its impact on blacks throughout the Muslim world (which regrettably continues in modern times). Unfortunately, the Islamic world continues to reflect systematic bias against blacks. In many nations throughout the modern Muslim world, blacks continue to be oppressed, enslaved, and denigrated. In India, the middle east, and a variety of regions throughout the Muslim world, the events that led Arab society from its relatively flexible early-Islamic state, to its later embrace of bigotry began with the rise of Islam itself.

BLACKS IN THE LIFE OF MUHAMMAD

Practitioners of the Islamic faith look to the life of Muhammad Ibn Abdullah as the best example of how to live one's life. Copious amounts of documents have been compiled detailing every minor motion of his life, and of his daily activities, with the goal that Muslims around the world, would mimic his example. For Muslims, studying his life, is the key to developing a deeper understanding of Islam. For our purpose, the record of his life, and his interactions with Africans living in Arabia, can be used to study the contours of African existence in Islamic society. Just as Muslims study his life to live a proper Islamic experience, we can study his life and treat his life as an example of typical life in early Arabia. His interactions with Africans are representative of the types of interactions that other Arabs would have had with Africans as well. A wealth of sources exist which detail his life, and daily interactions. The Koran is a recitation of his words, and documents called The Hadith are the record of his sayings and the minutia of his daily life-as reported by his closest companions. Scholarly studies, can be combined with these religious texts to help us understand the role of Africans in the development of Islam and Arabia. The patriarch, known as the Prophet Muhammad was born in approximately the year 570 A.D. (some sources say 571 A.D). His birth took place during "the Year of The Elephant"-which was named for the attack of the Ethiopian-Abyssinian army on the Kaaba in Mecca. During their attack, the Ethiopian Empire utilized African War Elephants, which created a spectacle so memorable that the event would be immortalized in the minds and (eventual) lore of the Arabs. The event was a major turning point for Arab culture, and however infamous the war may have been, it represents the interesting historical intercourse between Africans and Arabs. The event serves to remind us that Ethiopians, once created one of the most successful empires on earth, and held sway in Arabia. As the conquerors of portions of Arabia, they contributed marginally to the culture of Arabia, and affected the events on the peninsula. Infamy aside, the beginning of the new faith of Islam would find its origin and the birth of its founder, forever pegged to the actions of an African Empire. As the son of Amina and Abdullah Ibn Abdul Mutalib, Muhammad was born into a noble Meccan family, and like many noble families Muhammad's family would own a young Abyssinian slave-girl named Barakah Umm Ayman. The young girl was brought unusually close to the family, in part by the tragedies that the family would face. Muhammad's father died of an illness prior to Muhammad's birth, on a caravan trip between the cities of Mecca and Medina. It was Barakah that delivered the tragic news to the pregnant Amina. The young Abyssinian would nurse the future prophet's mother through her pregnancy, often sleeping at the foot of her master's bed. Barakah, was the first person to hold the new born Muhammad. And when Amina died, Barakah would raise the young prophet with his uncle Abu Talib. Muhammad would describe the Abyssinian as his "*mother*". Because she raised him, he would constantly refer to her as his "*mother, after my own mother*". She would care for him, until the end of his life. She would refuse to even marry, until after Muhammad married his first wife Khadija at the age of 25. Muhammad's relationship with Barakah would shape the young man and perhaps even influence his views on race. In this early pre-Islamic culture, the tribe, and one's place within it, were crucial determinants of one's place in society. Despite being born the son of nobles, and being well liked and respected universally throughout Arab society, Muhammad would grow up feeling estranged from society. As an orphan, on the fringes of Arab society, Muhammad would develop a kinship with the downtrodden and ostracized, like Barakah. And this affinity would be emphasized in his ministry. When the black Abyssinian was finally married to her first husband, Ubayd ibn Zayd, of the Khazraj tribe in Yathrib, she gave birth to her son, Ayman (Her name Barakah Umm Ayman, means mother (Umm) of Ayman). When Muhammad began to experience "visions" that he interpreted as revelations from god, Umm Ayman and her family, would be among the first converts to the new faith of Islam. After her first husband died Muhammad would tell men, "*should one of you desire to marry a woman from the people of Paradise, let him marry Umm Ayman*". In Islam, salvation is never guaranteed to a believer, as it is in Christianity. There were only a handful of individuals that Muhammad guaranteed, jannah- or eternity in paradise; Umm Ayman was one of this few. As one of the earliest converts to the new Muslim faith, she would suffer from the persecution of the Quraish tribe-one of the most powerful and militaristic tribes of pre-Islamic Arabia, and adamant opponents of the new Muslim religion. She would risk her life to uncover plots against the life of the new "messenger of Islam". When Muhammad was in Medina, she would travel on foot, through the harshness of the burning desert from Mecca (250 miles). When she arrived, with her sun scorched face, and blistered soles, burnt raw from the desert sands, Muhammad would greet her with "*Ya Umm Ayman! Ya Ummi*", which meant "*O Mother of Ayman! O My Mother!*" In his relationship with Barakah, we begin to understand the indifference that the central figure of Islam, Muhammad would display to race and the values he wished to see expressed in his new religion. But we can also begin to understand the role of race in pre-and post-Islamic society, and the various degrees of discrimination in early Arabia. In the study of Africans in history, the role of slavery often looms large. Africans as slaves is a favorite topic of academics, because it often fits into our preconceived notions about Africans and about the ancient world. In early Arabia, however slavery was not exclusive to Africans, just as it would not be exclusive to Africans after the advent of Islam. Because slaves were taken in inter-tribal warfare, many slaves in early Arabia, would have been Arabs. It may even be more appropriate to think of these "slaves" as war captives. In fact, the clear majority of slaves, in pre-Islamic Arab society were not African. Despite the example of Umm Ayman, the role of Africans then, was not exclusively as slaves. Now the Axumite state, exercised its dominance over major parts of Arabia and was widely respected. In the eyes of pre-Islamic Arabs, Ethiopian civilization was superior to Arab civilization. Its presence resulted in many black Africans living on the Arabian Peninsula in a variety of roles. They could be merchants, warriors, mercenaries, members of tribes, chiefs, or slaves. Other Africans would come to Arabia through various forms of commerce, which also included slavery. These Africans and their descendants would become a part of daily life and warfare in Arabia. We can look again, to the life of Muhammad to develop our understanding further.

MUHAMMAD'S BLACK GENERALS

Muhammad would embrace Africans in his new religion, and administration, but he would also welcome Africans into the most personal aspects of his life. As a young man, Muhammad and his wife would adopt a black son but he was not of African descent. Zayd Ibn Muhammad, is known by several names. Zayd Ibn Muhammad literally means, Zayd son of Muhammad, but he is also known as Zayd mawla Muhammad-which means Zayd, Protector of Muhammad (and Zayd Ibn Harithah-Zayd son of Harithah-who was his actual father). Zayd, was a dark-skinned child captured in a raid on a tribe. Zayd's actual ancestry is in question to some scholars, who prefer to argue that, while he had undeniably black skin, both of his actual parents were Arabs. However, the point is academic, as his very dark skin is a source of constant commentary, and Zayd would not have been recognizable as "Arab" in our modern context because of his appearance. Zayd is important both because of his progeny and because he represents the difficulty we face when we impose the fictional construct of race on the ancient world. There are many Afro Arabs in the early Islamic histories that are often misreported as Arabs. He is one of a very few whose black features were so pronounced that he is recorded as being as black as most Abyssinians. Most scholarly references to Zayd, identify him as a black person but also as an Arab. We can accept that Zayd's parents were themselves Arabs, but to both modern and ancient eyes, he was black. Like Antar the warrior poet, and many "Arabs" of the time, it is worth questioning if Zayd was the result of a mixed heritage. After the raid on his tribe, he was given, as a slave, to Khadija, the wife of Muhammad. Khadijah and her husband Muhammad decided to free the young boy, and chose to raise him as their son. He would live with Muhammad and his wife, in their home in Mecca. When Muhammad began to experience, what he believed were visions, his wife would be the first to accept his claims as legitimate. Khadijah would in effect, become the first Muslim convert, but their adopted black son Zayd would follow shortly thereafter. Some scholars suggest that Zayd- was the first male Muslim convert. This point is very controversial, and contradicted by MOST mainstream Arab scholars. Some traditions (the Sunni tradition) hold that Abu Bakr, Muhammad's father in law, was the first male convert to Islam, while other traditions (the Shia tradition) hold that Ali, Muhmmad's cousin, and son in law was the first male to convert. The controversy reflects politics in the Islamic world, as both Abu Bakr and Ali would both become Caliphs. In Islam, a great amount of esteem is given to those that converted to Islam early and the order that both men converted is of great significance. The right of both Ali and Abu Bakr to lead the Muslim community would become the basis for the schism between Shia and Sunni Muslims. It is reasonable then, to believe that the legitimacy of these leaders, as it relates to the order of conversion, colors the historical interpretation regarding the first male convert. Irrespective of the controversy, Zayd was at the very minimum one of the first males to convert to Islam. By the most traditional and conservative histories, Zayd would have been between the fourth and eighth convert to Islam. The value of Zayd's life, in our survey is that he, like Antar challenges our definitions of race. While Antar represents the highly prevalent trend of Afro Arabs living in Arabia, and contributing to pre- Islamic culture, during the life of Muhammad, Zayd represents those that we would call black in modernity. Zayd would become a military commander for Muhammad, as one of Islam's early generals. In fact, he was one of Muhammad's favorite military commanders. Despite the strenuous objection of Arabia's most powerful elites to serving under a black former slave, Zayd was placed in command of the largest Muslim Army ever assembled at that time. He would die, carrying the standard, in the Battle of Mutah, leading 3000 men toward Bosra in a raid against the Byzantine Romans. This was the first Muslim army in history to engage the Byzantines. As general his significantly smaller force fell to an army of nearly 200,000. Zayd was the first Muslim to die on foreign soil. An important part of his legacy was his marriage to the blessed Umm Ayman, which produced another black general, named Usama bin Zayd, who would also be important in the history of Islam (continued later).

When Muhammad began to receive what, he believed to be

divinely inspired visions, he would feel compelled to spread word of his new faith. Among the slaves that would flock to his new religion, would be Bilal ibn Ribah. Bilal was an African, and he was also a slave, but he would also be among the first converts to the Islamic faith. He too, would endure countless persecutions. His master was one of the most vehement opponents of the burgeoning faith, and one of the chief persecutors of new Muslims. When he found that he had a Muslim, in his own camp, he would beat Bilal viciously, and tie him down on the burning sands of the desert, placing boulders on his chest. His demand was simply that the black slave renounce his new faith. The Ethiopian refused, reciting over-and over, "One God", a reference to the familiar Muslim creed (There is no God but God). A fellow Muslim, Abu Bakr would purchase Bilal from his horrendous master, and Muhammad freed him. He would become one of Muhammad's most trusted Sahaba, or companions. Muhammad would name Bilal as the first Muezzin in the Islamic faith. In the Muslim faith, the Muezzin calls all Muslims to prayer, by singing a song from the top of minarets that typically surround mosques in Islamic communities. In the early days of Islam, there were no minarets and the Muezzin would physically travel throughout the city calling the faithful to prayer. In some sense, this person was the public face of the new religion. It was a prestigious position among early Muslims, and made a profound statement about the universality of Muhammad's new religion. Even more relevant to our study, is the fact that many Arabs, contested the choice of Bilal, using as an excuse, Bilal's inability to pronounce the Arabic letter "sheen" properly. As an Abyssinian, Bilal's first tongue was Ethiopian Geez, and as a result he would pronounce the Arabic "sheen" as "seen". Muhammad would tell the disgruntled Arabs that "*The 'seen' of Bilal is 'sheen' in the hearing of God*". While it is said that Bilal had a magnificent singing voice, the choice of Bilal was as much a statement about the importance of racial equality in Muhammad's new religion, as it was a recognition of musicality. Bilal would become one of Muhammad's most trusted companions. He would bear Muhammad's mace and spear in battle, and prove to be a steadfast friend. He would fight in the Battle of Badr, the Battle of Uhud, and the Battle of the Trench- which are some of Islam's earliest and most consequential battles. When the Muslims finally captured Mecca, Bilal would mark his place in history as the first Muslim to sing the call to prayer in Islam's holiest city. When Muhammad conquered the city of Mecca and entered the Kaaba to destroy the pagan idols of the Arab tribes, at his side (chosen from among all of Muhammad's followers) were Usama ibn Zayd (the son of Zayd and now commander of the Muslim army) and Bilal (as well as one member from the Querish tribe). As a companion of Muhammad, Bilal would help record the deeds and doctrine of Muhammad, and become a primary scholar of Hadith (or the detailed records of Muhammad's life, relied upon for proper worship by Muslims world-wide). He would also become an authority on the Koran. He would advise the future Caliphs and leaders of the Muslim community. There would be many black scholars of Hadith and the Koran, in early Islamic culture and many blacks would become religious authorities. Africans would have a significant role in developing early Islamic doctrines and attitudes, often identifying themselves with Bilal's legacy. It became very popular in western Africa, for black Muslims to link themselves with the history of Bilal. His life inspired conversions, and a sense of belonging within Islam for many African Muslims. It is even common for many black Muslims today and in the past, to take his name. There are numerous anecdotes in Islamic history, that allow us to understand early Arab perspectives on race. A famous incident, recorded by scholars like Ibn al-Mubarak in his books Al-Birr and As-Salah record a disagreement that occurred between Bilal and an Arab named Abu Dharr (a contemporary of Muhammad's). During the disagreement between the two, Abu Dharr hurled a racial slur at Bilal, shouting that he was merely "the son of a black woman". When news of the incident reached Muhammad, he told Abu Dharr, "*That is too much, Abu Dharr. He who has a white mother has no advantage which makes him better than the son of a black mother*". Abu Dharr was commanded to apologize to Bilal, and was rebuked for his prejudice. The affected Arab went to Bilal's home, where he placed his head on the ground and would not lift his head until Bilal had placed his foot on it. The two men, embraced, with Bilal forgiving the offense. The incident is revealing, as it eludes to the attitudes of early Arabs. It is clear, from this incident that racial divisions existed, or were developing. While not excluded from participation in the culture of early Arabia, and while black skin was not necessarily reviled (as ugly or distasteful), prejudice against non-Arabs existed. The marriage of Umm Ayman to an Arab is a representation of events that would have been common. African'would have been taken as wives and concubines, giving some of the population of early Arabia, a mixed heritage. We must consider that this racial diversity would have been the case for many Arabs. We can add to this picture of diversity, "Arabs" who had a similarly mixed heritage, but did not reflect their African roots in a pronounced way. While most scholars believe that Zayd Ibn Muhammad was the son of an Arab woman, and Arab father, his existence is an excellent example of the racial ambiguity that would have existed in early Arabia. Zayd was black in skin tone, and was a slave. And he was treated accordingly in Arab society. The anecdotes from Muhammad's life clarify the existence of the racial diversity that we can see reflected in the historical record. The anecdotes from his life also prove that by his time, some prejudice existed, in early Islamic culture. However, this prejudice is best understood as social or perhaps cultural, as opposed to purely racial. In each of the cases we have discussed, we can view the prejudice as a reflection of social status and cultural divisions; slaves versus freemen. We can also accept that disdain for blackness, was not a hallmark of pre-Islamic Arabia. We can best summarize early Arabia as reflecting prejudice, but not overt hatred or disdain for skin color. Our primary goal should be to understand that through Muhammad's example, blacks like Ubāda ibn as-Ṣāmit fought in the early battles of Islam and rose to become Emissary on behalf of the new Islamic order (to the Cyrus or Prefect of Egypt under the ruling Byzantine Empire); and Amar Ibn Yasir, was one of the highest ranking Companions of Muhammad and later became a renowned scholar and like many blacks contributed to the body of religious texts relied upon by Muslims today; over time even the highest roles were available to blacks like Muhammad al-Jawad who became the 9th Imam which is the holiest office for Shia Muslims referred to as Twelvers (for the 12 infallible Imams they venerate as the rightful successors of Muhammad). The contributions blacks made to the invention, propagation, understanding and eventual domination of Islam on the global stage is impossible to summarize in this text. The topic alone deserves a thorough dissection but in this context, gives us a broader understanding of the potential for blacks to assume roles of prominence within Islamic society.

SANCTUARY FOR THE FIRST MUSLIMS

In the early periods of Muhammad's ministry, the Muslims would be persecuted extensively by most of the Arab tribes, and merchant classes of Arabia. When the persecution of the Queriesh, Arabia's leading tribe, became too extreme,

Muhammad would command his followers to seek refuge across the Red Sea, in the Ethiopian Empire of Axum. The event is known as The First Hijra, and occurred in 615 A.D. The term Hijra- means the migration or flight, and it accurately describes the dire circumstances of the journey. Afraid, for their lives Muhammad's first followers would sneak away, at night, in a boat. Muhammad would not accompany them, because he was still under the protection of his respected uncle, Abu Talib. Muhammad would tell his followers that they would find sanctuary in the court of the African Axumite King. Many scholars point out the presence of the Ethiopian Bilal, in Muhammad's inner circle, and suggest that Bilal could have contributed to Muhammad's choice of Axum as a refuge for his followers. This is however, without independent corroboration and it remains a point of speculation. According to Islamic sources, The Negus of Axum-Al Najashi-was renowned for his sense of justice and piety. Muhammad would tell his oppressed followers:

"If you were to go to Abyssinia (it would be better for you), for the king (there) will not tolerate injustice and it is a friendly country, until such time as Allah shall relieve you from your distress."

The king of Axum, was reportedly, not given to narrow mindedness or cruelty, and Muhammad believed that the King of Axum would welcome the Muslims into his lands. Muhammad would send some of his closest family members, and followers, on this journey. When the Queriesh found out that the Muslims had fled to Axum, they sent two capable emissaries with ties to the Axumite administration. Amr Ibn Al-Aas was one of the ambassadors. It is worth noting that he was chosen for the mission because of his ties to the Axumite Court. He would go on to lead the conquest of Egypt in 640 A.D., establish its capital at Fustat and build the first mosque in Egypt (the Amr Ibn Al-As Mosque) after he converted to Islam. But in the early days of the faith he was instrumental in persecuting the first converts to Islam. He came to the Axumite court bearing gifts for the Christian Bishops and members of the king's retinue. He spent time in the court, inciting them with tales of this new foreign faith, informing the Bishops that the asylum seekers did not share their religion. He stirred the Bishops with claims that the insulting new faith, rejected the pillars of Christianity, and the traditional Arab religion alike. Using his connections, he arranged a meeting between the Negus himself, and the Muslims. The assembly gathered in a great hall where the Negus sat on his large throne. According to Arab sources, the King asked the Muslims *"What is that religion that made you abandon your people's religion and refuse to embrace our religion?"* Muhammad's cousin Jafar, was chosen to answer and he responded, *"O Your Majesty, we used to be a people of ignorance. We worshiped animals, ate dead animals, committed great sin, severed family relations, and acted according to the law of the jungle. We used to believe that survival was only for the fittest until Allah sent from among us a Prophet who was known for his noble descent, honesty, trustworthiness, and chastity. He invited us to worship Allah alone, and abstain from worshiping stones and idols. He ordered us to speak nothing but the truth and to render back our trusts to those whom they are due. Moreover, he ordered us to keep our ties of kinship intact, be good to our neighbors and abstain from what is forbidden. He ordered us not to commit evil, nor to say false statements, nor to eat up the property of orphans, nor to accuse chaste women of wrong-doing without proof or witness. Hence, we believed in him and in Allah's message to him. We worshipped Allah alone. We rejected that which we use to associate with Him as His Partners. We allowed as lawful what is haalal and prohibited as unlawful what is haraam. Consequently, we are harassed and abused by our people, who tried to turn us away from what Allah has sent down to the Prophet so that we may return to idol worshipping and the evil and unlawful deeds we used to do. We were oppressed, abused, and straightened in a way that prevented us from the proper worship of Allah. They even tried to turn us apostate. Therefore, we fled to your country and asked for asylum to escape oppression and tyranny"*. Jafar reportedly read the teachings of their Prophet to the Negus, who found them to agree with his beliefs concerning Jesus. In the most embellished versions of the tale, the Bishops, and the Negus, began to weep at the sheer beauty of Muhammad's sayings. The Negus vowed *"I will never surrender you"*, and guaranteed the Muslims asylum in his country. In a later meeting, the persistent Querish representative attempted to stoke resentment between the devout Christian monarch and the Muslims, by forcing the Muslims to recite their creed regarding Jesus. The trick did not work, and the Negus is reported to have come down off his throne, and used his mace to draw a line on the ground (or in some sources a stick) and pronounced *"I swear, the difference between what we believe about Jesus, the Son of Mary, and what you have said is not greater than the width of this twig"*. The Negus then ordered his Bishops to return the gifts of the Queriesh, saying *"God did not take a bribe from me when He restored my kingdom; therefore, I will not be bribed against Him"*. For the first time, since Muhammad's first revelations, the Muslims would enjoy the freedom to practice their religion. Islam, was still in its infancy and had grown up under a yoke of persecution. It was practiced in homes, and in secret. The Muslims would know freedom for the first time, in the lands of an African King. For the first time in history, Muslims would practice their new religion, unmolested, under the protection of an African Empire. This Christian King would nurture and tolerate the new religion, which was still in its infancy, and on the cusp of

258

being exterminated. We should consider the dramatic, historical impact of this king's actions. Historically, much of this event fits with established information about the Axumite Empire. Axum was a trading Kingdom, active on the Arabian Peninsula. The Axumites conquered Arabia in the 2nd, 4th, and 5th centuries, each time ruling for at least a generation. The fame of its kingdom would have been known in Arabia. As a trading Kingdom, the capital and cities of Axum were filled with many faiths. Traders from India, Arabia, the interiors of Africa, and Roman Egypt, would have all been present. There would have been Ethiopian Monophyte Christians, Roman Catholics, Hindus, and Buddhists in Axum. It is reasonable to presume that the King's religious tolerance would have been a habit developed because of commerce. In time the Muslims would return to the raging battlefields of Arabia, to suffer additional persecutions. While the anecdotes of African involvement in the affairs of pre-Islamic Arabia, give us an idea of the general state and reach of African civilization, we should understand that Africans, in large numbers would be directly involved in fighting for, and spreading the new Muslim faith.

BLACKS IN ISLAM'S EARLY BATTLES

Once the new faith began to grow, small skirmishes between the indigenous pagan tribes of Arabia, and the Muslims would become common place. As non-Muslims continued to persecute the new faith, Muhammad would differentiate himself from other spiritual guides, and permit his followers to fight back. The willingness to fight developed after-The Second Hijra. Only after the Muslims were forced to flee their homes for a second time, and were facing extinction by the forces arrayed against them, were Islam's first followers given permission to defend themselves. This historical event, occurred in 622 A.D, after the Muslims returned from the First Hijra or migration to Ethiopia. Persecution would force the Muslims to flee again but this time their prophet would flee with them, to a city called Yathrib-historically. Today, the city is known as Medina. Medina was a desert Oasis-city and trading outpost. Constant internal strife and conflict plagued Medina. Having heard of his honesty and fairness, Muhammad, was invited by the residents of Medina to mediate their conflicts. The residents of Medina agreed to accept his new faith, and submit to his judgements. An agreement was struck, and Muhammad was now a head of state. As a head of state, Muhammad would begin developing doctrines for war, giving his followers the right to resist oppression. At first, there were small skirmishes, but the battles would grow. The first significant battle was known as the Battle of Badr. The Battle of Badr, was a major turning point in the history of Islam. The Muslims were severely outnumbered, as their enemies in the Queriesh had 940 men while the Muslims only had 300. The Battle is often called "divine" because the Muslim's victory was believed to have been the result of divine intervention. Africans would fight with Queriesh (624-30 A.D), in this early battle, but they would also fight for the Muslims in the Battle of Badr. These early Islamic armies were small, and the presence of Africans was noticeable and felt. It is recorded that Muhammad noted this fact, during the Battle of Badr, stating that "*the Ethiopians went off throwing their lances*". A warrior, named Shaqran is remembered for his contributions in the Battle of Badr (some scholars suggest that he was an Ethiopian or dark skinned Persian). Africans would be present in all the major battles of early Islam, including the Battle of Uhud, which occurred one year after the Battle of Badr. An Ethiopian named Sa'ud would carry the banner representing the Queriesh Tribe. Carrying the Standard, was, for any tribe, a major honor, and it speaks to the level of African involvement in early Arabian military engagements and the value of the African contributions. Balancing this awareness with the ethnocentric character of early Islamic society, we should note that Queriesh, the most powerful tribe in Mecca would be mocked for allowing the African, Sa'ud, to carry their battle standard. Their peers would remark in a Poem:

You Boasted for Your Flag
The Worst Ground for Boasting
Is A Flag Handed Over To Sa'ub
You Have Made a Slave Your Boast
The Most Miserable Creature that Walks the Earth

In the battle, the Meccans were seeking redemption from their earlier defeat at the battle of Badr. During the battle the Muslims seemed poised for victory, until some of Muhammad's troops abandoned their posts in search of spoils. This created an opening for the heroic Khalid al Walid, who lead the Meccan cavalry into a decisive win which killed many Muslims and nearly killed Muhammad himself. Washi was an Ethiopian Warrior that achieved success in pre-and post- Islamic Arabia, by switching sides to join the Muslims at an opportune moment. At the Battle of Uhud, he fought for Queriesh, and killed the Prophet's Uncle, Hamza. At the Battle of Khandaq, Wahshi would again fight with Queriesh and again would kill another Muslim. When the Muslims took Mecca, he would join the Muslims. Several Years Later, he would fight in the Ridda Wars-which were designed to combat the apostasy of new prophets, after Muhammad's death and unify the Arab tribes under Muhammad's original structure. Wahshi would kill the greatest enemy of the Muslims, the "false" prophet-Musaylama. He would write later in life; "*I killed the best of men, after the Prophet, and then later the worst of them*". Other warriors included, an Ethiopian or Persian named Safina-freed on condition of serving Muhammad. Some argue that it was in these battles that Muhammad developed a high regard for the fighting capacity of Africans. As a head of state and pragmatic leader, it is easy to see how this Warrior Prophet would desire these capable African fighters in his growing army. Yasar ar-Ra'I was a Nubian that often fought with Muhammad in battle. The fame of individual African warriors is useful in developing a personalized understanding of these pivotal battles in Islamic history, but we should not allow the prominence of individual contributions to obscure the fact that they were not the lone African actors in these early Islamic dramas. Numerous Africans were involved in the early battles, and their contributions loomed even larger, in the early days of Islam. As Islam grew, even more Africans would join the cause, and they would factor in heavily in the first two centuries of Islamic expansion. While, Africans were comrades in arms in early Islamic armies, they would be subject to a growing bigotry among Arabs. In the early cultures of Arabia, there was always an emphasis on Arab authenticity and a prejudice against anyone that failed to express true Arab culture. For instance, Arabs that lived-in cities, were less authentically Arab, than the standard of Arabness-the Bedouin nomads of the desert. And blacks-no matter the relatively superior condition of African civilization-were also not authentically Arab. Yet, among pre-Islamic Arabs, Ethiopian civilization was seen as superior to Arab civilization. Arabs still maintained a natural sense of cultural pride, which expressed itself as a cultural prejudice. An interesting similarity can be observed by considering Arab attitudes towards Persians. Despite the clearly superior level of

Persian civilization, a distinct and vicious disdain against Persians would be expressed among early Arabs. We often think of prejudice as groups comparing themselves to, and then defining themselves as superior to another group. However, it is often the case that prejudice arises as a resentment to dominance, or as a natural pride in the indigenous culture. We should seek a balanced understanding that Africans would have been present in good numbers, contributing to the events and development of Arabia and Islam. They would have been confidants of the Islamic prophet Muhammad. They would have contributed significantly to the military culture of Arabia. Blacks and their descendants would have been members of Arabia's tribes (at times even becoming chiefs), and African Civilization would have been pivotal in shaping events on the Arabian Peninsula. Despite African contributions, in battle and in the protection of early Muslims, prejudice would continue to grow as Arab pride grew with the popularity of Islam. There is a sad irony in the fact that black Africans were held in higher esteem when paganism was the dominant form of religion in Arabia than they were after the rise of Islam. Black Africans would give their lives, faith, and allegiance to propagate a new Islamic civilization that would return their sacrifice by actively promoting anti-black sentiments. The status of blacks globally would decline in direct proportion to the growth of the new faith.

BLACKS IN ISLAMIC LITURGY

Muhammad's attempts to curtail racism among early Arabians, would also be reflected in his liturgy. Sermons, and Sura (chapters of the Koran) would reflect his efforts. The thirty-first chapter of the Koran, is called the Sura of

Luqman. Luqman- The Wise, whom some in early Arabia, and modern Islamic thought consider to be a prophet, was a real, pre-Islamic black figure in Arabia. The verses of the Koran recount the lessons he taught his son. They are some of the most profound, and meaningful verses in the book. Luqman could only teach his son, because no one in his tribe would listen to him because of his blackness. In the Koran, Luqman is described as perceptive, wise and blessed by God. It is said that he could see the inner meaning of things, and illuminate the truth of existence. According to the verses, an angel of the lord, came to Luqman, offering him the choice to become a king, or a wise man. Luqman, chose to become a wise man, however, slavers also captured him. While we must go to lengths to excise the mythologies, to assess the factual benefits of the story, there are considerable benefits to the liturgy of Luqman. The Koran proceeds to expound on his life, in slavery and the wisdom offered by Luqman to his son. The inclusion of Luqman's teachings, is an audacious example of Muhammad's attempt to challenge the Arabs of his century to focus on character. The inclusion of a black prophet, in Muhammad's "revealed" teachings was an attempt to close the cultural and ethnic divisions of Arabia. We must consider how stunning, and controversial it must have been to early Arabs for Muhammad to include the teachings of a black " prophet" in his " revelations", and perhaps how risky it might have been to challenge such closely held pathologies. The Sura of Luqman is also a tale about the basic humanity of all people, including slaves like Luqman. It is an implicit challenge to Muslims to treat their slaves humanely, if not free them and consider the character of the individual as opposed to his or her race or status. Muhammad would forcefully challenge nearly all the traditional hierarchies in daily life. Muhammad would systematically attack the divisions of race, class, gender, and tribalism. In the case of a black Muslim named Jowairbir, Muhammad saw an opportunity to tear down multiple barriers in pre islamic arabia. In the early days of Islam, immigrants from everywhere, came to hear about the new Islamic teachings. One such immigrant was a black male named Jowaibir. As an immigrant, Jowaibir did not have a home, or an occupation in Arabia, or roots of any kind. However, he was an earnest seeker of religion, who came to the region to observe the new faith, and consider its merits. When he accepted the Islamic faith he quickly gained a reputation for his honesty and integrity. Jowaibir, like most of the faith seeking immigrants, was homeless and Muhammad offered them housing in the early mosques. In time this situation changed and more suitable accommodations were made. According to Islamic lore, Muhammad inquired as to why Jowaibir had not taken a wife. The black immigrant immediately pointed out his condition of poverty, his status as a foreigner, his looks (Jowaibir is considered to have been very unattractive, and short), and his race. Muhammad would rebuff Jowaibir's concerns, and state firmly his intent to eradicate all the old divisions of class, race, and status. Jowaibir was a pious man, and in Muhammad's new order, the integrity of Jowaibir, or his Taqwa (virtue) was all that should matter. Muhammad very quickly suggested a marriage to Zalfa, one of the wealthiest, and most beautiful women in the early Islamic community. Her father Ziad ibn Lubaid, and his tribe were also known for their fickle bigotries. The tribe generally refused marriage to anyone of a lower class and anyone outside of their tribe. The father initially refused the marriage, and after a brief attempt at intimidation by the male members of the family, Jowaibir made it clear that the Muhammad proposed the marriage and it was not his own idea. The marriage eventually proceeded, and a home was purchased for Jowaibir and his bride. According to the religious records, Jowaibir was so overcome with joy by his new life that he neglected to be intimate with his beautiful bride on the night of their marriage. The poor immigrant, it is recorded, never even dreamed of owning a home in Arabia, or marriage. Jowaibir, was short, ugly, and black (his ugliness is not, at this point connected to his blackness). The couple lived in comparative luxury for the remainder of Jowaibir's life. He became a soldier and fought nobly in the Islamic armies, until his death. The story is instructive because it exemplifies the personal lengths Muhammad went to address the issue of race in pre-Islamic Arabia. However, proving the nobility of Muhammad on the issue of race is not our goal. Using his actions, we can further understand the role of race in Arabia. Muhammad's actions can be studied conversely to demonstrate that race was a divisive issue in Arabia. In early Islamic lore, there are many stories and fact based anecdotes that include Africans, and we are confronted with the fact that Africans were a strongly noticeable presence in early Arabia. However, we cannot and should not attempt to define a ratio of black representation on the peninsula. It is our inability to quantify black representation that makes it difficult to place these stories into context. We should not assume that blacks were an equal presence or a majority in early Arabia, or worse yet to declare that the original Arabs were black (as some Afro-centrists have done) but we should accept that they were prominent contributors to the society and to the growth of early islam. And thus, blacks played a pivotal role in the development of this part of the world. Muhammad's last sermon is especially illuminating, on the issue of race, and gender in early Arab society. On the Ninth Day of Dhul Hijjah 10 A.H, in the Uranah Valley of Mount Arafat, reportedly 140,000 people would gather to hear one final message from their prophet. Muhammad, for his part would deliver an urgent last message to his people, certain that he would not live to see another year, or make another address. The sermon, is a lengthy listing of issues he felt were most prevalent for the early community. Many of his points were a readdressing of earlier stated principles. In part, it reads;

"O People, it is true that you have certain rights over your women, but they also have rights over you. Remember that you have taken them as your wives only under God's trust and with His permission. If they abide by your right then to them belongs the right to be fed and clothed in kindness. Treat your women well and be kind to them, for they are your partners and committed helpers."

"All mankind is from Adam and Eve, an Arab has no superiority over a non-Arab nor a non-Arab has any superiority over an Arab; also a white has no superiority over a black nor a black has any superiority over white except by piety and good action. Learn that every Muslim is a brother to every Muslim and that the Muslims constitute one brotherhood."

There is an incredible irony, in this last sermon, in that two of the issues that would continue to haunt the Islamic world, would become women's rights, and prejudice in the Muslim world. It seems that the Muslims did not heed their prophet's warning. The last sermon hints at a severe racial conflict, that may have been burgeoning or could have been well established by this time. The need for Muhammad to address the issue of race, in his very last sermon speaks volumes. It is important to consider that these were his last words, to his community. This sermon represents those parts of his message that he felt his people should not be without, or those issues that he felt required review or dwelling upon. In the section regarding women, we know that Muhammad was deeply disturbed by the treatment of women in pre-Islamic Arabia. In this early culture, tribes would often bury female babies alive in the desert sands. Women were abused, severely beaten, and seen as a burden. They were the targets of criminal violence, and, as the father of several daughters-and no birthed sons, their plight was dear to Muhammad's heart. This concern is reflected in Muhammad's placement of the treatment of women, in his last sermon. Likewise, the mention of racial strife in his last sermon suggests that the conflict was similarly disturbing, and may have become an increasingly divisive issue. The comments towards Bilal, make it clear that prejudice existed, and the opposition to Bilal's commission as the first Muezzin suggests that early Arabs may have been sensitive to Africans in positions of power. The growth of prejudice then, could have been the expression of Arab fear, based on the threat of losing political and social power, rather than an expression of superiority rooted in the level of cultural development. After his death, the racial conflagrations would only grow with Islam, and the prejudice against blacks would grow proportionally with the new faith. However, Afro Arabs and blacks would continue to contribute extensively, especially in the immediate aftermath of Muhammad's death.

AFRO-ARABS & THE ISLAMIC EMPIRES

After Muhammad's death, the Muslim community would be led by an elected succession of leaders called Caliphs. The first four rulers would be called the Rashidun Caliphs or The Rightly Gudied Leaders, by Sunni Muslims. Their names were Caliph Abu Bakr (Muhammad's Father In Law, 632-634), Caliph Umar I (634-644), Caliph Uthman (644-656), and Caliph Ali (Muhammad's cousin, 656-661). There would be many wars between the early Arab tribes, in the immediate aftermath of Muhammad's death. There would also be wars against men that claimed to be new prophets, after Muhammad. The Islamic community would struggle against these "apostates" in the Ridda Wars. And there would also be controversy over the election of the Rightly Guided Caliphs. Some in the early Muslim community would express their belief that Muhammad's cousin, Ali should have been made Caliph immediately following Muhammad's death. They would consider the other Rightly Guided leaders to be usurpers. This argument, over the right of Ali to rule the Muslim community, versus the legitimacy of the elections that followed Muhammad's death, led to the reign of the first three Caliphs, and would form the basis for the formation of the familiar Sunni and Shia Muslim sects. Bilal the black Ethiopian, would serve as a trusted advisor to these early rulers, and other Africans would be involved in forming the new Islamic Empire, and in defining the contours of the new faith. Africans and their descendants would be present and prominent throughout Islamic society. The second Caliph, Umar I, is often reported as an Arab, but most scholars today-even those outside of the Afro-centric communities, acknowledge that he was of mixed heritage. Umar I, was the most effective of the Rightly Guided Caliphs, and one of the most effective Islamic leaders in history. We should however, be clear about, and not exaggerate his African heritage. Umar's father, Khattab ibn Nufayl, was the son of a black Ethiopian woman. The Caliph's father was effectively half black, and his grandmother, was of purely African origin. Our goal is simply to acknowledge the degree to which African blood coursed through the veins of many of Arabia's (and Islam's) most influential figures and to recognize the extent of African influence on the global movement of Islam. Umar's reign would lead to the bulk of Islamic conquests, and he would be primarily responsible for the expansion of an Islamic Empire, that would dominate much of the world (from the middle east to Africa and Europe). Most of the "

Muslim miracle" that displaced the powers of Rome and Persia, were conducted under his leadership. Although, the first Caliph, Abu Bakr would begin the wars to unify the Muslim community and tribes of Arabia, his reign would be brief, and Umar would literally alter the world with the expansion of his Islamic forces, in wars against the Byzantines, Persians, and Egyptians. Umar I, would come to power, and continue to incorporate blacks in his military. Notable warriors like Abu Bakra, would shine brightly in the Caliph's army. Africans were very important in the Islamic military before 750 A.D., which is during the major periods of Islamic expansion and conquest. Muhammad's adopted son Zayd, had a son of his own, with the African Umm Ayman. The child's name was Usama ibn Zaid. He was effectively the grandson of Muhammad, and he too was black. Muhammad thought very highly of both Zayd and Usama, and made both the primary commanders of the early Islamic army. Although Zayd died in battle leading the early Islamic forces, Usama would take his father's place as the leader of the Islamic forces. Under Usama's command, were the future caliphs, Abu Bakr, Umar I, and Uthman. It is worth noting that he was placed in command of the entire line up of future Caliphs, and many of Arabia's most important figures by the age of 16. Usama was even placed in charge of the famed Khalid al Walid, who would become one of Islam's most famous generals (he would later lead the crippling assaults against the major powers of the world). The Arab nobles expressed their displeasure at being placed under the authority of the black 16-year-old, and in a rare occurrence, openly defied Muhammad's order to report for duty under Usama. Many of the same "high born" Arabs had also opposed the appointment of Zayd, Usama's black-slave born father, as general of the primary Islamic army. Muhammad responded to their disobedience by saying,

"If you speak ill of his leadership, you have already spoken

ill of his father's leadership before. By Allah, he (Zayd) deserved to be a Commander, and he was one of the most beloved persons to me and now this (Usama) is one of the most beloved persons to me after him. " (Hadith 745 vol 5)

Muhammad made clear that Usama, like his father was far more qualified than any of the future caliphs, and even Islam's future generals to lead the Muslim army. It is worth pausing to consider that both Primary Commanders of Islam's early and largest armies were black. Among Muhammad's last commands before his death, he emphatically ordered his companions to "*Fulfill Usama's Command. Fulfill Usama's Command*". It is notable that Muhammad was so emphatic about this last command and testament, but it is also worth questioning why he felt the need to insist on this in his last moments of life. Usama was appointed the commander of a force, set to attack Rome and its territories throughout the middle east. When he was about to be dispatched (the leader of the Islamic community) the Caliph Abu Bakr, escorted Usama, walking alongside Usama's horse, while Usama rode. Usama found this to be inappropriate and insisted that the Caliph ride while he walked. It is recorded that Usama said, "*By Allah, you will ride and I will dismount*". Abu Bakr replied: *"By Allah, you will not dismount, and by Allah I will not ride. It does not harm me to get dust on my feet in Allah cause for an hour*". The Caliph then asked Usama for permission to allow (the future Caliph) Umar to stay in Medina instead of going to war. He asked, "*would you consider supporting me with Umar and leaving him with me in Al-Madinah*". Usama consented. The exchange is notable because of the status, reverence, and mutual respect between Usama, as a black Muslim and Abu Bakr. It gives us an idea of the complexity and flexibility of racial relations during this period. Upon leaving, Usama's army became the second army in history to engage the Byzantines (his father's was the first). Muhammad planned the battle prior to his death. Usama was ordered to attack Shem or Syria. His army was the first Islamic army to defeat the armies of Rome. His victories destroyed the mythology of Roman invincibility and paved the way for the conquest of Syria and Egypt. When many of the elders of Arabia refused to appear at camp and serve under Usama, many stated their fear that the Byzantines were simply too formidable to defeat. Usama empowered future efforts by conquering the fear of early Arabs, and crushing the myth of Byzantine invincibility. We can see in this event the surprisingly resilient resistance to serving under individuals who were both black and of "low birth". Usama would also be instrumental in one of Islam's greatest turning points, The Ridda Wars-to quell apostasy. After Muhammad died, many Arab tribes recanted their faith in Islam. They essentially disassociated themselves from the Muslim community, and refused to pay taxes to the central authority of the Caliph (the leader of the Muslim Community after Muhammad died). The New Caliph, endowed with authority to lead-was Abu Bakr. He wanted desperately to fulfill Muhammad's last command to move against the Romans. He sent out Usama-Zayd, who was hesitant to leave Medina undefended. On June 26th, 632 Zayd was ordered to leave camp. He marched to Tabuk where the rebelling tribes fiercely opposed him. He defeated them, and moved on towards Northern Arabia. There he encountered the Quza'a, another rebellious tribe. After bringing them back into alignment, he then moved on towards Dawmatu l-Jandal, which is modern day Al Jawf in Saudi Arabia. His efforts were instrumental in quelling the growing apostasy, and reuniting the Muslim community. He marched to Mu'tah (the site of the battle in which his father Zayd had been killed) where he fought the Christian Arabs and then returned to Medina. Usama is one of the most important generals in Islamic history. The Caliph Umar constantly referred to Usama as "*my prime*" or "*my commander*". On one noted occasion, when the Caliph Umar was dispensing payments to the Muslims, he chose to pay Usama twice the payment he gave his own son. When his son inquired as to the reason for this, Umar replied, to his son, "*Usaamah was more beloved by the Prophet, peace and blessings be upon him, than you were, and his father (Zayd) was more beloved by the Prophet, peace and blessings be upon him, than your father was*". The competency of Usama was noted among early Muslims who often said, "*We've never seen a safer army than Usaamah's*". Another black General in the Ridda Wars, to quell apostasy and rebellious Arab tribes, was Ammar ibn Yasir. Yasir's father was from Yemen, and his mother was a black slave, named Samiya, that married his father. Ammar was one of the first converts, approximately the fourth to sixth depending on differing traditions. He was considered one of Muhammad's best friends. Ammar received Islam early, and convinced his parents to as well. Both of his parents were still slaves, and their owner Abu Jahl hated the new faith. He would beat Ammar's father and mother (Yasir and Samiya). One day, Abu Jahl struck Samiya so hard, that he killed her. Ammar was forced to watch his mother die as he was branded on his back. By accepting Islam, Ammar's family became the first- entire family to convert to Islam. In being murdered for their faith, Ammar's family became Islam's first martyrs (or Shaheed). After being burned, and forced to watch the murder of his mother, Ammar would seek comfort from Muhammad. Because of Ammar's persecution, Muhammad would set a new precedence in theology by giving his followers permission to publicly deny their faith, if they were compelled to by persecution and threat of death. This is expressed in the often misunderstood, uniquely islamic concept of Taqiyya. Taqiyya is often misunderstood by non-Muslims to mean that Muslims may deny their faith in public to deceive their enemies. This is not what it means. Based on the story of Ammar, it simply means that under threat of death, one may renounce faith, if belief is maintained in the heart. It is also worth noting that this idea is only accepted by Shia Muslims, which comprise 20% of Muslims world-wide. The concept of Taqiyya has been used by Sunni Muslims to persecute and raise suspicions about Shia Muslims. The value of the story is that it gives us an example of the role of blacks in Islamic liturgy and lore. Ammar would be among those that migrated to Abyssinia. He was also (according to the Islamic scholar Ibn Ishaq) the first Muslim to build a mosque! Ammar was very close to Muhammad, and he would accompany him on all his public appearances. Muhammad said of Ammar, "***Ammar is as near to me, as an eye is near to the nose***". Numerous Hadith (which are documents that record the life and sayings of Muhammad, are studied rigorously, and form the basis of a great deal of theological study) were written by him. He is therefore responsible for writing and transmitting some of the documents Muslims use to understand their faith. He is recorded to have been one of Islam's most pious men. As a sign of his piety Islamic lore says that he kept his beard at least one fist long always. In Islam growing a beard is a measure of morality. We can take this to mean that he epitomizes Islamic virtue, which was (at first) not connected to or inhibited by his race. Sunni and Shia's respect him alike (which is rare). Shia Muslims consider Ammar to be one of the four pillars of the Sahaba or Companions of Muhammad. The Four Pillars are exemplars of true Muslim faith. The four men that comprise the group are Ammar, Salmon- (a revered Persian that was considered to be one of Islam's holiest men,), Abu Dharr, and Miqdad Ibn Aswad. In the split between Shia and Sunni Muslims, these four were most loyal to Muhammad's cousin Ali, whose right to rule the Islamic community was the basis of the Sunni, Shia split. After the prophet's death, Ammar would also fight in the armies to quell the apostates. When Ammar Ibn Yassir, was killed in battle, Muhammad's cousin Ali, held his head in his lap; and as life left the body of one of Muhammad's closest companions Ali is quoted as saying;

"We belong to God and to Him shall be our return. Whoever does not feel grief over the death of Ammar is not a Muslim. Oh Allah, be merciful to Ammar during that time when the Angels will question him in the grave. I did not witness with the Prophet a group of three, without Ammar being the fourth, or a group of four, without Ammar being the fifth. Ammar was not deserving of paradise only once; he deserved it on many occasions. The everlasting gardens that await him are countless because he was with the truth and the truth was with him and as the Messenger of Allah said, "It (the truth) accompanies him every which way he turns."

The Queriesh tribesman Amr Ibn Al-ass, had been sent to Axum, during the first Hijra to retrieve the Muslims out of the protection of the Christian king of Ethiopia. He had been chosen because of his connections to the court of the Ethiopian king. Amr is often called the son of Layla bint Harmalah. He is best known for his conquest of Egypt, an act which some scholars believe he undertook under his own initiative. By conquering Egypt, he dramatically expanded the dominion of the Islamic Caliphate. The highly-contested region was a world changing entree into the Mediterranean with dramatic global consequences. The first mosque in Egypt and Africa, was built by Amr and it still bears his name. The Amr Ibn Al-As Mosque is a major tourist destination in Egypt.

From 684-693, a Civil War would rage throughout the Islamic Empire. The war is known to history as the First Fitna and black soldiers would fight on all the sides involved in this First Civil War for the Islamic community. According to al-Baladhuri, an Ethiopian named al-Ghudaf operating independently seized the city of al-Anbar in Iraq, which was a major strategic location. He was a highly-respected warrior that was famous for his ability to raid caravans single handedly. The fracturing caused by the First Civil War resulted in the establishment of a new Caliphate authority called the Umayyads. Ibn az-Zubayr, refused to swear fidelity to the Second Caliph of this new Umayyad dynasty and incited rebellion against the new caliphate. Ibn az-Zubayr is regarded as the fifth Caliph (as a continuation of the old line of Caliphs before the rebellion established the new Ummayad line). Zubayr, amid this era of rebellion, had Ethiopian allies that served as his javelin corps. The Umayyads, which were the first Islamic Dynasty to reign after the first four Caliphs, utilized slaves in their war, and sent them against al-Mukhtar (who also led an insurrection against the Umayyads). Two of the slaves were killed; one of the slaves was Greek, and the other was an Ethiopian, which demonstrates the multiethnic use of slaves. Ibn az-Zubayr retaliated by killing one of the black Ethiopians in the service of the Umayyads in 692. Al-Hajjaj ibn Yusuf, a fierce ally for the Umayyads led an army which included numerous Ethiopians. After the civil war, Ibn al-Ash-ath revolted from 699-702 and blacks would aid in his effort. It should be noted that this was a major moment in Muslim history. This disjointed litany of activity is stated simply to highlight the presence and crucial role of blacks on all sides during the fracturing of the Islamic Empire and during its coalescence. By the 8th century the Muslim armies conquered whole regions that were once in the control of the Roman Byzantines. They dominated Armenia, central Asia, Egypt, the Persians, and Syria. And at every step African soldiers would have been involved. As Islam continued to expand, the internal politics of the Islamic community became more complex and confused with issues of theology. The election of the Caliph was a contentious issue from the outset of the death of Muhammad. The split between the sects known as Shia and Sunni, would erupt over this issue. According to

Shia doctrine Muhummad appointed his cousin, and son in law, Ali, as his successor. The Sunni, believed in and accepted the election of Abu Bakr, while those of the Shia sect consider his election to have been illegitimate. Ali would eventually be elected as Caliph, but Shia regard all the other Caliphs as an abdication of Muhammad's will. The Shia believe in the 12 imams, which are essentially composed of Ali and all his direct descendants. The Imam's in their view are the rightful heirs to Muhammad's authority. Each imam is believed to have been infallible, and divinely connected to and inspired by the will of God. The Shia believe that only the Imams can properly interpret the Koran and its esoteric meanings. After Muhammad died, Ali was the first imam. Each succeeding imam, was the son of the previous imam. In this lineage of 12 imams, several are African Imams, and two are black imams. The sixth imam, Jafar Ibn Muhammad, purchased, fell in love with, and then married an African Berber women. He trained his African bride, Hamidah Khatun to be an Islamic scholar. She was one of the most respected and revered women of her time. She bore the 7th Shia Imam, Musa al Kadhim, who married a woman known as Bibi Najmah, or Taktum (among a host of other names). Najmah, is believed to have been from Northwest Africa, in the Maghreb. Her precise race is a point of contention, as some sources suggest that she was black and even Nubian, while others argue that she was of another, unspecified African ethnic group. The 8th Imam, Al Reza, was the offspring of Najmah, and the son of the 7th Imam (whose mother was an African Berber). The life of Imam Reza is commemorated by the Imam Reza shrine in Iran. The 8th Imam, Al Reza also married a black African. His wife was called Sabikah, and she was definitively Nubian. Her son, was Jawad Al Taqi, the 9th infallible Imam. His body lies in a tomb in the Al Kadhimiya Mosque in Iraq. Many of the Shia Imams were born from Africans and slave mothers, because the Imams themselves encouraged Muslim men to marry their slaves. It may seem strange to a modern sense of morality, but this doctrine was intended to elevate the status and treatment of slave women. The 7th through the 11th Imams were born of slave women, although for our purposes, only two should be considered black African descendants.

In the first two centuries of Islam's expansion, Africans would continue to fight as warriors in Islamic armies. Africans would be significant partners in Islam, and the tradition of black women as active Muslims, merchants, scholars, brides and concubines and the interactions those stations produced would continue to result in prominent Afro Arabs. After the first four caliphs of the Rashidun dynasty, the Umayyad Dynasty would rule, to be followed by the Abbasid Dynasty. Prince Ibrahim al Mahdi-of the Abbasid Dynasty was black. Caliph Al-Muktafi (Muqtafi Li Arillah), and Caliph Mamun al Rashid (6th Caliph) of the Abbasaid dynasty were also black. Blacks would continue to grow in business, government, academics, and the arts. Men like Amr bahd al Jahiz would establish themselves as intellectual forces. Jahiz was a biological scientist, a religion philosopher, and a poet. He worked in Basra, Iraq and authored numerous texts. Irar B. Amr was the Governor of the Iraqi province, and a poet as well. Abu Abbad Mabad ibn Wahb was a famous 8th century musician. Africans and their Afro-Arab descendants were involved in every major motion and expansion of the Islamic Empire. Their roles cannot be overstated.

THE ISLAMIC SLAVE-TRADE

Despite the role of blacks as scholars, trusted companions, and soldiers active in the expansion of the Islamic faith, bigotries would grow against blacks, in direct proportion with African slavery in Islamic society. As Arab society began to interact with the world outside of Arabia, Islamic civilization would incorporate many outside ideas, sciences, and practices. The outside world would influence Islamic architecture, science and even the Islamic religion. Unfortunately, Islamic civilization would also adopt external attitudes regarding color and race. Blackness would now be despised, while white skin became a marker of beauty and status. Racism against blacks grew exponentially with the Islamic slave trade, and black slaves became preferred for certain tasks-as their skin made them readily identifiable in an Islamic empire that now stretched from Arabia, through Africa, and into Spain. There also seems to have been a desire to ethnically stamp Islam as an Arab invention. As Islam grew into numerous regions, Arabs were quickly outnumbered among converts, and the need to emphasize the origin of Islam as Arab, encouraged a level of ethnocentricity. Submission to Islam, very quickly became submission to Arab culture, and in many places, while converts would accept Islam-they would rebel in subtle ways against Arabization. In some cases, they would adopt the Arab language as the language of religion, and commerce, but they would alter the Arabic script to conform to their own language. Many African societies would take this approach, as well as nations in India, Persia and Asian Kingdoms. One can trace cultural and commercial connections in the old Muslim world, by these variations in calligraphic style and language. In some places, converts would express their indigenous language in an Arabic style of writing, thus refusing to bow entirely to Arabic linguistic demands. And in other cultures, variations would be as subtle as the thickness of the Arabic calligraphy. But the Arab claim to Islam would also be emphasized in other ways. Those that could claim ties to the heritage of Muhammad could also demand special privileges and treatment. As the power of the Muslim world grew, Arabs would see a variety of roles as beneath them. Everywhere in the Islamic world, the use of slaves would grow because of the perception that certain tasks were beneath Arabs. The ownership of slaves then, grew as a statement of status, as opposed to the demands of state building, which drove the later western slave trade. Owning large numbers of slaves was prestigious, in the Muslim world. Slaves would be used as elite guards, and viziers, and in any capacity that their presence could be a demonstration of wealth. Rarely were they used in hard labor, but as Arabs would come to look down upon labor roles, an ethnically diverse array of slaves would be taken. Whites would be taken from the Slavic regions of Europe. Whites were taken in such large numbers that their captivity would lead to the invention of the term "Slave", which is a corruption of the term Slav. Blacks would be taken from the near regions of Africa, by Arab slave raiders and often by black Muslim kingdoms against their black non-Muslim neighbors and tribes. The huge variety in African cultures worked against Africans, in terms of the slave trade. Because there is no definitively African identity, various groups had very little reason to see each other as related. This condition made enslaving one's neighbor, much more palatable. Non-Muslim groups and tribes actively raided and enslaved their neighbors, for wealth, resources, and traded goods- just as they would for later Christian slave traders. Wherever Islam grew in Africa, it created an interesting wedge between Africans. Religion-in the form of Christianity and Islam, has always been a double edged sword for Africa. The arrival of Islam offered the organized states which existed prior to the arrival of Islam, entry into a burgeoning-nearly world-wide system of commerce. Continued wealth and opportunity were among the advantages of the unifying nature of the faith. Beyond commercial opportunities, Islam, at least in theory offered an international brotherhood. Implicit in Muhammad's message were attractive notions about the one-ness of mankind, and this aspect of the religion has always been proposed as an incentive towards conversion. The Koran explicitly condemns tribalism, racism, and nationalism, but none of these divisive ideologies would be eliminated by the growth of Islam. In many ways racism of a different form, would grow under the new Islamic regime. As blacks continued to convert, they came to see themselves as members of this ideal of the Islamic brotherhood, but the ideal would never truly materialize. Instead, Muslims would use their faith in much the same way, later Christians would use their faith. Islam would be used to justify slavery, and justify notions of racial superiority. As black cultures converted to their own indigenous forms of Islam, in certain regions they began to see themselves as wholly separate and (in some cases) superior to other indigenous groups of Africans around them. They permitted and participated in the enslavement of closely related cultures around them, under the auspices that those being enslaved were not Muslims. We can see this explicitly in Swahili culture, in which Islamic urbanity and piety are used as markers of superiority to the surrounding "barbarians". However, the loyal participation of Africans and African kingdoms in the Islamic system, was never rewarded with true equality. Outside of Africa disdain and discrimination against black skin would grow and rigid systems of oppression would form. The Koranic prohibition against tribalism and consequently, racial solidarity, effectively (though not consciously) became a dogma that discouraged blacks from standing in unity with each other. And yet, the same doctrines ushered in a system of Arab supremacy. As loyal members of the Muslim Community, Africans would allow other blacks of non-Muslim tribes to be enslaved. As an important aside, this mirrors the events of later European Christians. Europeans too began by offering Christianity as an international brotherhood, promising that only non-

Christians would be enslaved. As new converts to Christianity many new rulers would permit the enslavement of surrounding pagan tribes or whole civilizations. Africans would then convert to Christianity to protect themselves against enslavement. The rapid subsequent conversion of Africans to Christianity would then cause Europeans to resend the exemption, almost immediately after it was made. The growth of the western slave trade would seed the germination of color conscious bigotry against black Africans, and lead to an inescapable structure of oppression. The evolution of events was a near perfect mirror image for Arab and European discrimination. For the Muslim world, it would take centuries before the pretense of not enslaving black Muslims would deteriorate entirely and blatantly racist dogmas to be established.

THE ZANJ REBELLION & EASTERN RACISM

Over time, as the institution of slavery grew in the Islamic world, the treatment of slaves worsened. While slaves were still primarily used in government, business, and domestic settings, a few plantation style camps of hard labor arose. East Coast Africans (also referred to as ZANJ) would be sold into slavery, and forced into the miserable salt marshes of Iraq. The deplorable working conditions and harsh treatment from their masters would provoke several rebellions. In 684-694, a charismatic black Zanj leader called Rabah Shir Zanj, or The Lion of the Zanj would lead the mistreated black slaves in revolts in Basra. These revolts, and the abuse that provoked them began within two generations of Bilal's life and move into the region. The success of these early attempts at revolution, was short-lived but in 867 A.D., a lasting rebellion would nearly crush the entire Islamic Caliphate. After several victories over the

Caliph's armies, the black Zanj, and their Bedouin partners would establish a new Islamic kingdom. The Zanj Rebellion would become famous throughout the Islamic world as a significant threat to the prevailing political authority of the Abbasaid Caliph-the central authority of the Islamic Empire. The Zanj would embrace a philosophy that contradicted the traditional standards that determined the authority to rule. The Zanj believed that heritage was not the measure of Islamic piety. The prevailing wisdoms of the Islamic Caliphate held that only those with ethnic, and blood ties to Muhammad were suitable rulers of the Islamic community. As slaves, the Zanj sought a more flexible system that allowed them to gain prominence in Islamic society. Their new capital would be called, The Elect City (or City of The Elect). Their capital, Al-Mukhtarah was followed by the conquest of Al-Ubullah, a seaport on the Persian Gulf, Ahvaz in Iran followed, with a subsequent decimation of the Caliph's army in Basra and the direct defeat of Al-Muwaffaq-the brother of the Abbasaid Caliph. The crushing defeats of the Caliph created a growing sense of momentum but the movement would falter from treachery within the Zanj community. The Caliph would bribe Zanj soldiers to defect and this tactic led to a fracturing that ultimately destroyed the movement. Following the Zanj Rebellion, stereotypes against blacks would grow in popularity. The early prejudice of Arabia, would metastasize into a malignant and pervasive bigotry. Islamic art would now depict blacks as inherently untrustworthy, demonic, and evil. Literature would warn masters of the sexual proclivities of African men, and poetry would serve as warnings to Arab masters with African male servants in their homes. Standing above the arc of history, we can see that early Arab Masters would eventually promote many of the same stereotypes and fears that their later European counterparts would promote. In time, a few Islamic Arab scholars would conjure ideas that were shockingly like later European scientists. Scholars like the famed Ibn Khaldun would argue that human beings came into their current racial forms because of the environment. He would identify temperature as the primary driver of evolution in various climates. In this early pre-cursor to the Theory of Evolution, the Islamic scholar, Khaldun would argue that tropical regions with warm climates produced darker skin tones. The heat in these regions, if excessive, he believed, discouraged the development of intelligence. Likewise, Europeans were in regions whose cooler climates were similarly, not conducive to the development of intellect. His work was a revision of some earlier theories that promoted the familiar idea that blacks were the cursed descendants of Ham. Like later Christians, some Islamic scholars would be among the first to misquote biblical sources and state erroneously that the Bible taught that blacks bore a curse that made them worthy of slavery. The theory would gain less traction in the Muslim world, but the seed was still planted and it gave birth to new racist ideas. Arabs would argue that they were superior to all races, suggesting that ignorance, and stupidity, were natural characteristics of both blacks and whites, because of the climates they lived in. It is important to note that whites in Arab eyes, were no better than blacks (although the value of white and black slaves and the adoption of white skin, as a preference in beauty suggest some differentiation). Whites, they believed also lived in climates that rendered them inferior to Arabs. While blacks were ignorant savages, burnt from being overcooked in the womb and fried in their inhospitable climates; whites were uncooked-unfinished barbarians, whose minds were slow and lethargic as conditioned by their cool climates. Arabs were of course, cooked to perfection. These ideas gained traction but met with an obvious problem. Arabs came from the same temperate regions as many blacks, and were in the same temperate environment as blacks. Adding to this obvious contradiction was the fact that so many blacks were academics, merchants, government officials and slaves of great stature. Ibn Khaldun, was himself friendly and familiar with the royal court in Egypt, in which black Africans were very prominent. There were simply too many blacks that displayed daily, their intellect and ability for these theories to be correct. Blacks comprised many of the offices of government. They were slaves, but they were exceptionally competent which made the argument of ignorance very difficult. Many African kingdoms were, now Islamic or semi Islamic and many of them were exceedingly wealthy, in some cases wealthier than Arab ruled territories. The wealth and prominence of these African kingdoms would persist. Arabs would have to explain away the existence of Africans and African states that clearly contradicted their claims to superiority. Ibn Khaldun would work to refine and resolve the obvious inconsistencies in his theories, while the popularity of these ideas grew throughout the Arab-Muslim world. Wedded to his theory of Arab supremacy, Ibn Khaldun would author the theories on climate induced intellect, and then revise them. He would resolve that the clear contradictions of powerful black empires, black intellectuals, respected black slaves, and government officials, could be explained by the "light of revelation". Arabs, he came to argue were the superior race, but blacks could be lifted from their natural state by the light of religion, which the Muslim faith brought. Thus, we see another parallel. Just as later Europeans would explain away-African cultural achievements by claiming credit for introducing civilization to Africa, Arabs would, have their own corollary which would predate the European mythology. They argued that Islam civilized the savage African, in the same way that Europeans would later argue Christianity could civilize the black savage. These unfortunate theories would creep into Islamic civilization within 200 years of its beginning on the Arabian steps. Centuries before the racial conflicts of the west, and the familiar and infamous supremacy theories of white evolutionists, Black Islamic academics would be forced to fire back at the racist dogmas being birthed by Arab scholars. By the 800's racist theories were being exchanged, with black scholars arguing for the superiority of blacks, and Arabs of their own. In the early 9th century, Al-Jahiz the famed black biologist and well respected intellectual would author "The Glory of Blacks Compared to Whites" as a response to the racism of his Arab counterparts in the scholarly world. He would boast about the Zanj Revolt, and the failure of Arab powers to conquer by force any African power. He would even remind Arabs that they had once been conquered by blacks. In the 12th century, Ibn al-Jawzi would pen "Illumination of Darkness Concerning the Merits of the Sudan and the Ethiopians". Both works were the ancient world's version of African apologetics, as black scholars were forced to push back against increasingly popular racist ideologies that were now pervasive throughout the Islamic world. Many of these black intellectuals were men, and black men endured most of the racism in the Islamic world. Fear of black men, because of the Zanj Revolt continued to feed distrust and bigotry in the eyes of Arabs. There was however, an equally interesting appreciation for African women throughout the Islamic world. African women had become a mainstay of sexual interaction in Arabia, pre-and post- Islam. And this appreciation continued despite the growth of disdain for black men. This appreciation was often displayed in the arts. An example can be found in the work of Al-Suyuti, a famous Egyptian poet of the 15th century. He wrote:

"Perl is the name of many a black girl
How amazing it is to have a black pearl
Night of union with a black woman is shiny bright
How amazing to have a night that is white"

The famed Arab poet Tuktum, wrote from a similar appreciation:

"I love black women for Tuktum's sake.
For her sake I love all who are black.
Show me anything with scent that's as sweet as musk,
Or better for resting than after dusk"

The Arab world can be perceived as torn between fear of black males, and the threat they posed to the singular ethnic dominance of Arabs, and a love for black women that continued to capture the imagination of Arab men, and bare numerous Afro-Arab sons. In a more realistic interpretation of history we must wrestle with the reality that Islamic slavery was not as brutal as the western slave trade. But whereas the beating and abuse of black men was a mainstay of the European slave trade, we can say the rape and use of black women as concubines was the most common feature of the Arab Slave trade. The propagation of racism throughout the Islamic Empire, as a response to the Zanj Rebellion, suggests that the hatred of blacks was a result of fear and a grudging realization that blacks could threaten the system of Arab privilege and dominance. The Zanj Rebellion would serve as a warning to Islamic Civilization, regarding the proper treatment of slaves. Islamic Civilization would reform the abuse of slaves, limit plantation style operations, harsh labor conditions, and discourage the physical abuse of slaves. But the Zanj revolt would also usher in the popularity of the peculiar institution of the African military slave.

THE BLACK MILITARY ELITE OF ISLAM

The Zanj Revolt would also spread the renown of Africans

as warriors, and it would lead to the growth of a particularly unique Islamic Institution. Early during Islam's initial growth, in the first two centuries of expansion, Africans in Islamic armies, were rarely slaves. But this would change after a time. The skill of blacks in the Zanj Revolt impressed many of the Islamic World's most powerful rulers. Whereas, later Europeans would avoid and fear the arming of their African slaves, leaders all over the Islamic World, would establish all black military corps, and personal guards. Blacks would continue as high ranking officials in government, eunuchs, domestic slaves, and concubines but they would also become critical backbones in the Islamic security apparatus. They would become close-protectors of royals, and in a few cases the core of their militaries. Slaves in general, and black slaves in particular were more trustworthy in sensitive positions than fellow Arabs. Despite Koranic prohibitions against tribalism, and sectarianism, Arabs would continue to maintain these divisions. Competition among various groups, both religious, political, and tribal, made the threat of betrayal a constant concern of Arab rulers. Black slaves and white slaves did not hold these ties, and could be trusted to remain loyal to their masters. The Abbasid Caliph Al-Amin formed a special Corp of Ethiopian Guards, called The Crows. Caliph Al-Muktadir depended on 7000 black soldiers in battle. In the 10th Century Ali Ibn Muhammad, the founder of the Sulayhi Dynasty in Yemen, would rely on 5000 Ethiopian soldiers to rise to power. It is worth noting that the only group to successfully resist the Sulayhi and their African warriors, were The Banu Najah. They were a royal family in a province of Yemen called Zubayd. The Banu Najah heavily utilized black soldiers but The Banu Najah were also the descendants of Ethiopian Slaves themselves. They were surrounded by a fierce force of 20,000 Ethiopian guards. This slave dynasty represents another fascinating aspect of African existence in Islamic civilization. Even as slaves, or their descendants, Africans rose to prominence, and power, and sometimes found themselves sovereign over states and governments.

In Egypt, in 868 A.D. a great Islamic leader named Ahmad ibn Talun would arrive in Egypt. He would be the first to set up a government independent from the Abbasid caliph. He would call his dynasty The Tulunid Dynasty. He was a descendent of the Mamluk heritage. The Mamluks were a warrior caste of Turkish military slaves. Talun seized Egypt's financial resources first, but he needed an army that would be loyal to him. He tried to bring in other Mamluks but they had to cross Abbasid territory which made them hard to come by. He brought in European slaves, which were combined with the limited number of Mamluks to make up a cavalry. Most his force however, would be composed of approximately 40,000 Nubians, used as infantry soldiers. Ibn Talun was impressed by the Nubian reputation for archery, which may have been informed by the early engagements of Islamic Armies with Christian Nubia, and the descendants of the Nubian Kushite era. His black infantry was so numerous that he built a special barracks for them. This African reliant Army maintained the independence of the kingdom until 905 A.D., when the Abbasids finally overcame them. After the fall of the Tulunid Dynasty, the Africans were incorporated into the Abbasid forces. This merger was a reasonably smooth integration, because the Abbasaids employed numerous Africans in their own army and in their personal Guard; The Crows.

In 935-969 the Ikhshidid dynasty came to power in Egypt. In order to be free of Abbasid control, the ruler would again lean on black African troops. This use of African soldiers was successful until the Ikhshidid fell to yet another group called the Fatimad's. The Fatimad's came from Ifriqiya, Tunis (in northern Africa). They were Shi'ite Muslims, that opposed the Abbasid Dynasty of Sunni Muslims. They considered themselves to be related to Fatimah, the daughter of the prophet Muhammad. They came to power in Egypt in the year 969 A.D. The dynasty would rely, even more heavily than the Ikhshidid, on African troops. The Fatimad army was composed of White Turks, Berbers, and Africans. But the number of Africans would dominate their military. The Fatimads imported thousands of Africans, from Nubia. Some sources suggest that they recruited 200,000 Nubians, while others place their numbers around a much smaller and unlikely 10,000. After their rise, the Fatimads would continue to diversify the racial composition of their military, and tensions would rise between black soldiers and their white counterparts of Turks and Monguls. During the reign of the Fatimad ruler-al Mustansir (1029-1094), the eighth Caliph of the Fatimad Dynasty, the animosities would come to a rolling boil. The Fatimad Caliph's mother was of African slave origin, and effectively governed the kingdom. She attempted to build an even larger African military force. She would attempt to expand the African role in the military, by allowing blacks to serve as cavalry. This expansion of blacks, as cavalry, caused an uprising amongst the Central Asian Turkish cavalry who felt displaced. Now in the Muslim world, the various corps of the military were often kept separate, and they were generally comprised of segregated groups. Africans were used as infantry, while Turks and Whites were used as cavalry. The rational for this segregation was based on the idea that competition for excellence would be more intense within the corps, if they were composed of singular groups. Blacks competing against other blacks, and whites in competition with other whites was believed to produce a superior military. Thus, the segregation, was not based on overt racial hostilities. However, the de-facto segregation, would eventually erupt in racial conflicts. The White Soldiers and Turks, would view the use of Africans as cavalry as an encroachment on their role. With their position threatened the Turkish Mamluks, and white soldiers launched a successful civil war. Africans would continue in the military but their role would continue to be limited to infantry. In time, the role of Africans would again grow in the Fatimad Dynasty. Their loyalty earned them high positions within the Fatimad Government and Palace. By the time of the last Fatimad Caliph, al-Adid, black eunuchs were very powerful in the palace and government. And black soldiers were still a major component of the military. When the famed leader-Saladin launched an attack against the Fatimad's, the black soldiers were the dynasty's most ardent supporters. They maintained their loyalty, and stood with the Fatimad's, long after others abandoned them. They opposed the overthrow longer than any other group. In 1169, Saladin was informed of a plot to remove him by the Caliph's chief black eunuch. Saladin acted swiftly, executing all the black eunuchs of the palace, and brought the prominence of blacks in the Egyptian government to an abrupt end. The role of blacks in the Fatimad Dynasty is interesting, because the Fatimad's enjoyed very close ties with Christian Nubia. It is tempting to see the significant incorporation of blacks in the Fatimad Court, as a factor in their close ties with the black Christian Kingdoms in the south. As trading partners both parties benefited from the relationship. The Nubians supplied the troops, that ensured the security and continued existence of the Fatimad dynasty. The Nubians also provided goods for the Egyptian economy while the Fatimad's reciprocated with an array of products. When the Fatimad's allies were fighting for their dynasty against Saladin, their black allies in Christian Nubia, would launch an attack to save the dynasty. They would however, fail. After a prolonged fight, Saladin was finally successful in defeating the black troops at "The Battle of Cairo". As a historical figure, Saladin is best known as one of the world's most astute military minds. He led the Muslim response to the crusade, and successfully expelled the conquering European armies. Despite his incredible military strategy, he is best known for being exceedingly merciful to the invading Crusader armies. When the Crusaders entered the middle east, and captured Jerusalem, they massacred numerous towns. At times, they engaged in cannibalism, and when they entered Jerusalem they slaughtered nearly every man, woman, and child in the city. Muslims and Jews alike were slaughtered indiscriminately. The crusader armies showed no mercy, killing everyone in their path, regardless of their religion. They even killed the city's Christian inhabitants, despite their common faith. When Saladin achieved victory over the crusaders, he spared the lives of the Christian Crusaders and their army. After breaching the walls of Jerusalem and brokering their surrender, not a single Christian was harmed. They were all escorted out of Islamic territory and returned home. This act of mercy, earned him a great reputation in Europe, and historical fame. Saladin, was not nearly as merciful against the Nubians. It is recorded that, in addition to killing all the black eunuchs and officers in government, Saladin, executed 50,000 Nubians and allies from the armies of Christian Nubia. He purged all blacks from the Fatimad military, and after this date, only whites were incorporated in the new Ayyubid military that protected his government. After the battle, traffic into Christian Nubia slowed, and Nubia headed into a slow decline, perhaps because of its hostile relationship with the new Ayyubid government. Although there is a considerable decline in reports from Nubian lands, some trade continued. But the Ayyubid Dynasty also pressured Bedouin Arab tribes, with whom they were in conflict, to move into the Nubian lands. The Bedouins were a destabilizing force that lead to the downfall of Christian Nubian civilization. At the end of three hundred years of Egyptian-Islamic history, three successive dynasties had risen on the backs of black militaries. That prominence was only interrupted by moments of racial strife between black and white soldiers. In the end, after purging Africans from prominence in Egypt, the Ayyubids would become increasingly demanding, on the Nubian kingdoms in the south. The Nubian Christian Kingdoms had always been isolated from the rest of Christendom. The good terms of their relationship with the Fatimads allowed Christian Nubia to continue its growth, wealth, and development. The loss of a friendly neighbor, lead to a decline in trade, which lead to a decline in wealth and quality of life. The Baqt treaty, which was once a mutually beneficial arrangement, became a significant burden on the Nubians. The encroachment of Bedouins further taxed the Nubians in the south, and Ayyubid interference in the political affairs of the Nubians resulted in the placement of puppets on the Nubian throne. The role of Africans regionally, and in Islamic militaries, was now at an end. Whether Saladin's actions should be seen in a racial context is debatable. It is very possible that this is a political drama and not a racial drama. The black regiments would have been loyal to each other-as a result of their relationships. The slaughter of the black eunuchs could be the execution of political enemies, and the suffocation of Christian Nubia could have simply been an attempt to cut off a regional opponent with a history of intervention and hostility. Elsewhere, in the Islamic Empire, Africans would continue to serve in Islamic Armies, and in Egypt (1498) they would enjoy a brief revival.

THE BATTLE OF THE THREE KINGS

As we survey the Muslim world and move deeper into Africa, we encounter the long history of black Africans in Morocco. The nation of Morocco has been led by several rulers, that by modern standards, were black. These leaders were responsible for some of the most consequential progress in the nation's history. They were historical actors, whose reigns held international influence and consequence. Black armies unified Morocco and elite black guards secured its monarchs. One of Morocco's most consequential leaders was the Sultan Abu al-Hasan Ali. During the 14th century, the Sultan Ali, would become one of Morocco's greatest rulers. He was known as, Al Sultan Aswad, or The Black Sultan. During his reign, (from 1335-1351) Morocco would achieve unprecedented progress. The black sultan would build many of Morocco's most famous cities. He would establish numerous madrasas or colleges, and Moroccan art, literature and culture would reach its peak because of his patronage. Sultan Ali, came to the throne, by evicting his brother from power. He was the son of an Abyssinian women, for whom he held tremendous affection. It is difficult to overstate the significance of his reign, and the international impact of his insatiable appetite and aptitude for conquest. The Sultan Ali, was exceptionally well known for his skill as a warrior and head of state. He was sought as an ally and defender throughout the Muslim world. During his reign, Spain or Al- Andalus (in islamic histories) which had been ruled by Muslims since 711 A.D was in danger of falling from Christian armies that were capturing territories by capitalizing on division caused by the competing Muslim kingdoms of Spain. When the Nasrid Dynasty- the last Islamic dynasty ruling a significant portion of Spain, was besieged by the Christian powers of Castile, Muhammad IV, the Muslim ruler of Granada would implore the assistance of the Moroccan Sultan. In 1331, after a two-month siege, Sultan Ali would retake Gibralter- a fantastic castle, of great significance, from the Christian Castilians. The Nasrid Dynasty was temporarily saved from its Christian enemies. Later, the sultan would again be sought for assistance in Spain, where his navy, would crush the combined naval powers of Castile and Portugal. His success however, would be short lived. The Sultan would end his career on the Iberian Peninsula-Spain, with a loss to Castile and Portugal, who had been brought into an alliance, because of the threat he posed. Ali, was also a unifier in the Muslim world. He joined the north African powers, with his own dominion through marriage, and war. His unification of his Moroccan territory, with Tlemcen and Ifriqiya- which were parts of north Africa, established an empire of tremendous size. His incredibly large empire drew the attention and respect of the entire Islamic world. His North African empire was so large, and so powerful, that the Mameluk Sultans of Egypt, relied on his protection. But his empire, at its greatest extent would be short lived. Bedouin Arabs, in North Africa would resist his attempts to transform them into members of his state. After the defeat, Ali would face hardship and crippling assaults. His previously acquired north African territories would fall (Tlemcen), and his throne would be usurped by his own son, Abu Inan or Faras. Defeat is never accepted by great men in history, and the Black Sultan, was no different. He would find himself, in the desert of Africa, in enemy territory, but he would raise an army and attempt to retake his territory. He would unfortunately fail. He would then raise another army to march against his son, but he would again, fail. The Sultan, whose reign led to the construction of Madrasas at Fez, and many of the nation's greatest monuments, would die in hiding. He is celebrated for his efforts to propel and polish Moroccan art, literature and culture to its greatest heights. His body was returned to Morocco by his son, Abu Inan. The tomb of his burial, as well as the tomb of his favorite European wife, are among Morocco's greatest treasures today.

In 1576 the Moroccan Sultan Abu Abdallah Mohammad II, would be deposed by his Uncle Abd al-Malik. To cement his place on the throne Mohammad II, killed his brother and forced his uncle, Al-Malik into exile under penalty of death. Al-Malik would return with an army supported by the Ottoman Empire. He would depose his nephew, who would in turn seek an alliance with the militant Christian King, Sebastian of Portugal. Sebastian of Portugal was anxious to expand the influence of his kingdom, and he would bankrupt his country by financing an army to oppose Al-Malik, in support of Mohammad II. At the "Battle of The Three Kings", all three leaders would be killed. Portugal would become the property of Spain, and Morocco would crown a new ruler. In Morocco, in 1578-1608, the brother of Al-Malik, Sultan Ahmad al Mansur whose mother was an African Fulani would become the new ruler of Morocco. The black Sultan Mansur, would order the Moroccan military to seize upon political instability in the West African Empire of Songhai. The black African ruler of Morocco would destroy the last great black West African Empire, to replenish his nations coffers which had been expended in multiple wars with European powers. Al-Mansur portrayed himself as an Islamic unifier. The rise of constantly competing Muslim powers fractured the global Islamic community, and Al-Mansur believed that he could halt the disintegration. Al-Mansur believed himself to be The Mahdi-the Islamic Messiah whose arrival was foretold in Muslim prophecy. To prove that he was indeed the Mahdi, Al-Mansur needed to act the part, displaying all the attributes ascribed to the Mahdi. He was already handsome (Islamic thought of the time associated piety with good looks). But the Mahdi would also be a man of uncommon charity. Al-Mansur would spend lavishly to prove his Islamic virtue. And as the defender of the faith, he would support military assaults against Christendom. The expenses however would drain his coffers. The seemingly inexhaustible wealth of Songhai, were an overwhelming attraction for the Moroccan King. His first attempt would end very badly, as the forces of Songhai easily expelled his army, but a period of political instability would create an opportunity for a second effort. The Sultan would install spies throughout the Songhai kingdom and receive regular reports in preparation of his attack. The black Moroccan Sultan would enlist the support of England's Queen Elizabeth I. She supplied advanced arms and soldiers to boot. Under the direction of a Spanish General, raised at court in Morocco, the combined troops of England and Morocco, would enter the region and plunge towards Timbuktu, the intellectual center of the Songhay empire. They would sack the city, and kidnap its scholars, who would be forced to serve the Sultan, in Morocco. They traveled the length of the empire burning and looting, town after town. They robbed the treasury of all that was there but could not find Songhay's goldmines. The cities and the empire would never recover. After his routing of Songhai, Sultan Ahmad al Mansur set up a black slave military force. He then forced its well-educated scholars to refine Moroccan culture and apply their intellects to improving his kingdom. Al- Mansur, is also the builder of El Badi Palace "The Incomparable Palace". The palace was considered a fairytale construction. It held 360 rooms, and a large courtyard, decorated with Italian marble and gold from the Sudan. Al- Mansur, The Victorious, also held extensive correspondence, with Queen Elizabeth I. It is worth noting that despite his status as The Black Sultan, Al-Mansur would decree that every black person in Morocco was subject to enslavement. The Afro-Moroccan confounds our modern notions of race as he willingly subjugated everyone that in a modern sense was like himself. His reign would end, when a new dynasty called, The Alouite Dynasty destroyed his precious Badi Dynasty. The Alouite King, was Moulay Ismail. He was also the son of a black woman. He was forced to deal with constant internal struggles, and issues of loyalty, in his own government. Between 1672-1727 the ruler, Mawlay Ismail (different spelling) could not depend on traditional forces so he acquired blacks living and working, in morocco. He built a force that some number at 150,000. They were called Abid al-Bukhara. They were infantry and cavalry. He gave them African brides to produce more warriors. This force became the primary force for imposing his control. He conquered most of modern Morocco with this force. His very successful reliance on Africans, would support his reign throughout the rest of his life. He ruled for 55 years, expanding the commercial ties of Morocco with Europe. He is credited for having made Morocco safe and prosperous, in the face of constant internal opposition. He also launched numerous holy wars. He was also engaged in discussions with Louis XIV, to attack Spain and England. The plans fell through because, Louis was not anxious to attack Catholics. Ismail's son (whom in a modern context is still black-African), Siddi Mohammad Ben Abdellah, or Siddi Mohammad III, would resurrect the use of a black military Corp which had fallen out of use in the struggles for succession after the death of Ismail. He forged partnerships and economic relationships with Denmark, England, Sweden, and Venice. In 1767, he signed treaties with Spain and France. In 1777, he was the first nation, to acknowledge the independence of the United States. His treaty with George Washington, is the oldest treaty in American history.

THE SIDDI OF INDIA & THEIR ISLAND FORT

By the early 7th century, Islam had come to the region of the Indian sub-continent. The region which includes India, Pakistan, and Bangladesh is broad and diverse. During the Islamic conquest of central Asia Islam was introduced to the region, but the region was largely governed by loosely connected Hindu kingdoms. The largest power in northern India was the Rajput, a Hindu power governed by the Rai dynasty. Now, hundreds of Hindu kingdoms ruled India, each carving out small but significant spheres of influence. As the unified power of the Islamic Empire continued its quest to expand the power and influence of the Islamic faith, the kingdoms of India would attract the attention of the Islamic Caliph. The Abbasid Caliph in Iraq would target the Rajput and timed his attack for a period of instability. His excuse for attacking would be an assault on his ships by Arab pirates that had found sanctuary in a Rajput kingdom. The ships were a gift to the Caliph Al Hajjaj Ibn Yusuf, from the King of Ceylon. When the Arab pirates attacked his ships, the Caliph would attempt to punish those that gave sanctuary to the fugitives. The caliph would send two expeditions, both of which would fail. Finally, he sent his son in law, Muhammad bin Qasim Al Thaqafi, in 712. This army would subdue the whole area of modern Pakistan, from Karachi to Kashmir. In his army were numerous soldiers that would come to be called, Habashi or Siddi, in India. Habashi means Abyssinian and it would become a common term for blacks in India. After the general left, the area would devolve into small Arab controlled states like Mansura and Multan. But while the influence of the caliph would decline, the influence and effect of Africans in Islamic India would only grow. The enslavement of Africans was never a popular trend in India. While there were imports of slaves from Ethiopian, Arab and Portuguese merchants at various periods, the institution of African slavery never gained the prominence it achieved in other places in the Islamic world, in India. The East African Zanj that entered the Indian subcontinent with Muhammad bin Qasim Al Thaqafi established a general impression of Africans as physically imposing and powerful warriors. They would be called The Habashi based on the Arabic term Al Habashi which meant Ethiopian. By 1100 A.D. these early Africans would gain the name Siddi, based on a new prominence in naval endeavors. The Africans would in time become expert sailors, and would establish themselves as the naval security force for the Muslim kingdoms. The famed world traveler Ibn Battuta would refer to them as the *"guarantors of safety on the Indian Ocean"*. They would ally themselves with the Moghuls, who were the descendants of Ghengis Khan's soldiers, who settled in the region, and established themselves as the dominant rulers. The Mongols entered the Islamic world as conquerors, disrupting the traditional powers and established themselves as an independent force. They were initially nomadic, but very quickly adopted the lifestyle, values, and religion of their Islamic subjects, and became known as the Moghuls. In time, they would become the dominant force in India, and in contrast to their largely illiterate and uneducated origins, they would become excellent rulers, as the progenitors of a highly-cultured kingdom. Their African allies would guard their naval flank, and serve in a variety of positions in Mughal governments. The Siddi, it should be noted were not slaves or mere mercenaries. They were a major political and military force. The commanding Siddi Admirals would demand 300,000 rupees for their services. While there were numerous Siddi kingdoms in the interior of India, because of runaway slaves and free blacks that turned their emancipation into opportunity by establishing kingdoms. The primary Siddi strong hold was the state of Murud Janjira. Janjira was an island fortress, from which the Siddi sailors deployed to secure the Indian ocean, and act in defense of their Muslim allies. The Siddi were allies of the Moghuls, but their enemies in the Maratha Empire would call Janjira, Habshan or The Land of the Habashi. By 1506 the Siddi were not just allies of the Moghuls, they were allied with the Mamaluks in Egypt, and the Ottomans. The Siddi were famous for their ferocious defense of their allies, and their own trading routes connected with East Africa. They also garnered acclaim for their successful defense against the Portuguese who attempted to disrupt the Indian Ocean spice trade by force and piracy, much like they had done on the East Coast of Africa. The Siddi repelled them on numerous occasions, displaying their sailing prowess and dominance over the Indian ocean trade. The Siddi formed an alliance with the Kingdom of Ahmadnagar, and numerous other kingdoms, in India. They carefully juggled the complex politics of numerous Indian powers. They would intervene politically and diplomatically to calm tensions between Indian Muslims and foreign Muslim kingdoms and their concerns in India. They would position themselves as attentive but fiercely independent kingmakers among the Indian empires. Their support or the lack thereof, was influential in the competitive power dynamic of ancient India. The Siddi and their navy secured the oceans for safe passage to the Hajj and the Umrah (Hajj is a mandatory pilgrimage to Mecca, whereas the Umrah is a smaller optional pilgrimage to Mecca). They made it safe for Muslims world-wide, to meet their spiritual obligation, and they ensured the security of trade for the Islamic powers in the area. Their naval supremacy made coastal shipping and trade safe, but also left trade entirely at the mercy of the Siddi. They would leverage that power over all the empires dependent upon them. Their protection of the seas made trade possible, and when they became displeased they were equally willing to make trade impossible. Various powers would attempt to wrench control of the fort from the Siddi, but each one would fail. The Dutch, English, Portuguese, and the powerful Indian Marathas Empire would all fail in their attempts to conquer the fort. In history, the fortress and the Siddi would gain a reputation as unconquerable. Massive mobilizations by the English were unable to unseat the Siddi from their throne, and in later history, the Siddi would strike out at the English and their territories in India. They would venture out of their fort and project their substantial power onto the mainland, and take Bombay from the English by force. The Siddi were not merely warriors, or mercenaries. They were a forceful power, and a hub of political influence in India. The powers they promoted, continued to gain influence, and those they opposed could suffer from their lack of support. Their rulers were patrons of the architecture, arts, and culture.

By the 1500's Africans were prominently featured in the political landscape of India. Africans were recruited as military slaves and administrators in government, like much of the rest of the Muslim world. Chingiz Khan was the prime minister of the Kingdom of Ahmadnagar, in 1575 during the reign of King Nizam mul-Mulk Bani. He was one of many Black Habashi in the Indian administrations. The Habashi warriors would support the King's son Murtaza I when he revolted against his mother, after the death of his father. In this pivotal political battle, the aid of the Habashi would be significant. During the reign of Murtaza II, the prime minister, Abhangar Khan would also be black. While early Siddi would ally themselves with the Moghuls, the most famous African leader in India would establish a different union and launch pivotal assaults that would dramatically influence the balance of power in the region. Born in Ethiopia, in 1550 Shambu would be known later in life, by his chosen name Malik Ambar. Malik, which means King was an aptly chosen moniker, as renowned Arab Historians like Ferista would call Ambar *"the most enlightened financier of whom we read in Indian history"*. He would become one of India's most consequential leaders, but he began his career as a slave. Like many Africans, he was pre-selected to serve as an administrator in the Islamic world. He was given an ample education in administration, in western Arabia. Malik developed a reputation for his brilliance and his several masters unanimously affirmed his phenomenal intellect. From western Arabia, or the Hejaz, he was sent to Baghdad, and then he finally settled in India's Deccan region. The Deccan is the plateau, which makes up most of the Indian peninsula, and for numerous years Ambar would prevent this region from falling into the hands of India's most powerful empire, the Moghuls. His skills and intellect would garner him respect and admiration, and he would be promoted through a series of powerful positions. The King of Bijapur would make Malik the commander of the Arab and Habashi troops. In 1590 Malik would rebel with a force of 1500 cavalry and infantry, most of whom, were similarly black. Malik's mobile army would hire themselves out to numerous rulers throughout the Deccan until Malik's ambitions became greater. After several years of fighting off the Moghuls, Malik would travel to the Kingdom of Murtaza II, and take control of the kingdom (Murtaza II had a black prime minister, and his administration also relied on African troops and officials). From this new seat of power, Ambar would continue to check the ambitions of the Mughul Emperor Akbar, who had been anxious to expand his sphere of influence. Emperor Akbar was an enigmatic and influential ruler. His building projects were monuments to Indian architecture, and his army would expand the Moghul Empire. Despite his skill as a ruler, The Moghul Emperor would suffer repeated defeats at the hands of the African Ambar, as would his successor the Moghul Emperor Jahangir. Jahangir was famously disdainful, of the Habashi in general, but he would be consumed with a particularly high degree of hatred for Malik Ambar. He made no secret of his frustrations resulting from Ambar's incessant interference in his plans. The tendency of Ambar to thwart the military advance of Akbar would leave the Emperor fantasizing about Ambar's death. But he would live out his reign only able to fantasize about the downfall of the Great Malik Ambar and his Habashi troops. He would never fail to refer to Ambar as *"the cursed fellow"* or *"the wretched Ambar"* or *"the black Ambar"*. The racial epithets were the clear result of Ambar's unfailing ability to repel the Moghuls and deny them dominion of the Deccan Region of India. Ambar would build an army of 60,000 armed with British artillery, and for 20 years he would continue to beat back the ambitions of the Moghuls. He would provide his soldiers with a proper education, and his faithful black guards would serve as his personal protectors. He would become the Regent of the Nizamshahi Dynasty of Ahmednagar. As regent, he would build the city of Khadaki which would become an ideal capital with canals, and outlying irrigation systems. Ambar was passionate about architecture. The city he built was a monument to his love of construction. He would fill his city with grand displays of his fascination. He would erect fabulous buildings, often out of black stone. The city is one of India's most popular tourist attractions. Ambar's passion for infrastructure would lead him to build the Neher, an impressive water system that was once believed to be an impossible feat. The Vazier Mullah Mohammad called the idea a fantasy! The project he declared would require Um-Re-Noh, "*the lifespan of Noah*" and Sab-Re-Ayub "*Ayub's Patience*" (Ayub is the Biblical Character Job), and Khazana Kharun- "*Kharun's Treasure*"! Ambar moved forward with his water system, completing it in 15 months, for a paltry sum. The system is still considered to be a modern miracle of logistics. He would prove to be a tolerant leader, by patronizing Hindu scholars, and granting land to Hindus. He would employ Brahmins to implement a sophisticated, progressive and sustaining system of taxation. He would have one of the greatest legacies of any ruler in India, and is widely considered to be the most consequential financier of public works, in Indian history. Malik Ambar would also introduce a new style of Guerilla Warfare into the region. He would mobilize a group of Hindu peasant farmers called the Marathas, and train them in the art of his Guerilla Warfare. The regions Islamic powers persecuted the farmers, some of which were in the habit of destroying

Hindu shrines and holy places. Ambar turned humble farmers into horseman, and warriors. Malik Ambar is often called, "The Military Guru of the Marathas". Ambar's contribution to warfare in the region, would have innumerable ripple effects throughout the course of Indian history. As soldiers under his direction, the Marathas would in time become masters of the sneak attack, and they would also go on to sell their newly learned guerilla services to other powers in the Deccan Region. Some of them would even turn against Ambar, and serve the Islamic Mughul powers that Ambar opposed. They would in time build their own great empire, conquering a vast stretch of territory, using Guerilla Warfare. They would expand upon Ambar's tactics and make them their own. The same Marathas would go on to harass black Siddi, using the skills that Malik taught them. We should note that, in the later wars that would consume much of the Indian subcontinent, the Marathas would be credited with being the sole power responsible for preventing India from becoming a part of Pakistan. The Marathas are often called The Saviors of Hinduism, for preventing the total consumption of India by Islamic and Christian powers. Malik Ambar's contribution to Indian history, has many such segues. Ambar, with his forces, would support the famous Mughul ruler, Shah Jahan, whose mother attempted to deny him the throne after the death of his father. His father was, ironically, The Moghul Emperor Jahangir, who hated Ambar. Shah Jahan, whose official title would become The Ruler of The World, is the most consequential ruler in the pantheon of Mughul Emperors. He presided over the Golden Age of the Mughul Empire. He is most famous for constructing the Taj Mahal. Malik Ambar is one of the world's greatest military leaders, and his contribution to Indian civilization is enduring.

RACE & ISLAM: AFRICAN OR ARAB

Africa, and Africans were instrumental in shaping the events that gave rise to the eastern world. Nubia: The Rise and Fall of African Empires was designed to correct the record and the popular misconception that African cultures were primitive and unaccomplished. A crucial part of correcting that record is recognizing that Africans ventured far outside of Africa as merchants, sailors, soldiers, scholars, and slaves. If we are to effectively change the perception about black civilization, we must reveal the massive role black empires played in shaping world events. We must also explain the role that blacks played in civilizations outside of Africa and in cultures where they didn't represent the majority. It was important to show what happened to Africans once they ventured outside of Africa, and to explain what became of their descendants. As intimate partners in the propagation of Islam, and as it's defenders (whether slave or free), they share in the bounty of Islam's accomplishments. We live in a culture that is much less familiar with the once grand Islamic empires. Many are simply unaware of the fact that in terms of wealth and trade, the center of the universe was once located in the East. Ignorance of this past makes it harder for readers to appreciate the accomplishments of black culture in eastern civilizations if they are not familiar with them. It was necessary to paint a new picture for most readers, of a world in which the Dark Ages stifled the development of the European west while the East flowered under Islamic dominion. In this Islamic world, black Africans held sway, and were pivotal to its rise. In assessing the role of Africans, we have included several individuals of mixed racial descent. It should be noted that with only a few instances (precisely two; The Caliph Umar, and the Moroccan Sultan) we have only included individuals that were at least half black. But to be intellectually honest, we must wrestle with the fairness and accuracy of even these inclusions. Does the simple fact of a slave mother, or consensual mother's African heritage, necessarily make an individual black? And does the lineage of a partially African person warrant collecting all the deeds of these individuals, into a collective of black racial accomplishments? Our quandary exists because race is an entirely fictitious construct that exists in modernity because of our prejudices and the need to categorize people for discrimination. Race is a construct that we struggle to impose on a past that would not have recognized it in the same way we do today. For instance, the Prophet Muhammad married a woman named Sawda bint Zam'a who by all accounts was very "black" or dark skinned. Sawda however was not "black" in the modern sense of having immediate African ancestors and yet in appearance she would have been described as black. There are many similar instances throughout history. Further complicating the issue is that the term "black" held numerous different meanings that differ dramatically from our modern usage. "Black" was applied to Caucasians that were swarthy. "Black" could refer to a menacing disposition or one who intimidates those around him. "Black" could also be describing dark skinned people but not necessarily men or women of African heritage as we would recognize them today. Additionally, not all "black" people as we would define them in modern society are dark skinned. In the effort to deny the existence of formidable black empires the bias of western society created absurd categories of race to facilitate a discrimination and distortion of history. We divided Africa into North Africa and Sub-Saharan Africa and we portrayed North Africa as a civilized and "white" culture, separated from "black Africa" below the Sahara. We depicted Egypt as a white or Arab civilization when all of the continent's cultures are simply African Civilizations. Their development was the result of a continent wide, cooperative feedback loop as the achievements of one culture spread from one edge of the continent to its farthest flung corners. We created this need to uncover African civilizations by denying their existence and we furthered that crime by creating a need for "black" men and women to prove that our civilizations were indeed our own creations. European scholars did not commit this grand theft of black achievement alone. Islamic scholarship cooperated in the falsification of history. A critical component of diminishing the achievements of "blacks" marked for discrimination was to recategorize mixed race men and women as if they were purely Arab. Thus, when a mixed-race person was inconsequential, they were condemned, ignored, forgotten, and categorized as "black" but if they rose to become generals, erudite scholars or even Caliphs they were labeled as Arab. Their contributions to history have been miscategorized and we should correct that record. These men and women are the descendants of those we currently identify as "black" or "African" and since it is their collective reputation that once bigoted historians called into question, it is their achievements that we should collect, laud and properly ascribe to them. It is worth discussing that many of the individuals that we have categorized as Afro Arabs, or the descendants of African heritage, would not have necessarily described themselves as "black". Some may not have ever even thought very much about their African heritage and still others would have resented the label of "black". We should consider the inclusion of the Caliph Umar I as an example. His father was the son of a black woman, and was therefore half black. The Caliph then, is only of African descent in this tertiary sense. We must ask if it is prudent to consider his accomplishments to be a part of black collective achievements. Would the Caliph have even seen himself as being black? The answer to the latter question is, surely not! Caliph Umar I, would never have described himself as black. How the Caliph saw himself is incredibly interesting, and it is a perfect window into the way that other Afro Arabs saw themselves. The Caliph was involved in an incident that is particularly relevant to our question. After the death of Muhammad, the "prophet's" daughter Fatima Zahra attempted to claim her dead father's lands, which were called Fadak and Khaybar. Both were lush oasis in modern day Saudi Arabia (i.e. Prime real estate). There was a controversy over Muhammad's intent, concerning his property after his death. The Caliph, Abu Bakr recalled that " *Allah's apostle said, WE (referring to himself) do not have heirs, whatever we leave is Sadaqa (for charity)*". Umm Ayman, Muhammad's black surrogate mother, was called as a witness for Fatimah Zahra. Before testifying, Umm Ayman requested that Abu Bakr, repeat what Muhammad once said about her. Abu Bakr accurately restated the "prophet's" words about Umm Ayman being like a mother to him, and that she was one of the few people on earth guaranteed Jennah or entrance into paradise. Umm Ayman, then testified that Muhammad had indeed, promised Fadak and Khaybar to his daughter, Fatimah. The future second Caliph Umar, whose effective grandmother was black, objected to the acceptance of Umm Ayman's testimony because she was not an Arab. One wonders if Umm Ayman was acting pre-emptively against the animosity she knew she would face as a non-Arab when she attempted to minimize the objections to her testimony by asking Abu Bakr to repeat Muhammad's words regarding her status. In this incident, we see that Umar, embraced fully his Arab heritage. His only racial or ethnic loyalty was to his Arab culture. Why then, should we categorize Umar I, or any person as an Afro Arab, and why should we consider their achievements as if they are a part of a black collective whole? In part, we should correct the record because our failure to do so would make us complicit in the racism that forced blacks to deny their heritage and emphasize their Arab lineage. We should also acknowledge Afro Arabs as a part of the African story, in part because they fit within our modern racial framework. In our current racial context, they are black and their achievements fit within the collective cultural accomplishments of black people or their descendants. Secondly, if we are to address misconceptions about African cultural accomplishments then we must correct the mistaken impression that Africans rarely left their continent. There is a persistent lack of awareness about the degree to which Africans travelled, sailed, and explored the world. The fact that Africans ventured outside of Africa is a critical part of their story. Uncovering their fate, and the fate of their descendants after leaving Africa becomes important to the narrative of African culture. If we are to see their history in the same way that we view the cultural accomplishments of other races then we must recognize the contributions of their descendants, even those that were born out of a condition of subservience and even those that were taught by their broader society to despise their own heritage. Our decision to include Afro Arabs in a discussion of African civilization is predicated upon the principle that we can and should recognize the contributions of oppressed minorities and slaves within a society. That fundamental principle is born out of a recognition that the refusal to recognize the contributions of minorities and slaves within a society would set as a precondition of recognition, that any group become the dominant force within a society to be recognized as contributing to it. It would essentially determine that blacks or their descendants could only be recognized as contributors to cultures outside of Africa, if they came to rule those cultures. Furthermore, our elitism would also be based in a sexism that refused to acknowledge the contributions of mothers within a culture. In early Islamic societies children were literally named after their fathers. The term " ibn" which was common in the full names of individuals, literally means, "the son of ". Islamic civilization was, and remains a patriarchal civilization, therefore what followed "ibn" was almost always the name of the father. The name of individuals like Zayd Ibn Muhmmad, literally translates into Zayd the son of Muhammad. The full name of Muhammad is likewise, Muhammad ibn Abdulluh, or Muhammad the son of Abdullah. As a modern culture, we have determined that any individual is equally, the son of his mother, just as he is the son of his father. We must therefore recognize the heritage of the mother, in categorizing these individuals if we wish to correct the record of sexism and not serve as propagators of gender bias. If we were to fail to do so, we would be bowing, not only to the racism in early Islamic culture that encouraged Afro Arabs to emphasize their Arab heritage as opposed to their African lineage; we would also be bowing to the sexism that forced them to favor the heritage of their fathers over their mothers. It is also impossible to know how many of these individuals felt about their African heritage, and how they felt about the discrimination that other blacks experienced in Islamic society. Did they feel conflicted? Did they crusade against it? Were they quiet defenders of their African heritage? Were they even raised by their African mothers? Or were they like Antar-The First of All Knights only accepted by their fathers after achieving fame in the Muslim community. These questions would require highly individualized answers and they create an impossible maze of inquiries that would make categorizing each individual impossible.

It is easy to discuss the role of blacks in Islamic society and be consumed by the injustices and inequalities, but we should acknowledge that for most black Muslims, there was opportunity within the Muslim Umma (community). Most did not have to fear that they would be accidentally enslaved or confused with subjugated blacks. A free, well-educated black Muslim could enjoy most, if not all the privileges of Islamic society. And they could climb the heights of hierarchy, generally unencumbered by discrimination, provided they accepted fully the process of Arabization demanded by the dominant Islamic culture. These individuals then, comprise some of the most outstanding contributors to Islamic society. Blacks would have been some of the most accomplished Islamic scientists, theologians, architects, physicians, and artisans in Islamic society. The universities of Africa would have produced stellar minds, that were in all ways, equal to all of those outside of Africa. Africa, with its possession of tremendous libraries and some of the largest book trades in the world, would have been a hub of intellectual development. These Africans would have certainly seen themselves as distinct from their Arab Muslim brothers, but they would have seen themselves as a part of the dominant Muslim society. And as the supplier of nearly 2/3 of the world's gold, the monetary system of the world was at the very least dependent on African gold. In the development of the Islamic Eastern world, which dominated the globe for nearly 700 years of history, blacks contributed to the development of all aspects of Islamic culture. As occasional enemies of the Islamic powerhouse, Africans were also some of the few that could successfully stand against its dominance.

CONCLUSION

The story of African civilization is an ancient tale that reaches back into the earliest moments in history. We chose to begin Nubia: The Rise and Fall of African Empires with the formal starting date of the Nubian Kushite Empire but that in no way represents the starting date for grand African empires or notable African societies. Kush for instance finds its roots in a settlement called Kerma. Kushite civilization didn't begin with Egyptian conquest nor was its development dependent on its interaction with Egypt. The first Nubians settled the Nile Region over 8,000 years- ago. They developed mud brick structures and incredible monumental architecture carved out of solid rock called "speo". Similar structures would not be created in Egypt for 2000 years, roughly during Egypt's New Kingdom period. Historians have given these Nubians the indescript name the "A Group" and they developed royal tombs two centuries before the Egyptians. It seems that many of Egypts funerary practices are related to customs developed elsewhere in Central Africa. Eventually, the early Nubians would build the City of Kerma, a cosmopolitan complex that was home to over 10,000 Nubians. Kerma was as wealthy and powerful as its contemporary, Egypt (2400 B.C). Their extensive buildings were framed by wood. They were round structures, gilded with stone flooring. Roads eased travel throughout Kerma, leading travelers to the Deffufa's; Kerma's 3-story high- ceremonial centers. Deffufas were filled with hallways and passages; Columns and walls were decorated with animal portraits painted in yellow, black, blue and red. Kerma's burial chambers were round subterranean complexes, that were 300 feet in diameter (the size of a football field). The mound was supported by underground chambers, rooms and a common hallway that linked them together. These incredible burial chambers, were clear pre-cursors to Nubia's pyramid burials. They were likewise constructed to bury their King's and usher them into the afterlife, as they took their riches, living cattle and servants into death with them. Nubians living within Egypt would also make meaningful contributions to Egypt as well. The Medjay for instance were an elite corp of the Egyptian military and many scholars credit them with making Egypt a major military power. The warrior nomads were recruited into the

Egyptian army around 2181 B.C. during Egypt's Old Kingsom. As desert scouts, and garrison troops the Medjay would man the massive forts protecting Egypt's borders with Nubia. They eventually became the royal guardians securing Egypt's palaces, monuments, and sacred religious complexes. Modern films often portray the Medjay as mysterious men in black clothing, while failing to acknowledge that the seemingly magical guardians of Egypt's monuments were Nubians. The Medjay even defended Egypt from total conquest during Egypt's Second Intermediate Period. The Hyksos were foreign invaders from Asia that conquered much of Lower Egypt, leaving the native rulers with only Upper and Middle Egypt to govern. The native-born Pharaoh Khamose led the effort to drive out the Hyksos invaders. In service to their Pharoh, the Nubian Medjay overran the garrisons of the Hyksos, expanding the territory held by Kamose. In response, the Hyksos tried to exploit a relationship they had with the Kushite King in the south, King Awoserre Apopi. The Hyksos King sent a letter, imploring aid from the Nubian Kushite but the letter was intercepted and Kamose secured his rear flank. The presence of Nubians on both sides (Nubian Medjay serving in Egypt, and Nubian Kush sought as allies for the Hyksos) of the conflict gives us an idea of the value of Nubians as allies. Kamose, in the past attacked Nubian Kush, retaking Fort Buhen and the Hyksos appealed to this offense and their mutual interest when courting Kush. The Hyksos Pharoh Apophis would write to the King of Nubia: *"Do you see what Egypt has done to me? The ruler who is in it, Kamose-the-Brave, given life, is attacking me on my soil although I have not attacked him in the manner of all he has done against you. He is choosing these two lands to bring affliction upon them, my land and yours, and he has ravaged them."*

Nubia or Kush was a grand kingdom, and power player from its earliest moments as Kerma. Because of modern scholarship, we now know that the Nubian system of Monarchy was the oldest monarchy in the world. The political structure of wealthy kingships in Nubia predated Egypt's monarchy by several generations. Nubian kingship begins as early as 3300 B.C, establishing a sustained monarchy earlier than any other in the world. The history of African Civilization extends much further than Kush or even Kerma. All throughout Africa researchers are still discovering new ancient empires. We discovered the mummified remains of a 3-year-old boy, given the name Uan Muhuggiag. The black child was mummified with a sophistication that Egyptian methods would not achieve for generations. Uan is the oldest mummy discovered in Africa and his remains were discovered 1500 miles away from the Nile Region (roughly the distance from Florida to Canada). The black child was the first evidence we found of a unified culture that spread across the entire central Saharan region. Before the Sahara region was an impassable desert, it was a lush and beautiful savannah. It was the home of a huge egalitarian society that seems to have been the source of inspiration for the "dog faced" God Anubis in Egypt as they depicted the worship of a similar deity and the dog faced masks they used to honor him. These incredible intersections show us the interconnectedness of all cultures and empires in Africa. It displays that no matter which ethnic group we see as dominant in an empire, like Egypt or Kush the effort to divide some cultures as resulting from a "black" influence and others as being the innovation of non-black "others" was always the misguided result of bigotry. All cultures in Africa were related and should be referred to as simply African. Every ethnic group, race and phenotype created high cultures within Africa's boundaries. They have all influenced one another, as the ingenious innovation of one culture, would have exploded across the continent, enriching cultures far and away. In the case of Uan's mummifying black culture with Anubis like deities, the pottery of this early black culture is even like pottery that would be found in the Nile Valley region much later. We are given even more reasons to revere ancient black cultures by the remains of an ancient African version of Stonehenge, called Napta Playa. It was built 1000 years before Europe's Stonehenge, near modern day Cairo (4000-5000 B.C). Napta Playa represents the world's first archeoastronomical device, proving that blacks in their earliest development were skilled astronomers. The stones are arrayed in relationship to Orion's Belt. They are organized in circular form to reflect the movement of the sky. The stones even match the distance of each star from the earth at a ratio of 1 meter to .8 lightyears. Some scholars believe that this is the source of Egypt's later developing astronomy cult. The cattle worship which took place at the site may have also inspired the Egyptian Cult of Hathor. In sighting these interconnections, we are not robbing Egyptians of the credit for creating their own culture. We are reinforcing the fact that one African Culture is connected to another. Their achievments feed upon one another. And the black empires of Africa were as ancient and accomplished as the cultures of any other group throughout the world.

Some readers may wonder why Nubia: The Rise and Fall of African Empires focused so much on Eastern cultures. Our modern culture focuses so intently on the development of western society that our book's focus on Eastern cultures, like Persia, Arabia, India, Judea, the Phoneicians, or even the Byzantines may seem odd. The reality is that during the

Dark Ages and during many of the periods for which we have reliable records of African Empires, the West was not the center of commerce or culture. The East was flowering while the West suffered from both an ice-age and the collapse of Rome as barbarian hoards literally tore the achievments of high European culture apart. It was in this universe that Africa's Empires thrived. African cultures perfected all the accoutrements of civilization. Art, architecture, literature, music, culinary arts, fashion, and science were as sophisticated in Africa as they were elsewhere in the world. When the East began to falter and the West began to rise, Africans would be taken from their homes by force to build the foundation for the Americas. The impression that our distortion of history has given us is that these Africans came to the Americas without skills. Africans brought their high cultures with them and they expressed their ample educations in a society that denied their talents and contributions. Africans hailing from huge agricultural communities became the source of knowledge for many European masters that were unfamiliar with the complexities of large scale agriculture. In some cases, slave masters would base their crop selection on the plants their African slaves held expertise in growing. Therefore, the culinary arts of these African cultures became the basis for much of our Southern and Latin American cuisine. African Muslims would be tortured into hiding their worship practices but many would continue adhering to their faith. The presence of Muslims among early slaves gives us an imprecise estimate of high literacy rates among early slaves. Some African Muslims were so well educated in their former lands that they memorized the Koran in its entirety. After being brought to the Americas, they would hand-write full recollections of the Koran to preserve their practice in the West. Some would even derive new Fiqh or Islamic

Laws, which was an incredible intellectual feat, to adapt their religion to their new circumstances and enslavement (Islamic law is derived from Greek Logic and can be deeply complex and intricate). They would even imbed their religion in unlikely creations. Modern scholars believe that the familiar call to prayer of the Islamic adhan, became the basis of Blues Music. The melodies, note changes, and stylistic vocal quivering are unmistakable hold overs from the same Islamic song once sung by Bilal. They would transform the Akonting (an African Instrument) into the western Banjo, creating a staple of country music. The Ngoni, and Xalam and over 60 other instrumental variants would form the backbone of black musical contributions to western music that oddly epitomizes southern culture while excluding the descendants of the Africans that gave birth to it. Blacks would bring martial arts like Tahtib (stick fighting), Nuba (African Wrestling), Musangwe, Dambe (Hausa boxing) and Engolo and transmit them into artforms like the Afro-Brazilian Capoeira. Their impetus to build civilizations would continue in the form of Maroon Cities which were built by escaped slaves. Once out of captivity, escaped slaves would follow the example of African cultures that built cities in the wild and thick forests of Africa. Maroons would often be built in seemingly inhospitable swamplands and forests to made them safe and hard to access by former slave masters and American authorities. These Maroon cities would often be formed by the union of escaped slaves and the culturally similar Native Americans. The linguistic education obtained by living in the multi-ethnic societies of Africa provided a flexibility that made these unions possible. Together the two would often out compete their white competitors in the early industries of trapping and hunting for furs and hides. By outcompeting white settlers, the Maroon cities would become economic threats and the U.S. Military would be called in to attack and crush these burgeoning Afro-Indian communities. The contributions of Africans to Western Culture are innumerable. In understanding those contributions, we understand that the Africans that were brought to the Americas represented the legacy of the societies they came from. The achievements of those cultures did not evaporate or disappear with their collapse. Their achievements were transmitted by their kidnapped descendants, forced to live in a new land. The black Africans that were brought to the Americas are a part of the story of African Empires. Nubia: The Rise and Fall of African Empires is ultimately the story of black civilization and culture, which is a tale that continues to write itself.

SOURCES AND RECOMMENDED READING

1) The Archaeological Survey of Nubia: Report for 1907-1908 By George Andrew Reisner
2) Letters from Egypt, Ethiopia and the Peninsula of Sinai By Carl Richard Lepsius
3) Cailliaud's Travels to Meroe and the White River By George Waddington
4) The Book of the Glory of the Black Race By Al-Jahiz
5) How Africa Shaped the Christian Mind: Rediscovering the African Seedbed of Western Christianity By Thomas C. Oden
6) The Ancient Arabic Poem of Antar 580 A.D. By Charles F Horne
7) The Hanged Poems By Imru-ul-Quais
8) The Art of Pablo Picasso 1906-1909, The African Period: The Amazing World of Art, Picasso Cubism Published By Unique Journal
9) The Sokoto Calpihate By Murray Last
10) Revolution in History: The Jihad of Usman Dan Fodio By Ibraheem Sulaiman
11) The African Calpihate: The Life, Works and Teaching of Shaykh Usman Dan Fodio (1754-1817)
12) The Kano Chronicle By Mervyn Hiskett
13) Journal of a Second Expedition Into the Interior of Africa: From the Bight of Benin to

Soccatoo By Richard Lander, Hugh Clapperton, Abraham V. Saleme

14) Narrative of Travels and Discoveries in Northern and Central Africa Vol. 2 By Major Denham Ham

15) The History of Bornu By Heinrich Barth

16) The History and Description of Africa Vol. 1 By Africanus Leo

17) High on the Hog: A Culinary Journey from Africa to America By Jessica B. Harris

18) African Empires: Volume 1 By J.P. Martin

19) African Cities and Towns before the European Conquest By Richard W. Hull

20) The Mughal Empire (The New Cambridge History of India) By John F. Richards

21) Malik Ambar: Power and Slavery Across the Indian Ocean By Omar H. Ali

22) African Elites in India: Habshi Amarat By Kenneth Robbins

23) The Benin Massacre By Boisragon Alan Maxwell

24) Women In African History- The Women Soldiers of Dahomey By UNESCO

25) Amazons of Black Sparta: The Women Warriors of Dahomey By Stanley B. Alpern

26) Ahmad al-Mansur: Islamic Visionary By Richard L. Smith

27) Benin, A Kingdom in Bronze: The Royal Court Art

28) The Art of Benin By Nigel Barley

29) Benin: Royal Arts of a West African Kingdom

By Kathleen Bickford Berzock

30) Benin: The City of Blood By R.H. Bacon

31) Lost Nubia: A Centennial Exhibit of Photographs from the 1905-1907 Egyptian Expedition of the University of Chicago By John Larson

32) The Nubian Pharaohs: Black Kings on the Nile By Dominique Valbelle

33) The Royal Kingdoms of Ghana, Mali and Songhay: Life in Medieval Africa By Fred McKissack

34) Medieval Europe By Chris Wickham

35) The Hidden Treasures of Timbuktu: Rediscovering Africa's Literary Culture By Alida Jay Boyce, John Hunwick, and Joseph Hunwick

36) Nubia: Ancient Kingdoms of Africa By Geoff Emberling

37) Ibn Battuta in Black Africa By Ibn Battuta, Said Hamdun & Noel King

38) Kerma and the Kingdom of Kush 2500-1500 B.C.: The Archeological Discovery of an Ancient Nubian Empire By Timothy Kendall

39) The Book of Hadith: Sayings of the Prophet Muhammad from the Mishkat al Masabih By Charles Le Gai Eaton

40) Africa's Discovery of Europe By David Northrup

41) Mansa Musa and the Empire of Mali By P. James Oliver

42) Sundjata: A West African Epic of the Mande Peoples By David C. Conrad

43) The Swahili By Mark Horton and John Middleton

44) The Periplus of the Erythraean Sea By G.W.B. Huntingford

45) Africa's Urban Past By David Anderson

46) Timbuktu and the Songhay Empire By John Hunwick

47) African Muslims in Antebellum America: Transatlantic Stories and Spiritual Struggles By Allan Austin

48) Leo Africanus By Amin Maalouf

49) Black Rice: The African Origins of Rice Cultivation in the Americas By Judith Ann Carney

50) Early Art and Architecture of Africa By Peter Garlake

51) Ancient Churches of Ethiopia By D.W. Phillipson

52) Prince Among Slaves By Terry Alford

53) Social History of Timbuktu: The Role of Muslim Scholars and Notables By Elias Saad

54) The Kebra Nagast (The Glory of Kings)

55) Narratibe of the Portuguese Embassy to Abyssinia During the Years 1520-1527 By Francisco Alvarez

56) The Rise of the Fatimids: The World of the Mediterranean and the Middle East in the Fourth Century of the Hijra By M. Brett

57) Race and Slavery in the Middle East: An Historical Enquiry By Bernard Lewis

58) Servants of Allah: African Muslims Enslaved in the Americas By Sylviane Diouf

59) Journal of a Second Expedition into the Interior of Africa By Clapperton

60) Narrative of Travels and Discoveries in Northern and Central Africa in Northern and Central Africa in the years 1822,1823 and 1824: V.2 by Dixon Denham

61) Saladin in Egypt By Ya'acov Lev

62) Saladin By David Nicolle

63) The Chronicle of Ibn al-Athir By D.S. Richards

64) Black Morocco: A History of Slavery, Race and Islam By Chouki El Hamel

65) Timbuktu Chronicles 1493-1599, Tarikh al Fattash By Christopher Wise

66) The History of al-Tabari By Tabari

.

Printed in Poland
by Amazon Fulfillment
Poland Sp. z o.o., Wrocław